TEACHER LEARNING AND POWER IN THE KNOWLEDGE SOCIETY

The Knowledge Economy and Education
Volume 5

Series Editors:
D.W. Livingstone, *Ontario Institute for Studies in Education*
David Guile, *Faculty of Policy and Society, Institute of Education, University of London*

Editorial Board:
Stephen Billett, *Griffiths University, Australia*
Zhou Zuoyu, *Normal University, Beijing, China*
Emery Hyslop-Margison, *Concordia University, Canada*
Karen Jensen, *University of Oslo, Norway*
Johan Muller, *University of Cape Town, South Africa*
Yoko Watanabe, *University of Kyoto, Japan*

Scope:
The aim of this series is to provide a focus for writers and readers interested in exploring the relation between the knowledge economy and education or an aspect of that relation, for example, vocational and professional education theorised critically.

It seeks authors who are keen to question conceptually and empirically the causal link that policymakers globally assume exists between education and the knowledge economy by raising: (i) epistemological issues as regards the concepts and types of and the relations between knowledge, the knowledge economy and education; (ii) sociological and political economic issues as regards the changing nature of work, the role of learning in workplaces, the relation between work, formal and informal learning and competing and contending visions of what a knowledge economy/knowledge society might look like; and (iii) pedagogic issues as regards the relationship between knowledge and learning in educational, community and workplace contexts.

The series is particularly aimed at researchers, policymakers, practitioners and students who wish to read texts and engage with researchers who call into question the current conventional wisdom that the knowledge economy is a new global reality to which all individuals and societies must adjust, and that lifelong learning is the strategy to secure such an adjustment. The series hopes to stimulate debate amongst this diverse audience by publishing books that: (i) articulate alternative visions of the relation between education and the knowledge economy; (ii) offer new insights into the extent, modes, and effectiveness of people's acquisition of knowledge and skill in the new circumstances that they face in the developed and developing world, (iii) and suggest how changes in both work conditions and curriculum and pedagogy can led to new relations between work and education.

Teacher Learning and Power in the Knowledge Society

Edited by

Rosemary Clark
Ontario Teachers' Federation, Canada

D.W. Livingstone
University of Toronto, Canada

and

Harry Smaller
York University, Canada

SENSE PUBLISHERS
ROTTERDAM / BOSTON / TAIPEI

A C.I.P. record for this book is available from the Library of Congress.

ISBN 978-94-6091-971-8 (paperback)
ISBN 978-94-6091-972-5 (hardback)
ISBN 978-94-6091-973-2 (e-book)

Published by: Sense Publishers,
P.O. Box 21858, 3001 AW Rotterdam, The Netherlands
https://www.sensepublishers.com

Printed on acid-free paper

All rights reserved © 2012 Sense Publishers

No part of this work may be reproduced, stored in a retrieval system, or transmitted in any form or by any means, electronic, mechanical, photocopying, microfilming, recording or otherwise, without written permission from the Publisher, with the exception of any material supplied specifically for the purpose of being entered and executed on a computer system, for exclusive use by the purchaser of the work.

TABLE OF CONTENTS

List of Figures and Tables ... ix

About the Authors ... xiii

Acknowledgements ... xv

Introduction: Teacher Learning and Power in the Knowledge Society ... 1
    D.W. Livingstone, Harry Smaller & Rosemary Clark

Introduction ... 1
The NALL/WALL Teachers' Project ... 6
Organization of Text ... 8
    Section A: Comparative Perspectives on Professionals' Work and Learning ... 8
    Section B: Teachers' Work and Learning ... 9
    Section C: Implications and Applications ... 10

SECTION A: COMPARATIVE PERSPECTIVES ON PROFESSIONALS' WORK AND LEARNING

1. Teachers and Other Professionals: A Comparison of Professionals' Occupational Requirements, Class Positions and Workplace Power ... 15
    D.W. Livingstone & Fab Antonelli

Introduction ... 15
Conventional Definitions ... 16
Review of Prior Research on Professional Work ... 17
Dimensions of Power over Work ... 22
Comparison of Specific Professional Occupations ... 23
    Demographic Variables ... 24
    Work Schedules ... 24
Professional Occupations' Control of Entry ... 25
    Control over Training for Professional Entry ... 26
    Association Membership ... 27
    Required Licensing ... 28
Professionalization and Workplace Power ... 29
Class Analysis of the General Labour Force ... 32
Class Analysis of Professional Occupations ... 35
Professional Classes and Workplace Power ... 37
Class Analysis of Specific Professional Occupations ... 38
Concluding Remarks ... 41

TABLE OF CONTENTS

2. Teachers' and Other Professionals' Learning Practices: A Comparative Analysis   45
    Fab Antonelli & D.W. Livingstone

Introduction   45
Review of Literature   46
Findings   52
    Job-Related Informal Learning   52
    Further Education and Professional Development Courses   56
    Workplace Power and Further Education   60
Integration of Further Education and Informal Learning   63
Concluding Remarks   64

SECTION B: TEACHERS' WORK AND LEARNING

3. Overview of Teachers' Work and Learning   69
    Harry Smaller

Introduction   69
Teachers' Work   69
Professional/ism: Autonomy, Power and Control of Teachers' Work   72
Schooling Reform   74
Teacher Knowledge   77
Formal and Informal Learning   79
Professional Development   81
New Teacher Induction   84
Conclusion   86

4. Full-Time Teachers' Learning: Engagements and Challenges   87
    Paul Tarc

Introduction   87
Canadian Teachers' Engagement with Learning   90
    Formal Learning   90
    Informal Learning   94
Teacher Perceptions of Changes in Working Conditions   98
    Perceived Changes in Workload Levels   98
    Teacher Stress   100
Inhibitors and Reactive Modes of Learning   101
Teachers' Learning and 'Autonomy'   103
Conclusions   108

5. Occasional Teachers' Job-Related Learning   109
    Katina Pollock

Introduction	109
Occasional Teachers	109
Growth in the Contingent Teacher Workforce	111
Teacher Workforce Hierarchy	112
Occasional Teaching, Authority and Learning	113
Types of Occasional Teachers	116
Internationally Educated Teachers (IETs)	116
Career Occasionals	117
Retirees	117
Occasional Teachers' Job-Related Learning: Formal and Informal	117
Formal Learning	118
Informal Learning	121
Teacher Workforce Hierarchy and Learning	124
Conclusion	125

6. Beginning Teachers   127
    Harry Smaller

Introduction	127
New Teacher Engagement in Formal Learning	129
New Teacher Engagement in Informal Learning	132
New Teacher Workload	134
New Teacher Stress at Work	136
New Teachers: Their Personal/Family Lives and Career Trajectories	136
Issues of Autonomy and Control for New Teachers	138
New Teachers: Possibilities for Innovative Learning Initiatives	140

SECTION C: IMPLICATIONS AND APPLICATIONS

7. Professional Control and Professional Learning: Some Policy Implications   145
    Rosemary Clark

Introduction	145
The Canadian Context: A Strong Unionized, Yet Strictly Regulated, Profession	145
Education Reform Agendas	147
Teacher Power in the Face of Reform Agendas	149
Necessary Policy Changes to Foster Teacher Professional Learning	151
We Need to Rethink Our Traditional Approaches to Formal Learning	151
We Need to Make Time During the Work Day for Informal, Ongoing Teacher Learning	154
Some Successful System-Wide Programs	155
The Ontario New Teacher Induction Program	155

TABLE OF CONTENTS

    The Teacher Learning and Leadership Program   157

8. Case Study: Job-Embedded Learning for Beginning Teachers in the Toronto District School Board   161
    Jim Strachan

Editors' Note   161
Purpose and Goals of the Beginning Teachers Program   161
Beyond Survival: The Retention Myth   162
Strategies/Actions Taken   163
Levels of Support   163
    Level 1: School-Based Mentoring   164
    Level 2: Family of Schools Mentoring   167
    Level 3: Central System Mentoring   169
Impact/Evidence/Results   170
Analysis: Personalization, Choice and Authenticity   171
Challenges and Learning   172
Summary of Evolution and Scope of TDSB Beginning
    Teachers Program   176

Conclusion: Reconsidering Teacher Learning and Power   177
    Rosemary Clark, D.W. Livingstone & Harry Smaller

Introduction   177
Teachers as Professionals and Professional Learners   179
Empowering Teachers for Greater Professional Learning   182

Appendix: Research Methodology   185

Who We Are   185
The Teacher Project Research Methods   186
    National Survey Questionnaires   186
    Time-Study Diaries   187
    In-Depth Telephone Interviews   188
    Focus Groups   189
    Face-to-face Individual Interviews   189
Research Limitations   191

Endnotes   195

Bibliography   201

LIST OF FIGURES AND TABLES

LIST OF FIGURES

Figure 8-1   Impact on student learning, years 1–5

LIST OF TABLES

Table 1-1	Demographic profiles of specific professional occupations, Canada, 2004
Table 1-2	Work schedules, Canada, 2004
Table 1-3	Advanced degrees required for professional occupations, Canada, 2004
Table 1-4	Membership in union or professional association, Canada, 2004
Table 1-5	Licensing for Professional Occupations, Canada, 2004
Table 1-6	Professional/Non-Professional Occupational Composition of the Employed Canadian Labour Force, 1983–2004
Table 1-7	Design work by professionals and other occupations, Canada, 1983–2004
Table 1-8	Organizational decision-making power by professionals and other occupations, Canada, 1983–2004
Table 1-9	Specific professional occupations by workplace power variables, Canada, 2004
Table 1-10	Employment class distribution, active labour force, Canada, 1983–2004
Table 1-11	Employment class by percentage with professional occupations, employed labour force, Canada, 1983–2004
Table 1-12	Organizational decision-making power by professional class, Canada, 2004
Table 1-13	Design own work by professional class, Canada, 2004
Table 1-14	Professional occupations and class locations, Canada, 2004
Table 2-1	Participation in job-related informal learning by employment class, 2004
Table 2-2	Participation in job-related informal learning by professionals and other occupations in general employment classes, 2004
Table 2-3	Participation in job-related informal learning participation by professional occupations, 2004
Table 2-4	Professional occupations by most important source of knowledge, 2004 (%)
Table 2-5	Professional class by informal learning topics, 2004 (% participating)
Table 2-6	Professional occupations by informal learning topics, 2004 (% participating)
Table 2-7	Degree attainment, further education course participation and proportion of job-related courses by employment class, 2004

LIST OF FIGURES & TABLES

Table 2-8	Degree attainment, further education course participation and proportion of job-related courses by general employment class and professional class, 2004
Table 2-9	Degree attainment, further education course participation and proportion of job-related courses by professional occupation, 2004
Table 2-10	Negotiating power by further education participation, 2004
Table 2-11	Sources of financial support for further education by professional occupation, 2004
Table 2-12	Helpfulness of further education and job-related informal learning to do job better by professional occupation, 2004
Table 4-1	Average weekly hours spent on courses/workshops, by seniority
Table 4-2	Average weekly hours spent on courses/workshops, by region
Table 4-3	Reasons for taking courses and workshops, by region
Table 4-4	Authority requiring courses and workshops, by region
Table 4-5	Time spent on all informal learning, by geographic region
Table 4-6	Content themes for teachers' informal learning
Table 4-7	Wider job-related issues
Table 4-8	Favoured modes of informal learning
Table 4-9	Teachers' perceived changes in workload over previous five years
Table 4-10	Overall workload change in past five years, by gender
Table 4-11	Overall stress-level change in past five years, by gender and seniority
Table 4-12	Overall workload change by overall stress level change
Table 4-13	Perceptions of change in teacher autonomy, by seniority
Table 6-1	Taken at least one course in past 12 months, by seniority
Table 6-2	Average hours per week of job-related formal learning, by seniority
Table 6-3	Teachers' engagement in types of formal courses, by seniority
Table 6-4	Plan to take courses in next few years, by seniority
Table 6-5	Planned courses are required, by seniority
Table 6-6	Costs of courses a factor in planning, by seniority
Table 6-7	Average hours per week of job-related informal learning, by seniority
Table 6-8	Teachers' engagement in informal learning, by seniority
Table 6-9	Average weekly hours of work, by seniority
Table 6-10	Teachers' perceived workload change in past five years, by seniority
Table 6-11	Overall stress-level change in past 5 years, by seniority
Table 6-12	Family responsibilities, by seniority
Table 6-13	Perceived change in workplace autonomy, by seniority
Table 8-1	TDSB retention of first year teachers
Table 8-2	TDSB Program Design
Table 8-3	How time release days are used by beginning teachers (1–5 years of experience)

Table 8-4	Evolution and scope of TDSB demonstration classrooms
Table 8-5	Beyond the workshop
Table 8-6	Models of mentoring
Table 8-7	Impact on student learning
Table 8-8	Summary of program

ABOUT THE AUTHORS

Fab Antonelli is Assistant Professor in Sociology at Mount Allison University in Sackville, New Brunswick. Prior to this, he taught secondary school in Ontario's public system. Building upon his experiences as a secondary school teacher, and working with government, federation, and community partners, his research primarily examines teachers' work and learning, curriculum reform, and democratic learning.

Rosemary Clark is retired from the staff of the Ontario Secondary School Teachers' Federation, where her many roles included policy analysis, teacher professional development, and directing and participating in a number of research projects. Her most recent books include *School law* (2007) and (as co-author) *Beyond PD days: Teacher work and learning in Canada* (2007). Since retirement, Rosemary has continued to do research and project facilitation for the Ontario Teachers' Federation and Ontario Ministry of Education.

D.W. Livingstone is Canada Research Chair in Lifelong Learning and Work at the University of Toronto, Professor Emeritus in the Department of Sociology and Equity Studies at the Ontario Institute for Studies in Education of the University of Toronto (OISE/UT), and Director of WALL (see www.wallnetwork.ca). His recent books include *The future of lifelong learning and work: Critical perspectives* (2008) (edited with K. Mirchandani and P. Sawchuk), *Education and jobs: Exploring the gaps* (2009), *Lifelong learning in paid and unpaid workplaces* (2010), and *Manufacturing meltdown: Reshaping steel labour* (2011) (with D.E. Smith and W. Smith).

Katina Pollock is an Assistant Professor in the Faculty of Education at the University of Western Ontario. She is also co-director of the Knowledge Network for Applied Educational Research (KNAER) and Faculty Director of the Joint Master's Leadership Program with the Thames Valley District School Board. Katina teaches in both the teacher pre-service program and at the graduate level. She has been a member of various research teams focusing on educational topics such as Work and Life-Long Learning (WALL Project), Urban School Poverty, Inclusive Leadership, Online Teacher Professional Development, and Information Communication Technology (ICT) in Innovative Schools. Her research interests include contingent teacher workforces, educational leadership, and policy. Recent publications include Marginalization and the occasional teacher workforce: The case of internationally educated teachers (IETs) (2010) and Hybrid courses and online policy dialogues: A transborder distance learning collaboration (2011).

Harry Smaller is recently retired from the Faculty of Education at York University in Toronto, where he taught in the graduate and teacher education programs for a decade. Prior to this, he taught in elementary, secondary and inner-city alternative schools in Toronto for three decades. His research interests include teachers' work and learning, teacher unions, schooling structures and streaming of students.

Jim Strachan has been working with (and learning from) children for 28 years as a social worker, classroom teacher of grades 2 to 8, and instructional leader for ICT. Currently on secondment to the Ministry of Education, for the past seven years Jim was the Program Coordinator: Beginning Teachers in the Toronto District School Board. Recent publications include *The heart and art of teaching and learning: Practical ideas and resources for beginning teachers* (2011) and *Flash forward: Rethinking learning* (2011).

Paul Tarc is Assistant Professor in the Faculty of Education at the University of Western Ontario. His research interests/initiatives in progressive and critical modes of education are articulated through 'post'-informed theories of representation, subjectivity and pedagogy. He has taught in K-12 schools in South America, South-East Asia and Ontario. His recent book *Global dreams, enduring tensions: International Baccalaureate (IB) in a changing world* (2009) uses IB as the focal point to historicize the 'international' of international education under globalization.

ACKNOWLEDGEMENTS

Our studies have been conducted under the sponsorship of the Centre for the Study of Education and Work (CSEW) at the Ontario Institute for Studies in Education of the University of Toronto (OISE/UT) (see www.learningwork.ca). CSEW itself is sponsored by the Department of Sociology and Equity Studies in Education and the Department of Adult Education and Counselling Psychology at OISE/UT. The CSEW mission is to pursue investigations of all aspects of learning that may be relevant to work. The research activities of CSEW have been funded primarily through research network grants from the Social Sciences and Humanities Research Council of Canada (SSHRC). The New Approaches to Lifelong Learning (NALL) network was funded by the SSHRC between 1998 and 2002. The Work and Lifelong Learning (WALL) research network was subsequently funded by the SSHRC from 2003 to 2008. The NALL and WALL teacher projects have been an integral part of these research networks from the outset. (For more information on our research group and research methodology, see the Appendix.)

Many members of CSEW assisted in the research reported in this book. CSEW co-ordinator D'Arcy Martin and CSEW secretary Rhonda Sussman, as well as NALL research co-ordinator Reuben Roth and WALL research co-ordinator Ilda Januario, played key roles in organizing the various activities in these networks. Both the NALL and WALL networks contained large teams of academic researchers, community partners and graduate students, most of whom are identified on the respective network websites (www.nall.ca and www.wallnetwork.ca). Many members of both networks provided valuable feedback on the design and development of our teacher projects. In particular, representatives of teachers' federations across Canada assisted in facilitating our surveys of their members over the years, and especially the Canadian Teachers' Federation (CTF), the Alberta Teachers' Association (ATA), the Nova Scotia Teachers Union (NSTU), and the Ontario Secondary School Teachers' Federation (OSSFTF). The cover photographs were provided courtesy of the Ontario Secondary School Teachers' Federation.

Both the 1998 and 2004 national surveys were conducted by the Institute for Social Research (ISR) at York University. Thanks for technical assistance are due to Doug Hart and Milosh Raykov, who conducted most of the statistical analyses for both the survey and the case studies, as well as to Fab Antonelli, Susan Stowe and Antonie Scholtz. Stephan Dobson undertook copy editing and formatting. The WALL international advisory committee included workplace learning researchers from several countries (Elaine Bernard, Stephen Billett, Keith Forrester, Veronica McGivney, Bernd Overwien and Kjell Rubenson), who offered valuable guidance throughout the project. We are most grateful to the many teachers who gave of their time to discuss their work and learning with us in the surveys and case studies.

D.W. LIVINGSTONE, HARRY SMALLER & ROSEMARY CLARK

INTRODUCTION

Teacher Learning and Power in the Knowledge Society

INTRODUCTION

I learned how to do pottery ... I found that I wasn't as technically able in pottery as I thought I would be ... [N]ot being able to do something that I wanted and being frustrated in that situation ... has made me more empathetic to kids who aren't naturally able in languages in the subjects that I teach ... I learned that ... I could learn a lot about cultures and I could learn a lot about people while I am teaching them something as well. (Mary, high school teacher, cited in Pankhurst 2009, p. 300)

By any definition, teachers are knowledge workers. In the school systems of modern societies, they have the primary responsibility to transmit formal knowledge to the next generation of workers and citizens. Teachers' work is among the most demanding and complicated of jobs focused on knowledge. To do their job well, teachers have to master the changing content and pedagogy of formal fields of specialized knowledge, develop empathic understanding with diverse groups of students and perform a multiplicity of other complex roles. But teaching is also among the most underappreciated jobs and the complexity of teachers' learning has been virtually ignored, for reasons that this book will examine, in comparison with other professions. A recent overview of teachers and teaching (Beijaard, Korthagen & Verloop 2007, p. 105) observed that: "It is remarkable that with so much attention being paid to student learning in schools, the issue of teacher learning has until recently drawn relatively little attention from researchers." There has been growing attention to some programmatic aspects of teachers' learning in some countries. In this book, we examine literature and trends worldwide, and use our Canadian empirical research data to deepen analysis of the global issue of teachers' learning. In this time when the processing of information has become more prominent than processing materials in so many peoples' lives, it is indeed ironic that so little is known about the learning processes of these knowledge workers who are so pre-eminent in the transmission of knowledge to others. The basic purpose of this book is to shed more light on the array of teachers' learning practices.

Since the development of industrial capitalism and mass schooling in the nineteenth century, public schooling and teachers have been targeted in virtually every economic crisis as both cause and cure (Curti 1935; Schrag 2007). The present study began in the context of an economic downturn and proposed major restructuring of schools in Canada, particularly the central province of Ontario.

R. Clark et al. (eds.), Teacher Learning and Power in the Knowledge Society, 1–12.
© 2012 *Sense Publishers. All rights reserved.*

From 1995 to 2003, the Conservative party in Ontario governed with a major part of its agenda focused on education reform in general and attacks on teachers in particular (see, e.g., Sears 2003). Similar to reforms in other state school systems, these challenges to teacher professionalism included legislation increasing teacher workload, an extensively revamped curriculum, mandatory teacher testing, and a compulsory professional development/recertification program which required each teacher to complete over a dozen formal courses every five years or lose their license to teach.

Human capital theorists continue to assert that more and better investment in formal education offers economic salvation. Such views ignore or evade growing evidence of a surplus of educational attainments in relation to job requirements, which suggest greater *relative* need of economic and workplace reform than educational reform (see Livingstone 2009). Nevertheless, general educational reforms and teacher training reforms are of vital importance and continue to preoccupy many people. Everyone supports the improvement of school systems to enhance human development. *Teacher learning and power in the knowledge society* aims to increase understanding of teachers as professionals and of some of the intricacies of their work and learning in these changing times, particularly in relation to challenges over control of their profession.

This book arose primarily out of concerns the editors shared in the mid-1990s about the limited usefulness of traditional formal professional development (PD)[1] for teachers and the lack of substantial studies of teachers' actual learning activities. For many years, in North America and beyond, substantial resources have been expended on further formal in-service training for teachers. With recent attempts to "reform" and "restructure" schooling, it appears that such efforts have been redoubled. Teachers are again presumed to lie at the heart of needed change. Therefore, change they must, and more PD is seen as the obvious way in which to affect this change. However, judging from numerous evaluations of program initiatives, surveys of school administrators and measurements of student success, much of this expenditure has been for naught.

The factors involved in the apparent failure of PD programs are complex. One could begin with a critical analysis of state schooling itself, and its apparent resistance to meaningful change, virtually since it was established over a century and a half ago (see, e.g., Labaree 1992; Lewis 1999; Popkewitz 1982). Similarly, one might begin with a critical analysis of the more recent schooling reform movement – the sources of this initiative, the reasons for its existence (curricular, pedagogical and political), and the varied definitions and expectations for success held by the diverse stakeholders, such as school administrators, school trustees, politicians at all levels, employers, university/college officials, parents, and students as well as teachers (see, e.g., Apple 1996; Hargreaves & Shaw 2000; Hatcher 2001). These expectations and agendas are very diverse and often conflicting. In that light, attempts to "develop" teachers to meet new, but very disparate, agendas, may in itself explain the antipathy to, and problems of, PD as we know it (OECD 2001; Slee & Weiner 1998; Vongalis-Macrow 2008).

At another level, however, we have been continually intrigued by and concerned with the ways in which teachers themselves have been portrayed in relation to the implementation of schooling reform and change. More often than not, in jurisdictions around the world, they have been seen as the bottleneck – the intransigent sector which cannot, or will not, adapt to needed change. According to this view, attempts to retrain teachers have failed, not because of the purpose, planning, form or content of the in-service learning provided, but because of the purported incapacity and/or resistance of teachers and their unions. However, as a number of international studies have shown, in some cases there have been good reasons why teachers have resisted specific imposed changes. In addition, even where teachers have readily accepted the change ideas being floated, the concomitant professional development programs often turned out to be less than successful (e.g., Lohman 2005; Darling-Hammond et al. 2009). In any event, there has been little dispute that teachers remain important knowledge workers. There is much less agreement about the wider social context in which they do their work.

The increasing prominence of information processing has led many observers to conclude that we now live in a "knowledge economy." For present purposes, it is sufficient to register the following social facts pertaining to all advanced market economies:

- declining minorities of jobs are in manufacturing and materials processing occupations and growing majorities of jobs and of tasks in jobs involve information processing with increasing amounts of the information being mediated by use of computers;
- growing proportions of jobs are designated as professional and technical occupations distinguished by forms of specialized knowledge;
- growing proportions of labour forces are attaining post-secondary education;
- participation in adult education courses is also increasing throughout the life course;
- as more married women enter the paid labour force, the significance of previously hidden unpaid household and community labours is increasingly recognized;
- with increasing recognition of information processing as a component of so many peoples' paid and unpaid work, recognition of the importance of lifelong learning in work has also increased and knowledge management has become a high declared priority of private corporations and governments.[2]

The debate over whether such social facts constitute a distinctive transformation to a "knowledge economy" still rages (e.g., Carlaw et al. 2006; Kennedy 2010). There is an increasingly pervasive general assumption that many people will have to intensify and document their learning efforts in order to keep up with the rapidly growing knowledge requirements of a new "knowledge economy" driven by economic utility and individual career motives (OECD 1996; Brine 2006). Others argue that we are already living in a "knowledge society," one in which the collective learning achievements of adults outpace the requirements of the economy as paid work is currently organized and that "the knowledge society dwarfs the knowledge economy" (Livingstone 1999b, p. 163). Sorlin and Vessuri (2011, p. 2) have recently observed that:

the two concepts imply radically different visions and ideals of the role of knowledge. Knowledge-based economies are growing all around us, but they do so without always acknowledging the democratic, ethical and normative dimensions of science and scientific institutions. The knowledge economy is market-driven and performs according to a market ideology, which stands in problematic but not necessarily conflicting relation to the norms and ideals of the knowledge society. The knowledge economies we live in suffer from a democratic deficit … [T]he democratic deficit needs to be addressed if academic life and culture should survive in the era of fierce global competition.

In terms of the work of teachers in school systems, these social facts and the debate at least suggest that an increasingly high priority is being placed on effective transmission/introduction of varied forms of specialized knowledge to current generations of students. Normal expectations for teachers now include having post-secondary degree-level teaching qualifications, engaging in continuing education activities to keep up with changing knowledge in their fields, and having a sufficient grasp of the changing cultural conditions of their students to effectively transmit needed knowledge to them. Aside from increased formal qualifications, these expectations may not have changed hugely from earlier periods. But it is probably fair to say that general expectations of teachers' own knowledge levels required for the transmission of vital knowledge to their students are higher than ever before.

With the increasing emphasis on information processing in recent decades, dominant models of work organization have come to stress the importance of commitment to lifelong learning for all workers. Such commitment is typically seen as involving increased collaboration and shared leadership among organization members, including the sharing or "capture" of workers' previously private or tacit knowledge, in order to enhance productivity (e.g., Senge 1990). Research on workplace learning has blossomed in this period (Malloch, Cairns, Evans & O'Connor 2010). But, with regard to teachers, it is probably fair to say that most studies of their learning have retained a programmatic nature focused on what teachers should learn in formal teacher training and professional development (PD) programs (e.g., Borko 2004).

There has been some recent empirical research that begins to focus on teachers' learning in their workplaces. Retallick (1999) notes that:

> The significance of the notion of workplace learning for teachers is profound. The idea of the school as an educative workplace for teachers (as well as students) represents a considerable advance on thinking about teachers' work. (p. 116)

The case studies of teachers' workplace learning by Retallick and colleagues (e.g., Retallick & Butt 2004) as well as several others (e.g., Lohman 2003; Jurasaite-Harbison 2008) have started to identify some situated learning practices and related organizational factors. Other recent studies have paid closer attention to how teachers learn through the activities they undertake when teaching classes

(Hoekstra, Beijaard, Brekelmans & Korthagen 2007; Maaranen, Kynäslahti & Krokfors 2008). Such studies are most welcome in beginning to identify some of the practices and factors involved in teachers' classroom-based learning; they may also point to bases of more effective linkage of teachers' workplace learning with formal teacher training and professional development programs. Jensen and her colleagues (2012), in another book in this series, provide extensive accounts of the learning processes involved in the professional learning cultures of novice school teachers, compared with those of computer engineers, nurses and accountants. But none of these studies address learning patterns among wider populations of teachers and other professionals or explicitly consider the influence of power on learning practices. This is the focus of the present study.

The present study, therefore, can be seen as a complement to these recent studies of teachers' paid workplace learning. But it begins from a wider perspective on both work and learning. 'Work' now includes 'earning a living' through *paid employment* in the production, distribution and exchange of goods and service commodities. But it also includes necessary unpaid work. *Household work* includes cooking, cleaning, childcare and other, often complex, household tasks. *Community volunteer work* sustains and builds social life through local associations and helping neighbours. All three forms of labour should be included in understanding contemporary working conditions for all workers, including teachers. The multiplicity of learning practices in each form of labour is also in need of study.

"Lifelong learning" is now widely regarded as essential to be an effective worker in the knowledge economy. But in generic terms, learning is the gaining of knowledge, skill or understanding anytime and anywhere through individual and group processes. Learning is the fundamental way in which our species has always coped with our changing environment and it occurs continually throughout our lives.

Several forms of learning can be distinguished in an *informal–formal continuum* ranging from spontaneous responses to everyday life to highly organized participation in official education programs. We all engage in *self-directed or collective informal learning*, explicit or tacit learning either individually or collectively done without direct reliance on a teacher/mentor or an externally organized curriculum. We also depend on *informal education or training* through mentors who instruct us without sustained reference to a pre-established curriculum in incidental situations. More formal learning includes instruction by teachers in *formal school systems* which now require continuous enrolment in age-graded curricula from early childhood to tertiary levels. Formal learning also includes *further adult education* with authorized instructors in a diverse array of further education courses and workshops in many institutionally organized settings, from schools to workplaces and community centres. Such continuing education, including professional development courses for working teachers, is the most evident site of lifelong learning for adults past the initial cycle of formal schooling. But it is now well documented for both adult learners generally and paid workers' job training specifically, that most of their learning occurs informally

(Tough 1979; Betcherman 1998). There is no compelling reason to presume that teachers or other professionals learn their jobs much differently.

Accordingly, the present study pays some attention to teachers' unpaid work as well as their paid employment conditions. More pertinently, the study documents a wide array of teachers' formal and informal learning practices and the interplay between them. These learning practices are related to changing general working conditions for different types of teachers. Prior to these accounts of teachers' work and learning, this study attempts to enhance general understanding of teachers' general work and learning conditions by offering empirically grounded comparisons with other major groups of professionals located across a wide global spectrum.

In sum, *Teacher learning and power in the knowledge society* offers: large-scale survey benchmarks to aid in situating teachers' work and learning in relation to other professionals; survey profiles and case study insights on different types of teachers' actual learning and work practices; and suggestive policy steps for improving professional development programs for teachers. In these respects, we hope to provide some broader contextual benchmarks for the emerging studies of teachers' learning in classroom settings and to increase appreciation of the complexity of teachers' work and learning in state schooling systems everywhere.

THE NALL/WALL TEACHERS' PROJECT

This study has involved extensive international literature reviews of prior research on work and learning relevant to teachers, including thematic analyses of professionalization, formal and informal learning activities, teacher knowledge, and the nature of teachers' working conditions and control over their own work. In addition to the recent emergence of exploratory case studies of teachers' workplace learning, there have been some insightful studies of the control of teachers' work (e.g., Ingersoll 2003). But there have been few studies of how teachers' working conditions and control of work relate to the array of teachers' learning practices.

The group of researchers contributing to this book – university faculty, graduate students and professional development field workers – first came together in 1997 to explore the complex issues related to teachers' work and learning. Since then, we have engaged in a number of empirical inquiries, all based on one dominant approach – *hearing out teachers themselves*.

Our journey has been broad, as we set out to explore the nature of teachers' engagement with learning, as well their opinions about this engagement and their own learning styles. We also inquired into the conditions of their workload, the social relations of their workplaces, and how these conditions may have affected their capacity to take advantage of meaningful formal and informal learning activities. Similarly, we also explored their perceptions about the nature and effectiveness of PD policies and programs.

The New Approaches to Lifelong Learning (NALL) network research developed an expansive conceptual framework for (paid and unpaid) work and (formal and informal) learning studies, and conducted the first national survey in the world of these forms of learning and work in 1998, as well as a series of over

30 exploratory case studies between 1998 and 2002. The Work and Lifelong Learning (WALL) research network conducted field research between 2003 and 2008. The WALL network further explored the array of learning activities of adults, relations between work and learning practices, and differences in these learning and work relations between socially disadvantaged groups and others. The WALL research team addressed these issues by conducting a large-scale, country-wide 2004 survey and 12 related case studies to provide unprecedented documentation of lifelong learning and work relations (see Livingstone 2010). The exceptionally large general population national survey conducted in 2004 (N=9,063) permitted unprecedented comparative analyses of the working conditions and learning practices of teachers and several other professional occupations. Closely related national surveys conducted in 1998 and 2010 found similar patterns of work and learning relations for the general labour force; however, their much smaller sample sizes (less than 2,000 respondents) did not permit reliable comparisons of teachers with other specific occupational groups.

The NALL and WALL Teachers' Projects have been an integral part of these research networks from the outset. Our data on teachers' work and learning were collected in a number of ways. In 1998, and then again in 2004, we conducted national surveys of representative samples of teachers – asking them to report on their involvement in formal and informal learning, their interests in further learning opportunities, and the nature and conditions of their work. These were the first large-scale national surveys ever conducted in Canada or elsewhere with teachers on this set of issues.

In addition, a small, purposive sample of regular full-time teachers recorded their work and learning over two weeks in time diaries, followed by in-depth interviews. Following the second national survey in 2004, focus group interviews were held across four provinces with randomly selected respondents. Finally, in 2007–2008, face-to-face interviews and focus groups were conducted with two different groups of teachers. The first of these were occasional teachers, including recent migrants with international qualifications, career occasional and retired teachers filling in on a daily basis. The second group included new teachers in their first and second year in the classroom. (For more information on our research group and the teacher project research methodology, see Appendix A.)

The general theoretical perspective that informs the NALL and WALL research networks posits an intimate connection between the exercise of workplace power and the recognition of legitimate knowledge. The greatest discrepancies between formal knowledge attainments and paid work requirements are expected for the least powerful, including members of lower economic classes, women, visible minorities, recent immigrants, older people and those identified as disabled (Livingstone 2004). These studies of work and learning have been inspired by contemporary theories of learning that focus on the learning capacities of adults outside teacher-directed classroom settings, such as Paulo Freire's (1970) reflections on collective learning through dialogue and Malcolm Knowles' (1975) work on individual self-directed learning. Both theorists stressed the active practical engagement of adult learners in the pursuit of knowledge or cultural change. Freire's projects generally illustrated the untapped and suppressed learning capacities of rural peasants. Subsequent empirical studies of self-directed learning documented extensive intentional informal learning among diverse social groups (Tough 1979).

This focus on learning in practical activity is consistent with earlier general theories of learning by experience which emphasized either the development of individual cognitive knowledge (Dewey 1916) or tacit knowledge (Polanyi 1966), as well as with the cultural historical activity theory of cognitive development which takes more explicit account of subordinate groups' socio-historical context (Vygotsky 1978). Each of these approaches to adult learning advances a conception of informal learning practices as situated in the everyday lives of ordinary people. This perspective has been increasingly applied in recent studies of workplace learning carried out in a number of countries (e.g., Lave & Wenger 1991; Engestrom, Miettinen & Punamaki 1999; Livingstone & Sawchuk 2004).

Applying this perspective in the NALL and WALL Teacher Projects, we first predict that there are important differences in the exercise of workplace power between professional occupations, and that teachers have relatively little power in terms of organizational control of their work. We posit that those in professional occupations with relatively little power are likely to be most dependent on continuing formal efforts to maintain recognition of their specialized knowledge to reaffirm their status and, therefore, may exhibit greater concern over participation in further education and PD. Some prior research focused only on teachers suggests that variations among them in decision-making power may be associated with differing capacities for teachers to engage in "organizational learning" or social processing of knowledge, measured in terms of staff development and instructional improvement provisions in the workplace (Marks & Seashore Louis 1999). But there have been few prior studies that have compared teachers and other professions in terms of their differences in workplace power and opportunities for participation in further formal education.

ORGANIZATION OF TEXT

The book is organized in three distinct sections. The first part situates teachers' general professional status and working conditions as well as their learning practices in relation to other major professional groups. The second part looks more closely at the working conditions and learning practices of both regular, full-time teachers and more precariously employed teachers. The final part addresses promising initiatives and prospects for more effective professional development programs.

Section A: Comparative Perspectives on Professionals' Work and Learning

Chapter 1 first explores the criteria that have conventionally been used to designate *professional status*. Standard criteria (i.e., university programs in specialized knowledge, association membership and regulatory licensing requirements) are reviewed. We compare teachers and several other major professional occupations, including doctors and lawyers, engineers, nurses, and computer programmers, in terms of these conventional criteria. But, in addition, professionals' negotiating and organizational powers are seen to be related to the class composition of these occupations. Class positions of professionals include: professional owners, self-employed professionals, professional managers and professional employees. Our distinctive general national survey data are used to develop profiles of the basic working conditions and workplace powers of these professions. Teachers are identified as predominantly professional employees with significantly less organizational decision-making power than some other major professional occupations. Evidence of recent class polarization of professional occupations and "deprofessionalization" of professional employees in terms of their workplace power is also offered.

Chapter 2 examines *formal and informal learning practices*, using comparisons of the same professional occupations and class positions with the national survey data. Teachers have among the highest rates of participation in further education. Further education rates are associated with negotiating power (based on ownership of firms for doctors and lawyers, high unionization for teachers and nurses). In addition, teachers are at least as likely as other professionals to engage in job-related informal learning. Teachers engage in both extensive formal learning and intensive informal learning to maintain their status as knowledge workers. But the integration of their formal professional development with their informal learning is found to be quite limited, perhaps partly because of their relatively limited organizational decision-making power. These general work and learning profiles of teachers and other professionals establish a comparative context for the rest of the book and, hopefully, for comparable studies in other countries.

Section B: Teachers' Work and Learning

This section provides the main empirical results and analyses of our case studies of teachers – a broad picture of teachers' engagement in their work and learning. The section begins with Chapter 3, a *review of literature* pertaining to teachers' engagement in their own learning, including theory and praxis of formal and informal learning, and a review of historical, descriptive, analytical and prescriptive literature related to the "field" of teacher professional development. Equally important is a review of pertinent literature examining factors which influence teachers' learning, including the social and material conditions of teachers' work, and the influences of professionalism and professionalization.

Chapter 4 presents a comprehensive profile of full-time teachers' engagement in their formal and informal modes of learning. It examines how teachers' shifting working conditions shape their commitments to and practices of learning and discusses limits of and possibilities for teachers' control over their professional learning. First, it presents teachers' participation in *formal learning* activities – workshops, PD days, lectures, seminars, courses, etc. – and teachers' perceptions about the quality and usefulness of these engagements. Then, by comparison, teachers' engagement in a broad array of *informal learning activities* is examined – one-on-one collaboration with colleagues, school administrators, students and parents; departmental and full-staff meetings; lunch room conversations; and individual and collaborative inquiries using print or online resources and networking. With all of these various learning activities, we are careful to acknowledge how the conditions of teachers' work in Canadian schools and classrooms mediate their capacity to engage in their own further education. Reactive modes of informal learning and the challenges and prospects for teachers' autonomy in their learning are discussed in the final sections.

Chapter 5 describes two clusters of teachers who generally hold less than normal status among their classroom colleagues overall. The first cohort consists of those who, even though fully certified to teach full-time in public schools in Canada, work as *"temporary" or "supply" teachers*. Many are employed only on a day-to-day basis, filling in for regular teachers who are ill or attending PD sessions; others hold at best a temporary contract ranging from several weeks to months. (While some have desired and intentionally selected this status, increasing numbers engage in this temporary activity while applying and waiting (hoping) for permanent teaching employment). The second group consists of those who *have recently immigrated to Canada* having engaged in their teacher education program in another country, and who are now teaching in Canada, either as permanent employees or as temporary teachers. As this chapter demonstrates, each of these groups maintain very specific interests about, and engagement in, their own further learning – which very much reflect the very specific work experiences which they encounter in their jobs. Based on data collected through surveys, interviews and focus groups, these issues are explored in this chapter.

Chapter 6 focuses on *new teachers in the system* – those in their first and second year on the job following teacher education and initial certification. This group received considerable attention in our research during its latter phases – partly because there had been increasing concerns expressed by a number of provincial governments and school boards over the globally recognized problem of a high drop-out rate of new teachers in their early years. For example, the Ontario government has provided considerable funds to school boards and teacher unions for targeted professional development for this group. For these reasons, it seemed useful to examine more closely new teachers' perceptions of the challenges they faced, their perceived learning needs, and the ways in which they had sought out and engaged in this learning. The data for this chapter were generated in large part through interviews and focus groups conducted with new teachers in the context of their engagement in professional development workshops and seminars specifically for their cohort – thus allowing us to focus on their emerging interests and needs for further learning.

Section C: Implications and Applications

The final main section consists of two chapters. Chapter 7 is devoted to implications for policy makers and professional development educators. Not unlike the situation in other state schooling systems, the Canadian teaching population has faced considerable government interference and dealt with reform agendas which have impacted their learning, as they have struggled for professional control. However, since 2003, the Ontario government has moved away from this approach to one more supportive of teacher professionalism, ceding more control over some professional learning programs to the teacher unions and teachers themselves. Thus, our research in this province has been able to synthesize what we heard from thousands of classroom teachers who have stated that they have benefitted from successful teacher development programs that are job-embedded, ongoing, based on teacher choice and continuous informal learning. Other recent studies support these conclusions (e.g., Darling-Hammond et al. 2009, Hargreaves & Shirley, 2009, Lieberman & Miller, 2001, and Broad & Evans, 2006). Several innovative programs which embody these principles, including the Ontario Teacher Learning and Leadership program, are briefly described as models.[3]

Chapter 8 provides a detailed case study of what we consider to be an innovative and successful model for provision of effective on-the-job learning for new teachers – a new teacher induction program which has been in effect for the past several years in one large urban school district (the Toronto District School Board).

The brief Conclusion to the book summarizes the main findings of all three sections and draws out significant implications, especially prospects for more integrated forms of formal and informal professional learning and more democratic decision-making beyond the classroom – findings which clearly have resonance for schools and teachers across the globe. It should be recognized that Canada represents a specific case in terms of its institutional history of educational development and particularly the relatively weak educational authority of a federal state regime in light of provincial governments' primary responsibility for provision of formal education. However, we believe that the findings of this study may well serve as a benchmark for further comparative research in many countries on the range of teachers' and other professionals' learning practices and the influence of professionals' power on these practices.

Various parts of this book may appeal to readers with different combinations of interests in research and practice. But *Teacher learning and power in the knowledge society* as a whole is intended to address the diverse stakeholders – teachers, school administrators and personnel involved with developing and implementing teacher professional development programs, faculties of education, university/college instructors and researchers, school board members and concerned citizens – who have an interest in making more effective connections between teachers' knowledge and its use and transmission in their workplaces. Different stakeholders may adhere to conflicting views of the demands of the "knowledge economy" or the potential of the "knowledge society." But, hopefully, increasing understanding of the learning practices of working teachers can encourage both genuine reforms of schools as workplaces and the creation of professional development (PD) programs that can link more effectively with teachers' continual pursuit of knowledge.

SECTION A: COMPARATIVE PERSPECTIVES ON PROFESSIONALS' WORK AND LEARNING

D.W. LIVINGSTONE & FAB ANTONELLI

1. TEACHERS AND OTHER PROFESSIONALS

A Comparison of Professionals' Occupational Requirements, Class Positions and Workplace Power

INTRODUCTION

Yes, I love being in front of the kids and I love to think that my work will have a positive effect on the people I come into contact with, especially the students. It's noble work. So, the noble nature of the work is what keeps me going. But I find that the type of compromises we have to make as teachers, and the limits put on us by the needs of bureaucracy and the administration are very stifling and defeating. We are increasingly asked to do administrative bureaucratic work that is time consuming and ultimately just drains us, and does zero in terms of helping our students in any way. (Moishe, teacher)[1]

Notions of professionalism have been problematic in occupations such as teaching compared with the classical professions of law and medicine (Hargreaves & Goodson 1996). Continuing debates about professional status have centred on technical knowledge content, control of entry to work, autonomy and accountability (Sachs 2003). Most recent comparisons of professional occupations have been quite ahistorical, ignoring the fact that notions of professional status have changed over time. "Professionalism" can also be used at the same time by different interests with quite different meanings: for example, notions of professionalism have been invoked by employers as a strategy of worker control and by employees to resist decreasing control of their work (Ozga & Lawn 1981).

Most prior comparisons of professions have focused on the strength of their claims to possess a specialized body of knowledge but ignored important aspects of underlying *relations* of workplace power that heavily influence any given profession's capacity to assert such claims. Our contribution starts with standard definitions and conventional criteria of professional status. We will offer a comparative empirical examination of these criteria, using a unique data set for several specific professional occupations, including teachers as well as doctors and lawyers, engineers, nurses, and computer programmers. But we will go further. We argue that class distinctions between *self-employed professionals, professional owners, professional managers and professional employees* must also be used in order to understand the limits of power for different professional occupations today. In fact, commonly recognized professional occupations differ widely both in class composition and extent of consequent workplace power. In particular, we will argue that teachers' contemporary professional status is intimately related to their predominant class position as employees.

CONVENTIONAL DEFINITIONS

A standard definition of a profession is an occupation that requires a specialized body of knowledge acquired by extensive academic preparation. Occupations with claims to specialized practical or spiritual knowledge have emerged in virtually all human societies with a division of labour – priests, witch doctors, apothecaries, court scribes, craft guilds and so on. Such claims often have been contested by sceptics and those with contending sources of knowledge. But occupational groups that have gained control over access to specialized training programs and development of a complex codified field of knowledge have been able to exclude many aspirants from entry into the field and also effectively mystify their professional field to the general public. Derber, Schwartz and Magrass (1990) cite the general importance of such appropriation of a field of knowledge as a key characteristic for the 'enclosure' of a profession, making access very difficult for others in society. Self-regulation by a governing professional association has also generally been regarded as the optimal means to control standards for entry into and adequate performance in professional practice.

The classical professions in medieval European society were divinity, medicine and law. In each case, full-time practitioners: (1) organized training schools; (2) formed associations; and (3) established regulatory bodies. The combination of these factors enabled such professions to claim overarching authority in their fields of knowledge, to make independent judgments about their work and to exclude those without such approved training and certification from legitimate practice in these fields. The status and power of divinity in secular societies now recedes. But medicine and law have continued to be generally recognized as the most fully developed professions in these terms, with widespread agreement that they are "callings" that require a specialized body of knowledge acquired by extensive academic preparation and that these occupations should be primarily self-regulating (Friedson 1986).

In early modern times, dentistry, civil engineering, architecture and accounting followed similar paths. With nineteenth-century industrialization, other specialized occupations began to claim professional status: pharmacy, veterinary medicine, nursing, librarianship, optometry, social work, and teaching. Throughout the twentieth century, these specialized occupational groups and others proceeded varied distances along paths of full professionalization with training schools, some form of group association and quasi-self-regulating bodies.[2]

With the growing centrality of information and knowledge production to advanced market economies, the opportunities for advanced training in strategic areas of specialized knowledge and for those who obtain such training to assert claims to professional authority have multiplied. The relatively new occupation of computer programmer is a pertinent case in point. There is much dispute over dividing lines between professionals and semi-professionals, as well as over which among all newer occupations deserve semi-professional designation. Indeed, there is an evident tendency in current advanced market economies for most occupations to want to designate themselves as 'professionals.' There could also be a counter-argument that current technologists could be considered as the skilled trades of the twenty-first century. For current purposes, we restrict attention to occupations whose claims to professional status are widely accepted by the general public.

Most of the prior research literature has distinguished professionals by relying on the aforementioned criteria: organized educational programs for advanced academic education; legitimate group associations; and self-regulatory licensing bodies.[3] In this chapter, we will first compare professional occupations in terms of these criteria and general working conditions. However, we will then go on to argue that additional employment distinctions that are historically and class-based distinctions be made among professional occupations in order to understand the differential capacities that professionals have to exercise power within their workplaces, whatever the popularly perceived status of the professional occupation *per se*. We will suggest that there are now four basic types of professionals: *self-employed professionals*; *professional employers*; *professional managers*; and *professional employees*.[4] Teachers in particular must be understood to be predominantly professional employees.

REVIEW OF PRIOR RESEARCH ON PROFESSIONAL WORK

Our literature review reveals few comparative studies of professionals' working conditions and job control. The few comparative empirical studies tend to be based largely on secondary analysis of evidence such as census classifications (e.g., Rowen 1994). Chan et al. (2000) conducted a rare comparative study of stress levels across six 'professions' and semi-professionals (emerging professionals) in Singapore: general medical practitioners; lawyers; engineers; teachers; nurses; and life insurance personnel.[5] This study concluded that stress affected each occupational group differently depending upon the hierarchical structure of the employing organization. Teachers, nurses and engineers experienced high levels of stress from their employers, leading these occupational groups to be "more psychologically vulnerable to the impacts of this problem than other professional groups" (Chan et al. 2000, p. 1431). However, they discovered that the source of stress varied across "professional occupations." The primary source of stress for teachers and nurses was employer-related, while lawyers mainly received stress from performance anxiety and client satisfaction. As we will see later, these differences in stress are likely a reflection of the employment class locations of these different professional occupations.

More generally, the literature on professionals' workplace power has been divided between those who argue that professionals are asserting ever greater control of modern workplaces and those who suggest that professionals are losing much of their control. These approaches can be termed *professionalization* versus *proletarianization* or *deprofessionalization*.[6]

Theorists who perceive the emergence of a 'post-industrial society' or 'knowledge-based economy' tend to see growing numbers of professionals with growing control of their work and the increasing centrality of their specialized bodies of knowledge in workplaces. There is much emphasis in the literature on the emergence of a 'knowledge-based economy,' with increasing discretionary thought being required of all workers to perform their jobs (e.g., Machlup 1980; Cortada 1998). Over the past century, capital intensification in most industries has put an increasing premium on human mediation of expensive machinery. The rise of the service sector has been contingent on increasing use of 'mental' as opposed to 'manual' labour. The proliferation of information technologies has now made a wider array of work tasks dependent on the self-monitoring use of workers' minds in the processing of ideas rather than material objects. Steelworkers, for example, are now more likely to be watching computer control panels than moving steel. In short, there has been a secular trend for the motives and learning capacities of the workforce to play a more strategic role in the capitalist labour process. In this context, Bell (1976) argues that the post-industrial society has placed professionals in a privileged position with increasing power because of the specialized knowledge they possess to contribute to this process. Unlike the proletarianization of craft workers in the nineteenth century, Bell argues, professionals have been able to secure their organizational position and independence because of the critical importance of their technical knowledge in the maintenance of modern organizations. Professionals bring a skill set that insulates their autonomy and preserves their immediate control over their work. Professionals are not dependent on the organization that employs them; rather they are individuals who possess a level of specialized knowledge that makes them increasingly valued and influential guides for society. In this context, teachers have frequently been characterized as doing highly complex and specialized work that requires increasing training and job autonomy (Sykes 1990).

Conversely, other theorists see professional occupations as increasingly fragmenting and falling into more constrained working conditions with less control and autonomy: a situation described as either *proletarianization* or *de-professionalization*.

The *proletarianization thesis* applied to white collar employees (Oppenheimer 1973; Derber et al. 1990) argues that the power of an individual to control his or her work is directly tied to the relation he or she has to the form of production. Over time, all employees (i.e., those without ownership control) will be reduced to the status of hired wage earners, completely dependent upon the selling of their own labour. The inability to own one's own work diminishes the ability for an individual to be involved in autonomous work. The proletarianization argument posits that all non-managerial employees over time will enter into a bureaucratized structure (Derber et al. 1990), lose control over the final product and find their work routinized and their skill levels diminished. As Oppenheimer (1973, p. 214) put it:

> The bureaucratized workplace ... tend[s] to replace in the professionals' own workplace factory-like conditions – there are fixed jurisdictions, ordered by rules established by others; there is a hierarchical command system ... The gap between what the worker does, and an end product, increases.

In a manner similar to the declining power of craft workers with the demise of medieval guilds, those in professional occupations today may be losing control over their specialized knowledge in the hierarchical structure of modern organizations. For example, Carey (2007) finds that social workers are increasingly subjected to deskilling and intensified workloads. Teachers have been characterized as workers who are subjected to increasingly simplified and standardized routines that permit very limited autonomy (Apple 1988). Derber (1983) postulated that the proletarianization of a professional occupation can occur both technically and ideologically:

> The lack of control over the process of the work itself (i.e., the means), incurred whenever management subjects its workers to a technical plan of production and/or a rhythm or pace of work which they have no voice in creating, can be called *technical* proletarianization ... The lack of control over the product can be reconceptualized more broadly as the lack of control over the ends of one's work. Called here *ideological* proletarianization, it will refer to the appropriation of control by management over the goals and social purposes to which work is put. (p. 313)

This argument emphasizes erosion of control over the products of professional work. Although professionals may still retain, for the most part, a modicum of technical skill and control over their immediate working conditions, control of the final product and goals of the organization have been lost to bureaucratized authority. Professionals, like craft workers in the past, are considered to have been placed in a position where their specialized knowledge or skill is used like a tool in the operations of the organization, leaving them without control of the overall operations of the organization and the final product.

The *deprofessionalization thesis* argues more specifically that professional occupations are experiencing an erosion of their control over their specialized knowledge (Haug 1973). Two key components of the deprofessionalization thesis are general technological standardization and the general advancement of knowledge of laypersons in society. In terms of technologies, recent case studies have found evidence that computerized administrative duties and standardized auditing of performance are impeding the provision of direct services to clients and undermining control over work (Easthope & Easthope 2000; Aziz 2004; Lewis et al. 2003; Carmelli & Freund 2004; Dickens et al. 2005; Lingard 2003). Even the most privileged professional groups are found to face increasing technical and commercial constraints on their self-regulation as well as increasing state regulatory procedures (Hanlon 1999). In terms of laypersons' knowledge, Haug (1975) presents the argument that growth of information technologies have allowed knowledge that was at one time kept distant from the general public to be stored and retrieved easily. A loss of control for professionals stems from the increasing level of knowledge of the general public. Essentially, it becomes difficult for professionals to enclose their control over a specialized body of knowledge and exclude the general public from an understanding of the profession when a growing proportion of this knowledge is no longer mystifying. Internet medical sites, for example, now allow people to type their symptoms into a database to reveal a list of potential ailments. On that same site, upon self-diagnosing his or her ailment, a person may then retrieve advice on how to treat the ailment. All of this does not require the family doctor and may be of benefit to people suffering from mild ailments. Toffler (1990, p. 8) even suggests that "the knowledge monopoly of the medical profession has been thoroughly smashed. And the doctor is no longer god ... In many other fields, too, closely held specialists' knowledge is slipping out of control and reaching ordinary citizens." In any case, according to the deprofessionalization thesis, a greater level of lay person intelligence makes specialized knowledge more accessible and professional status prone to greater public scrutiny and less public deference.

These contending claims of the increasing or decreasing control over their work and their specialized knowledge by professionals have typically been empirically supported by selective use of aggregated data on occupational distributions or case studies of particular professional occupations, with little comparative analysis of either professionals versus other occupations or the relative control of different specific professions. The dispute between professionalization and deprofessionalization claims persists in terms of tendencies toward control from within occupational communities versus control from above by employers and managers of the service organizations in which many "professionals" work (see Evetts 2003). But, as Terence Johnson (1977) has observed in a much ignored earlier contribution on the subject, these views have quite antithetical implications for professionals' place in the class structure of capitalist societies and neglect the dualism in the organization of knowledge as work. In his view, in advanced capitalist societies, those in professional occupations may play primarily a part of the global ownership and managerial functions of capital, or primarily be part of collective labour in a complex co-operative labour process, or be a combination of both. Professional occupational categories *per se* will not reveal the *class positions of professionals* without further examination of their relations in the production process.

Aside from Johnson's work, there is a significant body of prior conceptual literature on teachers' class position in particular. Three basic approaches have been identified (see Warburton 1986; Filson 1988): (a) schema that consider teachers as part of a *new middle class* or professional–managerial class serving to reproduce capitalist social relations in the next generation; (b) schema that focus on the *contradictory class position of teachers* as hired employees subject to intensification of their own labour at the same time as they play a role in shaping and controlling the future labour force of capitalism; and (c) those that claim that teachers are substantially *indistinguishable from other workers*, that "teachers are workers exploited like other workers by capital ... workers who have used professionalism strategically and had it used against them, that they have allied with organized labour ... (Ozga & Lawn 1981, p. 147). There is also a more recent critical assessment of such approaches that: (1) recognizes the increasing intensification of teachers' work simultaneous with public educational systems becoming more subordinate to interests of capital and teachers serving as agents of capital; and (2) attempts to resolve these contradictory emphases through a class analysis that recognizes "the significance of teaching as state employment, the growth of hierarchies within schools and the contradictory functions of education" (Carter 1997, p. 201).

All of Carter's points are relevant for the development of our approach to the class positions of teachers and other professionals. While a corporatizing trend serving capitalist reproduction may be currently ascendant, schools and other public institutions in capitalist societies must also continue to respond to democratic demands of the general public (Carnoy & Levin 1985). The growth of managerial hierarchies and state employment needs to be understood historically in relation to the development of professional occupations generally and teaching in particular.

The most important historical point about the development of professional occupations is that the most enduringly powerful ones emerged in the period of entrepreneurial capitalism. These professions had the capacity to sell their own goods and services containing their specialized knowledge, to own the proceeds/profits, and to hire others to assist in producing these products, as well as to self-regulate the training, recruitment and disciplining of members (e.g., physicians, lawyers, architects). In short, *they generally owned their own means of production*. During the expansion of industrial capitalist corporate organizations and the modern state, those professionalizing occupations emerging in substantial numbers with claims to specialized knowledge related to provision of goods and services – notably teachers – were much more likely to be directly regulated by and/or employed by the state and lack ownership of products. Also, as both private corporations and state bureaucracies grew, managerial hierarchies developed to direct the growing numbers of most professional occupations, especially the newer ones. Indeed, most professional occupations have become increasingly state regulated, even those classical professions that may still own their own firms or organizations in a legal sense.

Later, we will outline current class positions of professionals in 'knowledge-based economies' based on criteria of ownership of enterprise; authority over others in labour process; and specialized knowledge claims. We will also situate teachers and other specific professional occupations in these terms. But first we will offer a comparative analysis of the working conditions and power over their work for several professional occupations *per se*. Then, we will argue and demonstrate that prevalent relations in the production process need to be taken into account to explain the differences among such occupations in workplace power. As Erik Olin Wright (1980), one of the more creative contemporary class theorists, has demonstrated, any given occupational designation may contain people in diverse class positions. For example, a carpenter might be self-employed, might owe a firm employing carpenters and others, might be a manager or supervisor in a construction company, or he might be a hired skilled worker. It is reasonably clear that most professional or aspiring professional occupational groups include many people making efforts to construct their fields of knowledge to ensure the highest degree possible of control of their own work (see Derber, Schwartz & Magrass 1990). But, as we shall see, differential class composition places significant limits on the extent of this control, not least for teachers as an occupational group.

21

DIMENSIONS OF POWER OVER WORK

Power can be defined as the capacity to enable oneself and direct others to achieve desired goals. A basic distinction should be made between the *power to negotiate terms of provision of service or labour* (e.g., price, quality, type of product) and the *power to make decisions within the labour process of an organization* (Livingstone & Raykov 2008). These may be termed "negotiating power" versus "organizational power." Those who own their enterprises can negotiate terms of provision with possible clients; those who are employees must negotiate terms with their employers. Within organizations, owners have managerial prerogative; they may or may not delegate organizational power to employees.

Negotiating power for professional occupations has been conventionally treated as capacity to set terms for provision of services to clients while maintaining effective ownership of these services (e.g., doctors, lawyers). But for those in professional occupations who are employees, negotiating power has become limited to the extent to which they can bargain with their employers for workers' rights and benefits, typically through associations and unions.

Organizational power to make decisions within the labour process has two aspects: the degree of *individual discretion and autonomy* in conducting one's own labour tasks, and the *extent of authority one can exercise in relation to others' labours*. Once again, differences between owners of enterprises and employees should be distinguished. Those in occupations who own their enterprises have wide discretion in their own labour and managerial prerogative over the labour of others they hire. Those in professional occupations who are employees may have autonomy in their own labour tasks to the extent that their specialized knowledge and workers' rights have been negotiated with employers, but their organizational power beyond their immediate work stations remains delegated power from their employers.

Both *negotiating power* and *delegated organizational power* need to be considered in assessing the power of those who are employees especially, and therefore lack the prerogatives of proprietorial ownership. In the following empirical comparisons of professional occupations, we will examine negotiating power in terms of union and association membership strength, and delegated organizational power in terms of: (1) perceived choice in planning one's own work; and (2) reported participation in organizational decision-making.

It should be noted here that much of the recent literature on "teacher empowerment" (e.g., Bogler & Somech 2004) is fixated on personal autonomy (such as taking charge of one's own growth, feelings of self-efficacy), but ignores or underplays organizational decision-making and presumes participation in actual decisions about resources, types of programs, recruitment and so forth should be left to higher managerial prerogative. As we will see throughout this book, individual sense of workplace autonomy is very relevant for many teachers. But, in our view, sense of workplace autonomy for teachers and other professional occupations is best understood in the context of the negotiating power of their associations/unions and the extent of their organizational decision-making roles.

COMPARISON OF SPECIFIC PROFESSIONAL OCCUPATIONS

The empirical study of professionals has become quite complicated and difficult with proliferation of criteria and increasingly pragmatic definitions of what it means to be a 'professional' (Evetts 2006, p. 134). As noted earlier, our comparisons will focus mainly on occupations widely agreed to be professionals. In addition to teachers as the focal profession in this book, doctors, lawyers, engineers and nurses were selected for inclusion in this study because these are among the most commonly recognized 'professions.' In terms of the conventional criteria, all of these occupations exhibit high levels of specialized formal education and have well-established professional associations, but their extent of licensing control varies considerably (compare Friedson 1984). Doctors and lawyers have been able to establish clearly self-governing regulatory bodies with universal licensing requirements. Teachers' and nurses' regulatory bodies typically involve representation from other overarching authorities;[7] licensing (or certification) is now quite widely practiced, but unqualified teachers and nurses can be hired by schools and hospitals with minimal training in particular fields and in times of labour shortage. While engineers' possession of specialized knowledge is widely assumed, they often do not possess a formal licence in order to work. Those who have completed advanced academic training but who are not professionally certified are able to work provided they are supervised by a licensed engineer (see Professional Engineers of Ontario n.d.).

In addition, among now emerging professions, computer programmers over the past generation are perhaps most widely recognized as possessing a high level of technical skill and specialized knowledge. Post-secondary training programs in computer science have rapidly become required for entry into most programming jobs. While professional associations and licensing bodies may still be nascent, the current pertinence of computer programmers' specialized knowledge provides opportunities for members of this occupation to limit entry and develop self-regulation.

The empirical comparisons of professional occupations in this and the following chapter are primarily based on the only known population survey to date large enough to allow statistically significant comparisons[8] of the working conditions and learning practices of professional occupations. The 2004 Work and Lifelong Learning (WALL) survey included a representative random sample of the general Canadian adult population, over 9,000 respondents (see the Appendix for more information on the WALL survey). Many WALL survey questions were constructed to be comparable to the 1982–83 Canadian Class Structure (CCS) survey (Clement & Myles 1994). The CCS survey focused on issues of workplace power and comparable data will be used later to assess changes in workplace control between class positions over the 1983–2004 period. Our comparison of professional occupations begins with basic demographic features and work schedules drawn from the 2004 WALL survey.[9]

Demographic Variables

The demographic variables in Table 1-1 indicate clear gender differences among professional occupations. Engineering remains male-dominated, while the vast majority of nurses and teachers remain females. Majorities of doctors and lawyers are still males. So are most computer programmers. Majorities of many other aspiring professional occupations, such as health sector technologists, are predominantly female.

The age composition is similar across most of these professional groups, with an average age over 40. Computer programmers are somewhat younger and tend to have less work experience, reflecting the relative youth of this emerging professional occupation. Although the age profiles of the workers within each of the more established professions are similar, teachers and nurses tend to have somewhat more work experience (e.g., 46 per cent and 57 per cent respectively with over 15 years in the profession). This is partly related to the longer required training periods for doctors and lawyers who therefore begin their careers at later ages. Finally, the Canadian labour force remains predominantly white. Teachers are the most likely to be of white racial background – which may suggest somewhat greater racial bias in selection for teacher training programs and/or hiring processes. Computer programmers, the newest and least 'enclosed' of these specific professional occupations, are most likely to be from non-white backgrounds.

Table 1-1. Demographic profiles of specific professional occupations, Canada, 2004

Occupation	Sex (% Female)	Race (% White)	Age (average years)	Career (average years)
Doctors & lawyers	41	90	42	13
Teachers	75	95	42	15
Nurses	94	90	43	18
Engineers	17	81	40	10
Computer programmers	35	74	37	9
Other professionals	63	89	41	11
Total non-professional labour force	49	88	40	11

Source: WALL 2004 Survey (N=5,800)

Work Schedules

Comparison of work schedules finds that professional occupations are not very distinctive from the rest of the employed labour force in this respect. Over 80 per cent in most occupational groups worked full-time in 2004 and in the follow-up 2010 WALL survey – that is, over 30 hours per week – and at least two-thirds worked regular day schedules as opposed to alternating, night or irregular shifts. Teachers and nurses were more likely to work in part-time, short term and/or non-permanent positions than the other selected professional occupations.[10] Most professionals worked regular days. The most striking difference in terms of shift schedules is between nurses and the other selected professional occupations. Vast majorities of most professions – and nearly all teachers – work regular days, whereas the vast majority of nurses work rotating, split or irregular shift schedules and significant numbers work regular night shifts. This pattern is partly a reflection of the demands of patient care, especially in hospitals; however, most doctors with hospital responsibilities reported that they work regular days. In terms of average working hours of those working full-time, doctors and lawyers reported longer normal hours than the other selected professions. It should be noted that doctors and lawyers commonly have the capacity to bill clients for most of their work hours; conversely, teachers have been found to work more unpaid overtime than most other occupations and also tend to discount their class preparation time.[11]

Table 1-2. Work schedules, Canada, 2004

Occupation	Part-time (%)[12]	Regular days (%)	Ave. F/T hrs*
Doctors & lawyers	8	72	50
Teachers	18	97	43
Nurses	17	26	40
Engineers	5	87	44
Computer programmers	6	78	41
Other professionals	17	72	43
Total non-professional labour force	13	68	45
Total N	5,671	4,838	4,776

Source: WALL 2004 Survey (N=5,800)
* Full-time hours includes those working over 30 hours/week

PROFESSIONAL OCCUPATIONS' CONTROL OF ENTRY

The literature on professional work has been most preoccupied with the question of forms of control over entry into work (Derber et al. 1990; Friedson 1984, 1994). More recently, scholars have argued that increasing diversity of settings for professional work (Leicht & Fennell 1997) and the formalization of social control especially through state regulation (Evetts 2002) require more complex conceptions of forms of professional control. An ideology of professionalism as dedicated service and autonomous decision-making now appeals to many occupational groups; but the reality of many professional occupations is likely to be both more complex and more constrained (Evetts 2003). In the current comparative analysis, we will first examine negotiating power in terms the conventional criteria for control over *entry*: requirements for advanced academic education; association membership and certification to practice by regulatory bodies. Then we will offer comparisons in terms of the two aspects of organizational power: personal autonomy and participation in organizational decision-making.

Control over Training for Professional Entry

The most powerful professions have historically used the requirement of a high level of formal academic education as a primary criterion for entry into the profession and as a basis for subsequent claims to a greater degree of authority in relation to both other aspiring professional occupations and state regulation. Derber et al. (1990) cite the importance of formal possession of specialized knowledge credentials as a key characteristic for the 'enclosure' of a profession, making access difficult for others in society. University training programs have been the most pertinent vehicles for providing codified professional knowledge and of testing potential entrants to verify they have obtained a basic grasp of the body of knowledge of the respective professional discipline.

Table 1-3. Advanced degrees required for professional occupations, Canada, 2004

Occupation	Post-bachelor professional/graduate degree attained (%)
Doctors/lawyers	80
Engineers	33
Teachers	32
Computer programmers	15
Nurses	9
Other professionals	28
Total non-professional labour force	8

Source: WALL 2004 Survey (*N*=5,725)

Table 1-3 shows that doctors and lawyers have been far more successful than the other selected professional occupations in requiring a post-bachelor level professional or graduate university degree in their field as a basis for practices; eighty per cent have such degrees and most of the remainder are in the process of obtaining them. About a third of both engineers and teachers have such degrees but majorities in both fields are practicing their occupations with lesser formal qualifications, typically a bachelor-level university degree. (As we shall see in Chapter 2, most teachers have further specialized training but this is not recognized by completion of a further degree.) Only 15 per cent of computer programmers now have post-bachelor level degrees, but the majority of those practicing this occupation now have bachelor-level university degrees. Only ten per cent of nurses have post-bachelor university degrees; while bachelor-level degrees have become a requirement recently along with credential upgrading for older nurses, older nurses still rely on specialized practical training outside universities. Many aspiring professional occupations have imposed more stringent credentialing standards as a means of making entry qualifications more difficult and also to elevate public perceptions of the "legitimacy" and "worth" of the profession (Wynd 2003). But only doctors and lawyers, along with a few other long-established occupational groups such as architects, dentists and veterinarians, have been able to insist on post-bachelor professional or graduate degrees to qualify for entry.

Table 1-4. Membership in union or professional association, Canada, 2004

Occupation	Union member (%)	Professional association member* (%)	Professional association or union member (%)
Doctors/Lawyers	15	85	87
Nurses	85	78	97
Engineers	13	53	59
Teachers	90	50	95
Computer Programmers	17	14	29
Other Professionals	34	37	59
Total Non-Professional Labour Force	26	20	42

Source: WALL 2004 Survey (N=5,775)
* Professional association membership only asked if respondent indicated not a union member

Association Membership

In order to implement control over entry, any occupational group needs the organizational capacity to do so. All respondents to the WALL national survey were first asked if they were members of a union. If they were not, they were asked if they were members of a professional association. As Table 4 summarizes, doctors and lawyers are distinctive in having very high professional association membership and very low union membership. Doctors and lawyers have little apparent need for unions since they are commonly regarded as independent professionals with the right to private self-regulation rather than as employees. Teachers and nurses are distinctive in having very high union membership as well as majority professional association membership for those who are not union members. Teachers' and nurses' nearly universally union membership strengthens bargaining demands in negotiations with the public institutions that commonly employ both groups, while perhaps diminishing their claims to professional status in the eyes of those who regard unions as "unprofessional." Engineers have been the largest professional occupation in modern societies, with the skills most clearly needed for industrialization. But their dual origins in entrepreneurial–managerial work and skilled labour have long inhibited their ability to act as a cohesive group in support of their interests (see Collins 1979, pp. 159–170). Their very low union membership and modest professional membership proportions may be reflective of this continuing ambiguity. Computer programmers are distinctive in having very low proportions as members of either unions or professional associations, which may be reflective of their recency, diverse training programs and scattered workplaces.

Required Licensing

Self-regulation has been regarded as essential for a professional occupation to establish control over a field of practice. Regulatory colleges are able to set the requirements for entry into practice of the profession, as well as performance standards for continuing to practice. Regulatory bodies not only define the roles allowed to be performed by member professionals, but also have the ability to limit, control, and exclude others from entering into similar domains of practice. For example, as noted by Kelner et al. (2004) in their study of professionalization in Ontario's health care system, alternative health professions like chiropractors, midwives, naturopaths and homeopaths have faced very substantial challenges to legitimization of their skills by doctors. Recently, a number of these health-related occupations have been granted official status. But such status has come with tightly prescribed controls over the extent of their practice.

Table 1-5. Licensing for Professional Occupations, Canada, 2004

Occupation	License required to practice (%)
Nurses	93
Teachers	94
Doctors/Lawyers	89
Engineers	40
Computer Programmers	17
Other Professionals	48
Total Non-Professional Labour Force	37

Source: WALL 2004 Survey (N=5,775)

In Table 1-5, we see the extent of regulatory licensing among the selected professional occupations. Teachers, doctors, lawyers and nurses all report high levels of licensing at over 90 per cent, with most of their other practitioners in the process of obtaining official licensing. To continue to participate in these professional occupations, a person must obtain a license based upon completion of the criteria set out by the regulating college or government agency. Conversely, neither engineers nor computer programmers have yet been able to establish certification status as a normal criterion for practice by the majority of the members of their occupations. Recently graduated engineers must be supervised by licensed engineers for a minimum of four years prior to applying for certification and many continue to practice without achieving certification. Less than 40 per cent of engineers and less than 20 per cent of computer programmers were fully licensed practitioners of their fields in Canada in 2004.

Two points should be noted here. First, while nurses and teachers have similarly universal licensing requirements for practice as doctors and lawyers, this is not comparable to self-regulation. In Canada, only Ontario and British Columbia have professional regulatory colleges of teachers, for example (see Chapter 7). Secondly, licensing requirements to practice occupations are becoming quite widespread as many occupational groups are increasingly relying on credentials as primary entry criteria (e.g., real estate salespeople).[13] As we shall see, the credential society may be upon us but credentials and licences *per se* are no guarantee of greater control within the workplace for professional occupations.

PROFESSIONALIZATION AND WORKPLACE POWER

So what have been the actual general trends in the occupational composition of the labour force and in the workplace power exercised by its members? The professionalization thesis predicts that professional occupations are increasing significantly as a proportion of the labour force and that their workplace power is increasing accordingly. By contrast, the deprofessionalization thesis suggests that those in professional occupations are experiencing diminishing workplace power. Data from the 1983 CCS survey and the 2004 WALL survey offer some relevant estimates.

Table 1-6 summarizes the basic changes in professional-non-professional occupational composition over the 1983–2004 period. Consistent with the professionalization thesis, the proportion of professional occupations in the employed labour force increased slightly from about 17 per cent to 20 per cent. This marginal change is consistent with other analyses based on census data (Lavoie & Roy 2003; Bartel & Beckstead 1998). However, some occupational analyses distinguish between professionals and semi-professionals (see Pineo, Porter & McRoberts 1977). Undisputed professional occupations are established occupations that meet most of the above criteria for control of entry, including most of our selected professions as well as others such as architects, dentists and accountants. Semi-professional occupations include many that require training in advanced academic programs and are in the process of building associational strength to gain control of licensing requirements for practicing the occupation. In addition to computer programmers, prominent examples include early childhood educators, college instructors and medical technologists. According to the 1983 and 2004 national surveys, professional occupations made up about nine per cent of the employed labour forces in 1983 and eight per cent in 2004; semi-professionals increased from about seven per cent to 12 per cent during this period. The increasing numbers of semi-professionals might be considered a sign of increasing professionalization of the general labour force. But, as noted previously, there is considerable dispute over the categorization of these newer occupations as 'professional.'

Table 1-6. Professional/Non-Professional Occupational Composition of the Employed Canadian Labour Force, 1983–2004

Year	1983 %	2004 %
Professionals	17	20
Other Labour Force	83	80

Source: Canadian Facts Survey 1983 (*N*=1,759); WALL 2004 Survey (*N*=5,800)

In any case, the second pertinent question in this regard is whether these increasing numbers of professional and professionalizing occupations are actually increasing their degree of workplace power. As discussed earlier, power within the workplace can be estimated in terms of the extent to which people have the *opportunity to design their own work as well as the extent of participation in organizational decision-making* (i.e., making organizational decisions on such matters as the types of products or services delivered, employee hiring and firing, budgets, workload, and change in procedure).

In terms of control of design of their own work, Table 1-7 shows that professional occupations as a whole appear to have lost some of their relative autonomy during this period. In 1983, 85 per cent said they designed their own work either all or most of the time. In 2004, 71 per cent said so. In contrast, the rest of the employed labour force generally increased its extent of stated participation in designing their own work, from 39 per cent to 57 per cent.

Table 1-7. Design work by professionals and other occupations, Canada, 1983–2004

Design work	All or most of the time (%)	
Year	1983	2004
Professionals	83	70
Other Labour Force	40	57

Source: Canadian Facts Survey 1983 (*N*=1,484); WALL 2004 Survey (*N*=5,690)

In terms of organizational decision-making, as Table 1-8 summarizes, professional occupations generally were no more likely to report having organizational decision-making authority in 2004 (47 per cent) than in 1983 (50 per cent). However, the rest of the labour force generally increased its stated participation in decision-making from a quarter to about the same level as professionals (45 per cent). At the same time as professional occupations appeared to be becoming more prevalent, there appears to be greater general participation among other occupational groups in decision-making and *relatively* less organizational authority granted to professionals in general.

Table 1-8. Organizational decision-making power by professionals and other occupations, Canada, 1983–2004

Make decisions	On own or as part of group (%)	
Year	1983	2004
Professionals	50	47
Other Labour Force	26	45

Source: Canadian Facts Survey 1983 (N=1759); WALL 2004 Survey (N=5,505)

The general findings from these national surveys of respondents' subjective views of their extent of workplace power suggest that those in professional occupations have not increased their sense of power within the workplace during the past generation and may be experiencing some relative loss of control over opportunities to design their own work. Conversely, the remainder of the labour force may be experiencing a significant increase in their sense of workplace power. In other words, *the increasing proportion of professional occupations may be experiencing deprofessionalization in terms of workplace power.*

The extent of workplace power expressed by those in the selected professional occupations in 2004 is shown in Table 1-9.[14] In terms of opportunities to design their work, *teachers express a greater sense of discretionary control than any of the other professional occupations*. Teachers arguably are granted a relatively high degree of autonomy within their classrooms to deal with a complex array of issues, from curriculum delivery to student counselling, beyond the direct scrutiny of supervisory personnel. But smaller majorities in most other professional occupations, as well as in the labour force in general, said that they have opportunities to design their work most of the time. The finding that a sense of autonomy in designing one's own work is shared by majorities in all occupational groups suggests that an ideology of discretionary control has become widespread in the labour force.

In terms of organizational decision-making power, small majorities of doctors and lawyers as well as engineers indicated a significant role, compared with only minorities of teachers and the other selected professional occupations. The expressed differences between professional occupations and between professionals and the rest of the labour force in terms of decision-making roles are quite small, which may suggest that a modest degree of delegation of organizational power is becoming more widespread in the labour force and now does not distinguish very clearly between professionals and other occupations. In any event, these differences do not correspond very closely with differences in control of entry between these professional occupations. It is notable that, in both discretionary control in their jobs and decision-making roles, nurses express the lowest sense of organizational power. Most pertinently, teachers express the greatest discrepancy between personal autonomy and organizational decision-making power: the highest sense of design control of their own jobs but much less organizational decision-making power.

Table 1-9. Specific professional occupations by workplace power variables, Canada, 2004

Occupation	Make organizational decisions by self or as part of a group (%)	Design own work all or most of time (%)	Difference between columns 1 & 2
Doctors & lawyers	61	74	13
Engineers	57	72	15
Computer programmers	42	66	24
Teachers	42	89	47
Nurses	35	51	16
Other professionals	50	73	23
Total labour force	46	60	14
Total N	5,548	5,756	N/A

Source: WALL 2004 Survey (N=5,725)

In summary, the findings from these national surveys confirm the prediction that a (very slowly) growing proportion of occupations are assuming features of professional status, most notably in terms of some of the basic criteria for control of entry. But the variations among specific professional occupations in these terms remain large. Moreover, professionalization in these terms has not lead to an increasing sense of power *within* the workplace for professional occupations generally; rather, the remainder of the labour force has gained a greater sense of power while sense of power among professionals generally has remained similar to the level it was a generation ago. Other bases of workplace power are presumably involved. A class analysis of professional occupations may be a useful way to clarify the apparent contradiction between occupational professionalization and workplace deprofessionalization tendencies. The following class analysis of the general labour force is intended to provide a context for the later more specific class analysis of professional occupations, including teachers.

CLASS ANALYSIS OF THE GENERAL LABOUR FORCE

The purported death of classes based in workplace relations in advanced industrial societies has been heralded for generations. The decline of manufacturing employment with large concentrations of industrial workers and their labour unions, and the expansion of a diverse array service sector jobs, have inspired various arguments that the production process itself is extremely unlikely to generate class groupings with any social force, because of very diverse employment conditions, high occupational mobility and new, experience-diversifying technologies (e.g., Kingston 2000, p. 227). In contrast, we argue that classes stemming from relations between capitalist owners and hired employees are continually created and modified, and that we need to understand these underlying class relations in order to make sense of the *differential* powers of professional occupations, for example.

The basic class division in market economies proposed by Marx (1867) was between the owners of means of production and those who offer their labour to make a living. This division was qualified by his recognition of the existence of a shifting array of middle classes, including self-employed craftsmen and farmers, and the emergence of foremen and managers as well as those excluded from employment. Since then, scholars have identified a growing complexity of the structure of occupations and power. But Weber's (1928) later occupational class scheme was grounded in a similar tripartite distinction between the "market capacities" of those who owned property, those who possessed specialized skills, and those who possessed only their own capacity to labour, which was implicitly manual. More recent employment class models have often been derived from Marx, Weber or both. In the current analysis, we begin with a conceptual framework that examines the distribution of power in advanced market economies in terms of an underlying employment class structure that, similar to Marx and Weber, identifies positions based on ownership of property, other positions based on the provision of paid labour to produce goods and services, and middle classes in positions with formally delegated managerial authority or recognized specialized knowledge. Credential society approaches have argued that some professional and skilled occupational groups exercise greater power over external labour market exchange relations, thereby enabling job shaping possibilities and job-related learning activities (Collins 1979). But they have not explicitly recognized employment class differences among professional occupations.

The conceptual model of general employment class positions used to begin the research in this book is grounded in these ownership, delegated managerial authority and specialized knowledge distinctions.[15] Eight main employment-based class groupings are distinguished: *large employers, small employers, the self-employed, managers, supervisors, professional employees, service workers, and industrial workers*. Among owners, large employers include owners of substantial capital and corporate executives who oversee investment in companies and corporations with multi-million dollar assets and many employees. Small employers, typically family firms or partnerships, tend to have exclusive ownership, small numbers of employees and continue to play active co-ordinating roles in the labour process of their firms. The self-employed remain in control of their small commodity enterprises but are primarily reliant on their own labour.

At the other end of the class hierarchy are those workers without substantial ownership claims and devoid of official supervisory authority or recognized rights to exercise specialized knowledge. This includes industrial workers who produce, distribute or repair material goods. It also includes service workers who provide a widening array of sales, business, social and other services, similarly without recognized supervisory authority or task autonomy. Between employers and those workers at the lowest level of an organizational authority structure, other employees tend to have mixed functions. Managers are delegated by owners to control the overall labour process at the point of production to ensure profitability but may also contribute their labour to co-ordinate this process. Supervisors are under the authority of managers to control adherence to production standards by industrial and/or service workers but may also collaborate directly with these workers in aspects of this work. Professional employees have task autonomy based on their recognized specialized knowledge to design production processes for themselves and others and to execute their own work with a high level of discretion, and are sometimes subordinated to employer prerogatives. Furthermore, in advanced capitalist economies, the state has become a major employer and most state employees' power is not negotiated with or delegated directly from owners of capital. Rather, their power relations are with elected representatives and upper managerial civil servants who are supposed to act on behalf of the needs of all citizens, including the reproduction of capital and the democratic demands of other citizens. Teachers, it should be noted, are now largely state employees.

As noted earlier, these general employment class positions based on relations of ownership, managerial authority and recognized specialized knowledge are distinct from specific occupational classifications; but they obviously overlap with them. Those with the professional occupation designation of doctor, for example, could be small employers, self-employed, managers or "semi-autonomous employees" (see Wright 1980).[16] If these general class divisions are not considered, employment class effects are likely to confound more specific analyses of workplace power among professional occupations as well as others.

One of the clearest illustrations of the structural effects of differential employment class powers on job definitions and designs is the almost total absence of analytical attention to assessment of the capacities of business owners to perform their jobs.[17] Business owners generally have the managerial prerogative to impose competency assessments on subordinate employees, without any reciprocal privilege. Beneath the level of ownership, the less distinguishable managerial authority one holds, the more prone one tends to be to the competency assessments of those above. The assessments that owners make of hired managers are rarely known to lower level employees. Professional employees who are recognized as attaining specialized knowledge in established fields at least remain likely to have more autonomy over performance of their designated job tasks than industrial and service workers. (The extent to which teachers who are professional employees are widely recognized as having specialized knowledge to guide children will be addressed later in the book.)

Estimates of the general magnitude of these employment classes are provided by Table 1-10, which summarizes composition and changes over the past generation in Canada. Between 1983 and 2004, large and small employers grew slightly to make up around five per cent of the labour force while the self-employed increased to about 15 per cent. Managers doubled to over ten per cent of the labour force. Professional employees increased by half to make up over 15 per cent of the labour force. Conversely, the proportions of industrial and service workers declined substantially from being the majority (42+23=65 per cent) to a minority (27+19=46 per cent) of the entire employed labour force. It should be stressed here that classes are relational phenomena rather than static categories. In particular, many professional employees in occupations currently designated as "semi-professional" are engaged in contests with employers and government agencies to attain full professional status or at least to resist further deprofessionalization. In terms of the argument for general professionalization of the labour force, the evidence indicates that professional employees in general increased from about 11 per cent to 16 per cent between 1983 and 2004. The trend is in the posited direction but they still made up a small proportion of the labour force.

Table 1-10. Employment class distribution, active labour force, Canada, 1983–2004

Employment class	1983 (%)	2004 (%)
Large employers	<1	1
Small employers	4	6
Self-employed	11	15
Managers	5	11
Supervisors	4	5
Professional Employees	11	16
Service workers	42	27
Industrial workers	23	19
Total	100	100
N	1,758	5,437

Sources: Canadian Facts Survey 1983; WALL Survey 2004. See Livingstone and Scholtz 2010

CLASS ANALYSIS OF PROFESSIONAL OCCUPATIONS

A shortcoming of prior analyses of professional occupations and workplace power is that they tend to treat professional occupations as homogeneous groups and for the most part ignore employment class positions. Professionals who own either large or small enterprises possess ultimate control over both their own work and the goals of the organization. Self-employed professionals without employees have full control of their own work, although they may now contract themselves to larger enterprises at times. Professional managers, without the privilege of ownership, lack the power of complete control over the direction of the organization but do possess a relatively high level of decision-making control within the organization compared with professional employees. Professional employees' relatively high level of specialized knowledge to perform the job makes them more difficult to replace than most other non-managerial employees. But they remain similarly vulnerable as sellers of labour without control over the final product/service.

Table 1-11 estimates the distribution of professional occupations among employer, self-employed, managerial and professional employee classes in 1983 and 2004. The small sample size in 1983 permits only limited trend inferences. While other census-based analyses confirm that professional occupations overall have increased somewhat as a proportion of the total employed labour force (see Lavoie & Roy 2003; Bartel & Beckstead 1998), our findings suggest that the distribution of professional occupations across employment classes may also have altered somewhat.

As noted previously, professional employees increased (from 11 to 16 per cent of the total labour force). But Table 1-11 suggests that professional employees may have declined as a proportion of all professional occupations (from 62 to 52 per cent of all professionals), while the proportion of self-employed professional occupations has increased (from seven to 15 per cent). There may have been some increase in the general proportions of the self-employed class who are professionals (to 21 per cent from 12 per cent) and some decline in the proportion of managers who are professionals (from 40 per cent to 30 per cent). But the main conclusion to be drawn from this class analysis is that there is *no definitive trend* in the professionalization or deprofessionalization of the class structure. The overall proportion of more dependent professional employees in the labour force overall has increased at the same time as the proportions of more independent self-employed among professional occupations themselves has also increased.

Table 1-11. Employment class by percentage with professional occupations, employed labour force, Canada, 1983–2004

Employment Class	1983 % of professionals within this employment class	2004 % of professionals within this employment class	1983 % of all professional occupations	2004 % of all professional occupations
Large/small employers	15	19	5	6
Self-employed	12	21	7	15
Managers	40	30	26	27
Professional employees	17	20	62	52
Total %	100	100	100	100
N	1,758	5,397	309	1,085

Sources: Canadian Facts Survey 1983; WALL Survey 2004

The proportions of the self-employed class, and perhaps of the employer classes, with claims to specialized professional knowledge grew. Business owners may have thereby enhanced their managerial prerogatives and the self-employed became somewhat more likely to base their entrepreneurial claims on specialized knowledge. However, the rapidly growing general ranks of managers may not have increased their relative capacity to co-ordinate the work of professional employees by having similar specialized knowledge claims. Conversely, those who remained professional employees became increasingly vulnerable to overarching direct control or influence by employers, self-employed consultants and managers who also had acquired claims to the same specialized knowledge. *There are virtually as many professionals now in employer, self-employed and managerial classes as there are professional employees.* These class differences surely should be considered when analysing the workplace power of those in specific professional occupations.

PROFESSIONAL CLASSES AND WORKPLACE POWER

The current general differences between professional employers, self-employed professionals, professional managers and professional employees in terms of self-reported workplace power are summarized in Tables 1-12 and 1-13. Predictably, the differences in organizational decision-making control are quite pronounced. As Table 1-12 summarizes, virtually all professional employers have substantial decision-making control, unless they choose to delegate it to managers. Most self-employed professionals have decision-making control alone or with partners of their self-account businesses, unless they are working as consultants for others. About two-thirds of professional managers make significant organizational decisions, usually as members of a group. In clear contrast, most professional employees report no direct decision-making role and those that do have one are most likely to be part of a consultative group. Professional employees clearly have significantly less organizational decision-making power than employers, self-employed and managers, whether the latter are professionals or not.

While the smaller sample size for 1983 again limits detailed trend inferences, it appears that professional managers may have become more involved in organizational decisions over this period (from 54 per cent to 64 per cent) while professional employees' involvement may have declined somewhat (from 45 per cent to 32 per cent). As Table 1-12 suggests, professional employees by 2004 were little more likely than service and industrial workers to perceive themselves as having a meaningful organizational decision-making role.

Table 1-12. Organizational decision-making power by professional class, Canada, 2004

Professional class	Make decisions (yourself) or as member of group (%)	No direct decision making role (%)	Total (N)
Professional employers	(39) 84	17*	65
Self-employed professionals	(43) 61	39**	152
Professional managers	(14) 64	36	278
Professional employees	(8) 32	69	553
All professionals	(16) 47	53	1,048
Other non-managerial employees	(8) 21	79	1,771

Source: WALL 2004 Survey (N=5,800)
* Delegated to managers
** Consultants for other businesses

Opportunities to design one's own work also differ by professional class position but not in such a pronounced way as organizational decision-making. As Table 1-13 shows, professional employers almost all design their own work all or most of the time. Three-quarters of self-employed professionals and professional managers also design their work most of the time. Professional employees feel they are somewhat less able to design their work, but two-thirds say they do so most of the time. It should be recalled that, as per Table 1-9, about 60 per cent of all workers now say they can design their work most of the time. In a labour force in which a majority of workers now report they design their work most of the time and very few indicate no opportunities to design their work, professional employees are not distinct from most other workers in this regard.

Table 1-13. Design own work by professional class, Canada, 2004

Professional class	Most or all of the time (%)	Sometimes (%)	Never (%)	Total (N)
Professional employers	90	10	0	68
Self-employed professionals	75	22	4	167
Professional managers	75	24	1	295
Professional employees	64	33	4	563
All professional occupations	70	27	3	1,093

Source: WALL 2004 Survey (*N*=5,800)

In terms of extent of control over design of their work, limited comparison with the smaller 1983 survey suggests that professional employees generally may have experienced some decline in immediate control over design of their daily tasks. There is some indication that professional owners, self-employed professionals and professional managers have retained or increased their control.

Overall, there is support here for the deprofessionalization thesis in terms of professional employees experiencing an erosion of their organizational decision-making power and work design control. Conversely, professional employers, self-employed professionals and professional managers appear to be gaining greater workplace control over professional employees and retaining control over the remainder of the non-managerial labour force. In short, we see indications of increasing workplace power for professionals with ownership prerogatives as well as for those professionals with official managerial functions, but decreasing workplace power for professional employees.

CLASS ANALYSIS OF SPECIFIC PROFESSIONAL OCCUPATIONS

The professional occupations selected for this analysis differ widely in the extent to which they have ownership of the organizations in which they work. As Table 1-14 shows, about two-thirds of doctors and lawyers have ownership status, most operating either as small employers or self-employed. None of the other professional occupations in the study have more than 20 per cent with ownership status; most of these are self-employed without employees. Only among engineers are there even significant numbers of small employers (nine per cent), while the other professional occupations, including teachers, report two per cent or less of respondents holding employer status. The fact that most doctors and lawyers own their own firms or practices gives their professions significantly more economic power than most other professional occupations.

Table 1-14. Professional occupations and class locations, Canada, 2004

Professional class locations	Doctors & lawyers (%)	Engineers (%)	Computer Programmers (%)	Nurses (%)	Teachers (%)	Other professionals (%)
Professional employer	41	9	2	1	1	5
Self-employed professional	23	8	16	3	3	19
Professional manager	18	43	28	31	16	33
Professional employee	18	40	54	65	81	43
Total	62	97	127	95	124	700

Source: WALL 2004 Survey (*N*=5,800)

All of these professional occupations contain significant numbers of professional managers to co-ordinate and control the work of both professional employees and other non-managerial employees. Engineers are just as likely to be managers (43 per cent) as employees (40 per cent), while the percentages for other professions with managerial positions are lower (between about 16 and 31 per cent). Computer programmers are more likely than nurses or teachers to be self-employed (16 per cent) which probably reflects the relative openness of entry to this new field. But a small majority of programmers (54 per cent) are professional employees.

Teachers and nurses are distinctive in this comparison in remaining mostly professional employees. Most are employed by public sector organizations without any prospect for ownership of their practices. Over 80 per cent of teachers and about two-thirds of nurses are professional employees. Nurses may be more likely to assume managerial positions (31 per cent) but often under the authority of doctors. In this respect, teachers and nurses are not much different in employment class terms than industrial and service workers – except for their specialized knowledge claims. Teachers' specialized knowledge claims will be examined in more detail in later chapters.

Simply viewing professional occupations in terms of general claims to authority in their fields of knowledge misses the underlying class dimensions of ownership control and managerial authority or conflates them with claims to specialized knowledge. The extent to which respective professional groups succeed in achieving self-regulatory authority over a field of professional knowledge continues to be intimately related to gaining legal ownership. Doctors and lawyers ability to form private practices and partnerships continues to enable the enclosure of their professions, codification of their knowledge, promotion of their importance to the general public and self-regulation of their fields. Engineers' mixed employment class composition, with a few business owners but most evenly split between managerial and non-managerial class positions, continues to inhibit both association development and claims for professional self-regulation. Teachers and nurses now tend to be well organized in occupational groups but, given their dominant class position as employees, there is continuing priority within these groups to act as employees' unions bargaining with their employers rather than establishing self-regulating professional field claims with the general public. Computer programmers have highly topical claims to specialized technical knowledge that enable some to establish their own small businesses. But they currently have little associational strength to achieve self-regulation and wider legal ownership of their services. In sum, the class position of professional occupations is fundamental to success of their claims for full professional status. The dominant class position of teachers and nurses as employees continues to undermine such claims.

The fact that minorities of teachers and nurses indicate any role in organizational decision-making (see Table 1-9) is clearly related to their prevalent class position as professional employees. However, as Table 1-9 also summarized, being able to put one's own ideas into practice is not closely related to ownership or managerial position. Again, teachers report the *highest* level of design discretion among all these professions for putting their own ideas into practice. Behind classroom doors, teachers have to make continual decisions about a very complex array of tasks. Teachers engage in activities that range from teaching and assessing to counselling and coaching. Many of the decisions rest solely with teachers and need to be made on the spot with little time for consultation or reflection. In this respect, there is considerable discretionary control in the daily activities of teachers. But, as noted previously, the relatively great autonomy of teachers over classroom space contrasts markedly with their lack of organizational decision-making power. As argued by Reid (2003), the apparent control that teachers have over their immediate space must be tempered by the clear lack of control over their curriculum, classroom structure/size, course loads, among other organizational decisions that have considerable influence over their daily work lives. The following quote from a teacher expresses a common concern over work intensification and the lack of control over organizational decision-making and its impact on everyday job processes:

[There is] seemingly never-ending struggle to provide better education with less resources, or with increasingly fewer resources. We are discovering and learning more and more things about what good teaching practice and good education mean, but simultaneously we are provided less and less money and resources towards this. What ends up happening is that those of us teaching are expected to do a lot more. It's becoming more and more clear what good

education looks like… the quality of education and how things can get better. At the same time, governments are starving public education. Classroom and curriculum that is coming out is so convoluted. And yet, we neither have the time nor the training to try to digest it. Boy, I don't know where else to go.
(EJRM, Moishe, 2005)

At least among teachers, who are very predominantly professional employees, the deprofessionalization thesis is supported by substantial empirical evidence.

CONCLUDING REMARKS

Prior studies of professionals' status and power have tended to focus on conventional criteria of control of entry into the specific occupation: advanced academic education, association membership and licensing requirements. Proponents of the growing influence of professionals as leaders in an emerging knowledge-based economy tend to assume that advance on these criteria will lead to fuller recognition of professional status. However, most of these studies tend to ignore the fact that we live in an advanced capitalist society in which economic class relations still have a major influence on what occurs in paid workplaces. Ownership of the means of production, whether by large corporations or small firms, still counts. The fact that doctors and lawyers (and a few others including dentists and architects) can command direct fees for their services, own their own business firms or practices and often employ others is hugely consequential for their status as fully developed professions. The superior professional power of doctors/lawyers is mediated by their self-regulating professional association membership (i.e., over 70 per cent exclusively association members and few employee-based union members) but grounded in the prevalence of proprietorial class positions (self-employed or employers). The struggle by increasingly more knowledgeable progressive popular forces for socialized provision of human services, notably medicare and public education but also legal services, led to increasing state funding and regulation of such services through most of the twentieth century. Conflict over socialized versus privatized provision continues, as well as conflict over control of the specialized knowledge contained in such services and the consequent professional status of their providers. Doctors and lawyers have also faced much more extensive oversight of their services (Krause 1996). But, with the negotiating power of their self-regulating associations, many continue to be paid their fees and retain prerogative over their use, as distinct from most other professionals who are paid salaries determined in negotiations with their employers and are more prone to challenges to their knowledge and status.

Even though many other professional occupations may also have specialized post-secondary education credential requirements as well as widespread association memberships and licensing, most others remain subordinated to either private employers or managers in public institutions. Engineers and computer programmers are typically hired experts in private firms and are empowered in their workplaces largely through high demand for their technical expertise. But their very limited ownership of their services coupled with lack of organizational strength and licensing regulation seriously limits their professional power. Teaching and nursing have few prospects for general ownership of their services, typically work in public institutions under control of bureaucratic state administrations, and are mainly professional employees in female-dominated fields, with even more limited prospects for full professional status, even if they become managers of those in their own field.

Professionalism certainly needs to be understood partly in terms of the degree of technical skill and unique knowledge to perform particular specialized work, as well as the conventional entry criteria. But the relationship of this specialized work to employment class positions rather than to specific occupations *per se* should be considered both in assessing the power the profession is able to exercise in the workplace and in understanding the limited success many occupations have had in asserting their claims to full professional status. At the same time, ownership of one's own work in itself is no guarantee of professional status. Consider the many highly trained visual artists whose works compete with unschooled amateurs in the private marketplace and who remain among the poorest paid of all occupations because of the lack of associational strength.

Teachers in particular have to exercise a high level of technical and social skills in their complex pedagogical work with often diverse groups of students. But they lack sufficient control over their occupation to convince much of the general public that they deserve full professional status. Teachers also contend with popular notions that others could teach much of their curricular content to children if they only had the time. Teachers are employees, not self-regulating except in a few jurisdictions where self-regulatory bodies have been created and remain highly subject to governmental intervention (see Chapter 7). Teachers do hold distinctive control within their own classrooms in relation to their students. But such control is continually in jeopardy because of organizational decisions made outside the influence of classroom teachers.[18] Educational practices such as standardized curricula, testing and reporting, bigger classroom sizes, and increased administrative duties, just to name a few, have an enormous impact upon the immediate workspace of teachers. If teachers' strong sense of discretionary control within the classroom is to retain much substance, they may need to exercise greater influence over the organizational decisions made outside these walls. Otherwise, teachers, like many other professional (and semi-professional) employees are in danger of losing more control over their *immediate* workspaces.

Further comparative studies are surely needed. However, it should now be appreciated that both the professionalization and deprofessionalization theses are serious simplifications with regard to the workplace power of current professional occupations. The evidence presented here suggests that professional occupations are gradually increasing as a proportion of the labour force. But it also suggests that increasing class polarization of professionals is occurring: on one hand, professional employers and self-employed professionals are gaining relatively greater workplace power; on the other hand, professional employees are losing workplace control and facing continuing challenges to asserting wider claims to professional status. Teachers are clearly on the losing side of this divide. Perhaps

C. Wright Mills (1951, p. 129) was right when he observed that "School teachers … are the economic proletarians of the professions."

FAB ANTONELLI & D.W. LIVINGSTONE

2. TEACHERS' AND OTHER PROFESSIONALS' LEARNING PRACTICES

A Comparative Analysis

INTRODUCTION

Do we want to be blue collar or do we want to be professionals? ... If you are ... going to be a professional, then you have to take responsibility for professional learning ... even though there may be moments when you put on your blue collar and thump around, and start to want to refuse to do these things. I just am not sure that it should really be this or that. I think that you can do both, to some degree. But a lot of people will almost argue that they need to shut down their professionalism, their professional development because, you know, we're without a contract, we're not doing anything. So ... it's almost like being bipolar, I guess ... Learning with colleagues is really important, the biggest problem is that you are just going hell-bent for leather and sometimes you really don't have the chance to sit down and have that dialogue ... It's really tough to say when informal learning will come into play, but it does. The amount of informal learning a teacher uses is probably huge, probably huge! (Neil, Secondary School Teacher)[1]

The purpose of this chapter is to provide an extensive comparative analysis of professional learning. As Chapter 1 has documented, professionals depend greatly on formal education entry credentials for their legitimacy. Professionals are also widely assumed to engage in continual learning to upgrade their specialized knowledge and skills to remain current in complex and changing jobs. We posit that, since professional occupations remain highly dependent on recognition of specialized knowledge, continuing participation in further job-related *formal* education (usually called "professional development") is likely to be higher than in most other occupations. As noted in the Introduction, workplace learning can be seen as occurring on an *informal-formal continuum*, with much of it taking place informally (see Betcherman 1998: Livingstone 2009). All workers are likely to require continuing learning in relation to changing job conditions, so we expect that the incidence of job-related *informal* learning will be quite extensive among all occupations. Most of the attention in this chapter will be devoted to comparing formal provision of professional development for teachers and other specific professional occupations and by class positions of professionals.

We will also examine relations between professionals' (negotiating and organizational) power and variations in further job-related formal professional

R. Clark et al. (eds.), Teacher Learning and Power in the Knowledge Society, 45–66.
© *2012 Sense Publishers. All rights reserved.*

development. As noted in the Introduction to the book, our general theoretical perspective posits that, other things being equal, greater power is associated with more opportunity for formal professional development. The threshold for professional occupations' participation in continuing formal education courses is now relatively high because continuing re-legitimation of specialized knowledge through re-certification is now widespread among most professions; in addition to the increased role of the state in standards regulation, the growing recognition of the role of formal knowledge in contemporary work has led to heightened certification requirements across the board (Evetts 2002). Professionals who are predominantly in proprietorial class positions (i.e., self-employed or employer) and in self-regulating associations should have managerial prerogative to take further formal education courses at their own discretion. Whereas, among professional employees, the greater negotiated bargaining power *with* their employers and the more delegated organizational decision-making power *from* their employers, the greater opportunity there is likely to be for participation in formal continuing professional development courses. For example, as Chapter 1 documents, teachers have high negotiating bargaining power through their unionization but typically tend to have low delegated organizational decision-making power from school boards and principals. Teachers are highly reliant upon their unions for negotiated power in the workplace and their professional development provisions. We expect that variations in delegated organizational power may also be associated with teachers' professional development provisions but in more secondary ways.

This chapter reviews the prior research literature on professional learning and then presents the findings from our national surveys of the workplace learning activities of doctors/lawyers, teachers, nurses, engineers and computer programmers, other professional occupations and the rest of the labour force as well as by class positions of professionals.

REVIEW OF LITERATURE

Prior empirical research on professional learning suffers from two basic limitations. First, many studies either conflate formal and informal learning or focus on one to the exclusion of the other. Secondly, learning practices are rarely considered in the context of working conditions, particularly power relations. In addition, previous studies have dealt primarily within individual professional occupations. Very few studies to date have explored comparisons in learning across professions (see Cheetham & Chivers 2001). Two studies of note (Gear et al. 1994; Eraut 1997) examined professional learning across professions, but did not delve into the potential links between workplace conditions *per se* and forms of workplace learning. As well, no prior studies have explicitly explored the different class positions of professional occupations in relation to learning.

Cheetham and Chivers' (2001) extensive comparative study helps inform further research in terms of the *informal* learning practices of a sample of professional occupations. Much of Cheetham and Chivers' study was an exploration of patterns of informal learning (method of delivery and content of subject material) across 20 professional groups. Although not explicitly comparing professional occupations in terms of organizational structures, Cheetham and Chivers (2001) hint at differences in workplace environments as a major influence on the ways professionals learn and their ability to implement what they have learned into their everyday work practices. But the most general findings of their study stressed commonalities across the selected professional groups in terms of their informal learning practices. What surfaced as a very common thread among the professional groups was their ability to learn the unique and site-specific practices essential for their work among colleagues as job-embedded learning (Cheetham & Chivers 2001). More specifically, the authors found that the professional groups they studied learned most effectively through a combination of experiential and interactionist workplace practices. Interviewees would refer to being more "rounded professionals" after they had experienced and struggled through the early part of their career and dealt with difficult clients (or "diverse classrooms" in the case for teachers), or situations that made them apply past knowledge and experiences quickly and creatively. Not surprisingly, those respondents who were better able to manage their daily work practices in the early years of their professional careers were also in a better position to apply prior learning to their workplace practices. Participants in this study generally reported that colleagues were the best source of information for navigating through the profession and daily work routines. Some differences were found among professional occupations in the ways they took up learning as well as preferred methods for job training. For example, professionals in church and dentistry occupations differed in the worth they placed on "pre-entry experience," with the clergy valuing lived experience as an important element of work within the profession. Dentists felt that previous lived experience was of little importance to their work and instead the technical aspects of performing their work took precedence.

But studies focused on informal learning practices of professionals have been relatively rare compared to studies of formal professional development. In addition to Cheetham and Chivers (2001), and the earlier smaller comparative studies of Gear et al. (1994) and Eraut (1997), most prior studies of professionals' informal learning have focused on individual professions (e.g., Lave & Wenger 1991; Gopee 2002; Billet 2003). Most commonly, these studies have examined the practice of collegial learning, citing the benefits of support mechanisms within organizations – including but not limited to mentoring, job shadowing, and learning groups or communities. These support networks in some cases provided greater opportunities for learning than did more formal learning programs. Both Cheetham and Chivers' (2001) study as well as some others have discussed the importance of networking within formal PD sessions. Group PD sessions provide a space for professionals to congregate and compare notes on the way things are done in their specific situations. For teachers, it seems that this is a highly valued component of PD sessions. Because pedagogical practices are dependent upon specific and unique classroom scenarios – such as curriculum content and student needs – teachers often face disparate and varied classrooms that demand equally varied pedagogical practices.

Some of the most recent studies of teachers (e.g., Hoekstra et al. 2007) emphasize the importance of informal learning in the pedagogical practices of public school teachers. Working with a teacher population not involved in formal professional development programs, the authors were able to explore the "active learning" in which Dutch teachers participated, most notably at the classroom level. Specifically, the authors chose to examine the informal learning teachers undertook through the processes of their classroom teaching. Through self-directed and in some instances tacit learning, teachers were able to learn a great deal from the interactions with students, particularly as it relates to what works well in the classroom. This type of informal learning involves considerable experimentation and reflection to determine best practices for various settings and scenarios. For the teachers involved in this study, many learned through what did *not* work in the classroom, accordingly adjusting their practices to better suit the needs of students.

Both Maaranen et al. (2009) and McNally et al. (2008) view the importance of informal learning among new practicing teachers in shaping their pedagogical practices and stress its value over more formal avenues for learning. Maaranen et al. (2008) look at teacher candidates who were employed as classroom teachers prior to and during their time in teachers' college. The beginning teachers in this study noted the invaluable experience of classroom teaching (the informal, self-directed aspects of their learning), an experience helping to inform the formal learning that took place in their program. The self-reflective and collegial moments of learning experienced while working in their schools helped teacher candidates explore and uncover the nuanced and irregular aspects of teaching so critical for developing classroom practices. McNally et al. (2008) echo many of these sentiments of collegial learning, while adding an emotional learning and coping component to beginning teachers' experiences. They viewed the supportive elements of mentoring and collegial support as it pertains to the emotional elements (such as performance anxiety) related to the work. In this way, the self-reflective learning of pedagogical practices was, in part, understood through interactions with colleagues.

Jensen (2007) compares the general, mainly informal learning practices of four professions (teachers, nurses, accountants and computer engineers) and finds that learning is mediated through the practices of the organization and the profession as a whole. General findings indicate that professionals in the first six years of employment understand knowledge expansion to be essential for their career development, with members of all professions citing a need to keep "current" with knowledge, almost as an obligation to a self-perceived "professional standard." As well, Jensen finds the learning that took place across the professional groups was consistently tied back to practice. Effectively, Jensen is suggesting that professionals adhere to a professional ethos (a standard they think is associated with the profession). At the same time however, their "self-regulated learning" is mediated by the demands placed upon professionals by associations, organizations and the public to remain current in their understanding of professional expectations and practices. Knowledge on its own is not seen as relevant unless it can be tied to their everyday work practices. Tied to the idea of practicality, Jensen discovers that the participants from the four professions she studies often cite feeling unable to completely understand everything they would need to fully participate in their profession. Jensen notes that in Norway, where the study took place, professionals do not have rigid standards for knowledge attainment set by professional associations, resulting in a less restrictive environment for knowledge acquisition. The perceived limitless expanse of opportunities for knowledge attainment by professionals controls both their desire for learning and the approaches to obtain and implement new knowledge. Respondents in her study cite an inability to "know everything" and instead simply learn "enough to get by."

Overall, the increasing number of studies that have attended to informal learning among professionals have found it to be very extensive, highly reliant on work colleagues and not very different in basic patterns between professions. In these respects, research on informal professional learning merely replicates what has been known for some time in general research on workplace learning (see Betcherman 1998; Livingstone 2009).

In contrast to recent studies that have focused on expansive informal learning among professionals, most prior studies have stressed the drive for greater formal learning credentials. Freidman and Phillips (2004) argue that formal professional development programs are a way for professional associations to assure the public that its members are up to date with current knowledge and can be trusted. They also noted that some professionals have felt the bureaucratic process and accountability measures associated with formal professional development programs were, in fact, a threat to their autonomy. Rather than be in control of their knowledge base and relational workplace practices, professional development programs initiated by a governing body outside of the control of workers were viewed by some as simply another control mechanism. For example, Hodkinson and Hodkinson (2004) examined the differences between two teachers in England on the ways they took up learning in the workplace. The authors identified that teachers will perform individual learning as a response to external factors (e.g., curriculum change). Changes were perceived to originate out of the hands of teachers, leaving the teacher in a reactionary position to participate in PD. Although the authors were not implying that teachers regularly practice reactive learning, it is worth noting that teachers because of the lack of control over their organizational practices can sometimes be placed in coping positions regarding their professional development. The authors see formal PD in England as primarily regulating professionals, tying their learning to financial accountability, and utilizing arbitrary outputs to measure return on investment and generally acting as a mechanism for control of professionals, rather than an impetus for professional growth, general interest, and self-actualization (Hodkinson & Hodkinson 2005).

Expanding upon the idea of restricted agency, Tikkanen (2002) examined the learning of older IT workers and noted that, in their respondents' opinions, 'new learning' or reorganization of work may be a façade. Rather than feeling powerless in their learning, older IT workers and engineers in Tikkanen's (2002) study felt that many of the suggested workplace changes were simply a reorganization of old ideas. One experienced engineer, following the wishes of his clients, described his work as "organizing old bricks in new ways" (Tikkanen 2002, p. 92). As another engineer put it, "when you have done planning work for over 20 years, in every problem situation you can surely come up with ten different solutions" (p. 92). To an extent, the agential opportunities to put their own learning into practice were tempered by the wishes of the client and the organization.

Daley's (2001, 2002, 2005) comparative explorations of work and learning of nurses and other professions examined the integration of learning within professional practice in relation to organizational change and rationalization. Daley's studies compared the working arrangements of nurses, social workers, teachers and lawyers and related these differences to the ways they engaged in formal professional development. These studies found that engagement in formal PD activities and subsequent implementation of knowledge gained from PD varied considerably across occupational groups because of the unique workplace practices associated with each profession, notably *their job autonomy*. For example, lawyers indicated that the autonomous nature of their practice resulted in the structure of their firm having little influence over their use of knowledge. Nurses, on the other hand, described the structure of the hospital as a "hurdle" and indicated that to implement new learning in their practice they often had to circumvent organizational rules (Daley 2002, p. 85). Hart and Rotem (1995) also observed the irregularity of nurses' work scheduling – as documented in Chapter One – and found this led to particular difficulties for nurses in finding time for formal learning opportunities. These findings relate in several ways to teachers' experience, as we will document in later chapters. However, the power relations within organizations that may lead to different formal PD practices were not much explored in most of the prior research studies.

One common theme found in the literature on formal professional development was the obstacle of 'client satisfaction' as a structural element of work that limited the opportunities to bring what was learned into practice. 'Client satisfaction' could be loosely defined as the interactions professionals have with the people and or public they serve. Often professionals cited "working around" organizational rules or learning more than was expected because of a commitment to serving the needs of their clients (Daley 2001, 2002; Svensson, Ellstrom & Aberg 2004; Ryan 2003). Daley's (2002) study found that professional workers often saw their occupation as a calling. One nurse reported: "The idea of nursing as a career ... I guess that's what I really see in it for myself. This is my calling" (Daley 2002, p. 82). The perception by professionals that they could be doing a disservice to their profession was compounded by the fear that clients would be receiving an "inferior" level of care if they did not continually keep up to date with current practices. Similarly, teachers are often compelled to go that "extra mile" in order to bring effective pedagogical practices in classroom for student success. The tie of learning to client satisfaction seemed to both empower and limit these professionals. In one way, professionals expressed that the learning was serving a personal purpose, helping to fulfill a desire or calling; however, this commitment to clients also acted as a restrictive and controlling agent, prompting many professionals to give and extra effort despite already being stretched too far.

Many of the studies dealing with client satisfaction noted that professionals would complete the learning process of formal PD sessions by implementing what was learned with their clients to determine the merit and worth of the new information/practice. In a way, the client acted as a check. As Daley (2001, p. 50) notes: "Thus, a major component of how knowledge becomes meaningful in professional practice is determined by how the professionals' perspectives change through client interactions. In this study, it was evident that professionals did change how they viewed their practice following significant client interactions." However, as noted in Chapter One, client satisfaction likely has been a greater preoccupation for professionals who are proprietors and whose organizations' success is dependent on positive client response, as distinct from professional employees, who may express greater concern with employer-imposed conditions they must "workaround" to serve clients adequately.

While some of these prior studies allude to issues of organizational control or agency and learning, the relationship between professionals' power and learning practices has rarely been articulated. Marks and Seashore Louis (1999) have posited a link between teacher empowerment and more effective learning. With greater freedom and control by teachers in their everyday workplace practices, there is some evidence of more democratic and effective learning in the classroom. However, much of their study focused on institutional features of "organizational learning" as currently constituted in many private businesses and corporations, and overlooks the organizational power relations that can limit knowledge attainment and implementation. As a consequence, the authors advocate "stronger leadership," indicating that "organizational learning also requires strong and sometimes directive leadership in the articulation of organizational goals in ways that are meaningful and evocative for all participants" (Marks & Seashore Louis 1999, p. 714). This is a problematic recommendation since power is considered to derive from outside and above rather than from the classroom teacher, potentially jeopardizing the "democratic organization" so necessary for "democratic learning." As well, Marks and Seashore Louis, like most other research on formal PD, ignore the self-directed and informal learning practices that are increasingly recognized as integral for effective professional learning.

In sum, prior studies of professionals' continuing learning have found that professionals tend to be highly involved in continuing formal professional development courses and are similarly highly involved in informal collegial learning practices. Prior studies for the most part have paid little attention to differences in formal continuing education and PD between professional occupations, between professional classes, and between professionals and other workers. The few comparative studies of professions have stressed a widespread imperative for formal upgrading and recertification courses, as well as high motivation to confirm new knowledge through relations with colleagues and clients. But there has been little attention to differences in power among professional occupations that may affect their respective learning activities, not to mention the varied power dynamics between class positions of professional occupations (e.g., self-employed, employers, managers, and employees). Recent general studies of workers' intentional *informal* learning practices confirm that informal job-related learning practices are very widespread over the entire labour force, including both the most highly formally educated and the least formally educated workers (Livingstone 2009). Since display and affirmation of certifiable specialized knowledge is central to professionals' legitimacy, we expect that their participation rates in further education will be greater than the rest of the labour force. But we also assume that some differences in opportunities for *formal* professional development are associated with the differential power of specific professional occupations and the class positions of these professionals.

FINDINGS

Using the general 2004 WALL survey data,[2] we present comparative analyses of the formal and informal learning practices of those in different general employment class positions, in different professional class positions (i.e., professional employers, self-employed professionals, professional managers and professional employees), and in the specific professional occupations of doctors/lawyers, teachers, nurses, engineers and computer programmers. We will first look at patterns of participation in job-related informal learning. Then we will examine formal learning, primarily in terms of job-related further education courses and formal professional development.

Job-Related Informal Learning

As Table 2-1 shows, those in all employment classes exhibit very high levels of reported participation in job-related informal learning. Over 80 per cent in all classes indicated that they engaged in intentional informal learning activities related to their jobs within the past year. Estimates of average hours devoted to such learning activities per week are also very similar among different employment classes (Livingstone 2009). These figures only reflect the learning activities that people recognize on brief reflection and undoubtedly underestimate the full extent, or represent only the tip of the "iceberg," of workplace learning activities. The richness and complexity of informal workplace learning is now being documented in a widening array of studies (e.g., Malloch, Cairns, Evans & O'Connor 2010), including fuller analyses of the general findings from the WALL 2004 survey and related case studies of learning in diverse forms of paid and unpaid work (Livingstone 2010). Professional employees in general may be marginally more likely to report engaging in intentional informal job-related learning than some other employment classes. But the central point is that virtually all workers are continually engaged in informal learning practices in the course of experiential change in their work.

If we compare professional and non-professional members of relevant employment classes, as in Table 2-2, again we find few differences. Self-employed professionals may be slightly more likely to report engaging in intentional job-related informal learning activities than self-employed non-professionals (91 per cent versus 77 per cent), but once more the vast majority of all self-employed are so engaged.

Table 2-1. Participation in job-related informal learning by employment class, 2004

Employment class	Informal job-related learning (%)
Large Employers	87
Small Employers	88
Self-Employed	87
Managers	92
Professional Employees	92
Supervisors	88
Service Workers	84
Industrial Workers	84
Total Labour Force	87

Table 2-2. Participation in job-related informal learning by professionals and other occupations in general employment classes, 2004

Employment Class	Informal job-related learning (%) Professionals	Other Labour Force
Employer	84	85
Self-employed	91	77
Manager	89	84
Employee	80	71
Total labour force	84	78

Table 2-3. Participation in job-related informal learning participation by professional occupations, 2004

Occupation	Informal job related learning (%)
Doctors/lawyers	90
Engineers	89
Nurses	89
Teachers	89
Computer programmers	91
Other professionals	86
Other labour force	78
Total labour force	80

Finally, Table 2-3 compares teachers, other specific professional occupations, and the rest of the labour force in terms of participation in job-related informal learning. There is no discernible difference between the reported participation rates of any of the professional occupations. Those in professional occupations may be marginally more likely to report engaging in intentional informal job-related learning than the rest of the labour force as a whole. But the basic pattern is that the vast majority of workers in all occupations, as in all employment classes, engage in substantial informal job-related learning practices in their work.

The most common finding of the prior research on professionals' informal learning has been the pertinence of collegial learning. Table 2-4 provides survey estimates of the most important sources of knowledge for professionals and the rest of the labour force. The most striking finding is the small proportions who consider formal training programs to be their most important source of knowledge, around ten per cent or less in most occupations. Most rely heavily on informal learning, either in their own independent efforts or with co-workers. The majority of doctors and lawyers find their own independent learning efforts to be most important. Engineers and computer programmers are also more likely to rely on their own efforts than on co-workers. Teachers and nurses report almost an even split in respondents who report their most important learning is from co-workers and those who consider their own independent learning as most important. But professional employees generally and teachers and nurses in particular are much like most other employees in relying heavily on more experienced co-workers to develop their working knowledge.

Table 2-4. Professional occupations by most important source of knowledge, 2004 (%)

Most important source of knowledge	Co-workers	Independent efforts	Training program	Combinations
Doctors & lawyers	18	61	7	14
Teachers	36	39	5	20
Nurses	35	30	14	21
Engineers	31	47	9	13
Computer programmers	30	47	11	12
Other professionals	24	51	8	17
Total non-professional labour force	27	42	16	15

The relatively high reliance of doctors and lawyers on independent efforts may be related to working in small independent practices or firms, or their position as employers of others with prerogative over employees, as well as the presumption that their expert knowledge does not require assistance by subordinates. The finding that teachers and nurses report that co-workers are equally important to their own efforts in developing their working knowledge is consistent with the finding from a growing number of empirical studies of employees documenting the centrality of mentoring from other experienced employees in a wide array of workplaces (see Betcherman, Leckie & McMullen 1998; Center for Workforce Development 1998). As a new teacher in a public secondary school put it:

With on the job training, it was somewhat helpful [laughter] in terms of me doing my job ... I had a formal mentor last year ... There were other people on the job who were not my formal mentors who, you know, did a significant

amount of mentoring for me and helped me in my job. It can be quite helpful.
(Goranna, secondary school teacher)[3]

We suggest that the more subordinated that professional or other workers are in their work organizations, the more likely they are to rely on other experienced subordinate employees or those with greater managerial authority to learn their jobs, and the more challenging it may be to integrate their formal and informal learning practices. We can further suggest that collegiality among fully developed professions like doctors and lawyers who also own their practices may focus on various matters of self-regulation such as fee structures, while professionals who remain employees may be preoccupied with more clearly identifiable learning tasks such as helping each other to cope with changing working conditions mandated by their employers.

Table 2-5. Professional class by informal learning topics, 2004 (% participating)

Informal learning topics	Professional employers	Self-employed professionals	Professional managers	Professional employees
New job tasks	68	73	74	64
Computers	70	66	72	64
New equipment	64	58	61	56
Organizational or managerial skills	52	46	60	39
Budgeting or financial Management	48	42	42	21
Teamwork, problem solving	52	55	66	68
Work conditions & workers' rights	40	27	42	41
Politics in the workplace	43	23	40	39
Language & literacy	20	33	26	32
Health & safety	39	35	64	50

Particular occupations and employment classes will obviously vary in the pertinence of specific topical knowledge required to meet changing job demands. When we examine the actual *content* of job-related informal learning, differences do emerge depending upon professional class. Table 2-5 shows that some learning topics like 'learning new job tasks' or 'learning about computers' have similar participation rates among professionals regardless of their class position. However, professional owners and managers participate at higher rates in informal learning topics that deal with organizational/managerial and budgetary skills. Self-employed professionals are less likely to be interested in learning about workers' rights or politics of the workplace. Managers and employees participate at higher rates in learning topics that deal with workers' rights and health and safety in the workplace. Professional managers consistently report similar or greater participation in all work-related informal categories compared with owners and employees. It appears that managers, because of their mediatory role within workplace relations, must develop their knowledge in a relatively wide array of workplace learning topics.

As for specific professional occupations, it is to be expected that they devote more time in informal learning that relates to their specific types of work. As Table 2-6 shows, computer programmers report very high levels of learning informally about computers. Teachers report very high levels of informal learning on language and literacy issues, also hardly surprising considering the amount of their work time teachers devote to teaching language and literacy skills to students. Nurses, who frequently deal with potentially hazardous work situations, cite health and safety as their most prevalent work-related informal learning topic. Conversely, nurses and teachers report the lowest levels of participation in 'budgeting or financial management,' a consequence of their almost exclusive position as employees. Doctors and lawyers report relatively low levels of participation in 'teamwork and problem solving' learning. Again, this may be attributed to presumptions of superior expert knowledge and managerial prerogative over their employees.

Further Education and Professional Development Courses

Formal educational attainment has tended to reproduce pre-existing class standing. Families in higher employment class locations have been much more likely to send their children to university than families from lower employment classes (Curtis, Livingstone & Smaller 1992). Table 2-7 shows that current employment classes continue to be quite highly differentiated in terms of the proportion attaining a university degree: about half of professional employees and around a third of all large employers and managers, contrasted with ten per cent of service workers and four per cent of industrial workers. But completion of some form of post-secondary certification has grown rapidly in recent decades among younger people who still only get working class jobs (see Livingstone 2009).

Consequently, the long-established association between higher school attainment and greater participation in further formal education courses may be playing a somewhat diminishing role in the cycle of class reproduction. Table 2-7 also shows that the gap in further education participation between large employers, managers and professional employees, on the one hand, and service and industrial workers, on the other, is significant but is now much smaller than their differences in educational attainment. The further adult education gap appears to be decreasing as service and industrial workers have significantly increased their post-secondary education attainments, especially through community colleges (Livingstone 2002, 2009). In 2004, two-thirds of employers, managers and professional employees took further education, but around half of service workers and 40 per cent of industrial workers also did so. This is not to suggest that service and industrial workers' participation in further education can overcome prior exclusion from post-secondary schooling but rather that ore of these workers are completing some form of post-secondary schooling and continuing their further formal education, whether or not they have been able to use it to get jobs.

It should be noted here that the vast majority of participation in formal further adult education has been found to be job-related and therefore not very distinguishable from general participation in further education (e.g., Peters 2004). As Table 2-7 shows, around 80 per cent of further education in all employment classes is in job-related courses. Both figures will be presented in the following tables.

Table 2-8 goes beyond the general employment class analysis above to compare the formal educational attainments and further education participation rates of different professional classes. The majority of professional employers have at least an undergraduate university degree. Self-employed professionals, professional managers and professional employees have slightly lower levels of university degree completion. But all four professional classes are distinct from the rest of the general labour force in having much higher levels of university-level formal education. Each of these professional classes is also distinct from non-professional members of their general employment class positions: professional employers are three times as likely as other employers to have a university degree, as are self-employed professionals compared with the professional self-employed; professional managers are at least twice as likely to have university degrees as other managers. Professional employees are distinguished from working-class employees primarily on the basis of their advanced academic education, so it is not surprising that they are at least five times as likely as working-class employees (i.e., service and industrial workers) to have a university degree. But the fact that substantial and growing numbers of those in working-class positions, as well non-professional fractions of employer, self-employed and managerial employment classes have obtained university degrees should be noted. As suggested by advocates of the deprofessionalization thesis (see Chapter 1), the claims of those in professional class positions to exclusive specialized knowledge are weakened by the existence of growing numbers of other workers with versions of advanced formal education, knowledge that had been a primary basis of professionals' status claims.

As we expected, those in professional class positions have higher rates of participation in further formal education than the general labour force. As Table 2-8 summarizes, three-quarters of professional employers have taken a further education course in the past year, followed by lower proportions of professional managers, professional employees and self-employed professionals, respectively. The rest of the labour force generally has somewhat lower participation rates in further education, around 45 per cent. The gap in further formal education is much narrower than in levels of initial schooling, but professionals still have greater participation rates than the rest of the general labour force and also compared to non-professional fractions of all employment classes. Further education may be helping to close the gap between professionals and the rest of the labour force but only very gradually.

Table 2-6. Professional occupations by informal learning topics, 2004 (% participating)

Informal learning topic	Doctors & lawyers	Teachers	Nurses	Engineers	Computer programmers	Other professionals	Total non-professional labour force
New job tasks	66	75	71	70	81	68	57
Computers	71	78	63	75	90	65	56
New equipment	55	57	75	70	64	51	59
Organisational or managerial skills	33	48	42	61	54	49	45
Budgeting or financial management	38	25	17	36	32	37	34
Teamwork, problem solving	49	66	71	68	69	62	56
Work conditions and workers' rights	45	36	51	42	29	37	45
Politics in the workplace	40	32	46	32	26	38	32
Language & literacy	25	71	24	28	23	30	18
Health & safety	50	53	76	64	29	48	59

Table 2-7. Degree attainment, further education course participation and proportion of job-related courses by employment class, 2004

Employment class	University degree (%)	Further education participation in past year (%)*
Large employers	35	67 (86)
Small employers	23	46 (79)
Self-employed	22	46 (78)
Managers	34	68 (87)
Professional employees	46	67 (88)
Supervisors	14	54 (85)
Service workers	10	52 (78)
Industrial workers	4	41 (87)
Total labour force	21	53 (84)

* Percentage of job-related courses are in parentheses

Table 2-8. Degree attainment, further education course participation and proportion of job-related courses by general employment class and professional class, 2004

Employment class	University degree (%) Professional	University degree (%) Other labour force	Further formal education (% yes)* Professional	Further formal education (% yes)* Other labour force
Employer	57	18	77 (81)	42 (80)
Self-employed	46	15	56 (81)	43 (78)
Manager	48	20	70 (87)	57 (87)
Employee	45	7	65 (88)	46 (84)
Total labour force	47	14	66 (86)	50 (83)

* Percentage of courses that are job-related are in parentheses

Table 2-9 summarizes the formal educational attainments and further education of those in the selected professional occupations and the rest of the labour force. In terms of formal educational attainments, virtually all doctors/lawyers and teachers have university degrees, compared to over 80 per cent of engineers and nearly 60 per cent of computer programmers. Slightly less than half of nurses have university degrees. But only among doctors and lawyers do majorities have post-bachelor degrees.[4] About a third of engineers and teachers have post-bachelor degrees, compared to 15 per cent of computer programmers and less than 10 per cent of nurses. Clearly, doctors' and lawyers' associations have been *much* more successful than the other selected professional occupations in requiring advanced formal education for entry, while engineers and teachers have been more successful than computer programmers and nurses.

Table 2-9. Degree attainment, further education course participation and proportion of job-related courses by professional occupation, 2004

Occupation	Any university degree (%)	Post-bachelor degree (%)	Further formal education (% Yes)*
Doctors/lawyers	96	79	64 (84)
Teachers	94	32	65 (85)
Engineers	82	33	45 (96)
Computer programmers	58	15	47 (79)
Nurses	47	9	67 (90)
Other professionals	64	28	55 (86)
Other labour force	24	8	39 (83)
Total labour force	35	13	43 (84)

* Percentage of courses that are job-related are in parentheses

However, participation rates in further education generally and (job-related) formal professional development in particular are more similar between these professional occupations. Nurses are just as likely as doctors/lawyers and teachers to participate in further education (about two-thirds), and somewhat more so than engineers or computer programmers (less than 50 per cent). Around 40 per cent of the non-professional part of the labour force is also participating in further education and most of this participation, as noted above, is job-related (around 80 per cent). These small differences in further education rates are unlikely to make up for the large differences in formal educational attainments between employment classes or the large differences in post-bachelor degree attainments between doctors/lawyers and the other selected professional occupations.

Workplace Power and Further Education

General research on relations between workers' power and intentional learning practices has found that higher levels of negotiating power (as indicated by union or association membership) as well as greater delegated organizational decision-making roles are associated with higher rates of formal further education (Livingstone & Raykov 2009). The current findings on further education rates also suggest some differential effects of workplace power among professional occupations. Most notably, as Table 2-10 shows, greater negotiating power appears to be associated with higher rates of participation in further education. Doctors/lawyers, nurses and teachers, all of whom have nearly universal membership in either professional associations or unions, have majority participation rates in further education. Engineers and programmers, who have much lower membership rates, also have only minority participation rates. Doctors' and lawyers' negotiating power comes distinctively from their very high membership in self-regulating professional associations without need for dependence on union membership. Nurses and teachers depend very predominantly on high union membership to deal with their employers. Engineers are much less likely than doctors/lawyers to be in professional associations, programmers even less so, and very few engineers or programmers are in unions; therefore, their collective negotiating power for further education provisions is more limited.

Table 2-10. Negotiating power by further education participation, 2004

Occupation	Union or professional association member (professional association without union) (%)	Further education (%)
Doctor/lawyer	87 (72)	64
Teacher	95 (5)	65
Nurse	97 (12)	67
Engineer	59 (46)	45
Programmer	29 (12)	47
Other professional	59 (24)	55
Other labour force	42 (15)	39

Doctors and lawyers, with their high levels of certification and professional association membership, are expected by their self-regulating colleges to frequently confirm the currency of their specialized knowledge. But, as predominantly employers and self-employed, they typically have wide discretion in their choices for professional development studies. The similarly high further education rates of teachers and nurses are consistent with their high levels of certification and requirements of both their colleges and their employers to continually upgrade their knowledge. But, as predominantly employees with near-universal union membership, they are typically expected to take more standardized forms of retraining. Engineers' and programmers' lower rates of further education are consistent with their more limited associational strength and certification requirements. As such, they are less encouraged or compelled by their negotiating power than these other professionals to participate in further formal recertification studies.

Differences in perceived organizational power may also mediate participation in further education among professional occupations. Among professional occupations generally, 70 per cent who design their work most of the time have taken a further education course in the past year, compared to 47 per cent of the smaller proportion who never do so. Among teachers, those who feel they have a great deal of personal choice in doing their jobs are more likely (72 per cent) than those who feel they have little choice (53 per cent) to have taken a further education course in the past year. Similarly, the small numbers of teachers who have delegated organizational decision-making roles are more likely (82 per cent) than others to have taken a course. If we focus on those teachers who were excluded from further formal education (that is, they wanted to take a course but were unable to do so), they are predominantly found among those who are excluded from any meaningful organizational decision-making role. It should also be noted that course participation is higher for full-time permanent teachers (69 per cent) and lower for part-time temporary teachers (50 per cent) who generally have the least organizational power.

Although teachers and nurses participate in further education at similar rates to doctors and lawyers, there are substantial differences in accessibility of further education associated with their different class locations and organizational power. Among professional occupation respondents to the WALL survey, nurses and teachers are more likely to cite barriers, such as the expense of the course, the inconvenience of the time and place of the course, as well as the lack of employer support, as obstacles to further professional learning. Conversely, doctors/lawyers reported low levels of concern over matters such as cost, inconvenience, or support as obstacles to further education. Clearly the negotiating and organizational powers of doctors/lawyers afford them better control over their time, as well as the financial means to support further formal learning.

Differences in sources of financial support for further education are summarized in Table 2-11. It should be noted here that the extent of employer support has generally been much greater for professional and managerial employees than for other working-class employees (Livingstone and Scholtz 2010, p. 37). Consistent with their dominant class positions as proprietors, doctors and lawyers mainly self-finance their further education, whereas most other professionals are more likely to rely primarily on employer support. But teachers may be only marginally more likely to rely on employers than to have to self-finance their further education.

Table 2-11. Sources of financial support for further education by professional occupation, 2004

Occupation	Employer (%)	Self (%)	Other (%)
Doctor/lawyer	24	55	16
Teacher	44	40	16
Nurse	47	30	23
Engineer	66	24	10
Programmer	55	38	7
Other professional	51	33	16
Rest of labour force	53	33	16

As in the prior research on professionals' further education, the most common obstacles expressed by professional employees in our related case studies were structural impediments involving their employers. A computer programmer described his experiences with professional development in terms of the control over the timing, content and use being in the hands of management:

You have to take courses and its part of your manager's job to ensure that your education plan is set and that you do the courses. They have something called an individual development program that you do around the beginning of the year ...like it might not be your fault, it could be your manager's fault for saying, "No, you've been too busy, you can't go on that course," etc., it looks bad on him as well. So, it's like a team effort between you and your manager to get the education. (Isaac, computer programmer)[5]

A teacher explained the organization of the school and the profession that presented obstacles to her teaching and learning:

If I could walk into my job and teach children, I would be satisfied. But the extra layer of working with the administration ... is stressful, people get hypersensitive about issues. Just in delivery of the curriculum, how much freedom you have. With the administration ... I don't think they understand how my program can be successful. (Signe, secondary school teacher)[6]

INTEGRATION OF FURTHER EDUCATION AND INFORMAL LEARNING

As the prior tables show, those in professional occupations and professional class positions generally exhibit the most consistently high levels of participation in advanced schooling and further education courses. Given the sheer pervasiveness of informal workplace learning, professionals should have the greatest opportunity to integrate their formal and informal learning practices, whereas those in working-class jobs with little advanced schooling and lower rates of further education must rely relatively more heavily on continuing informal learning. However, this does not guarantee that such integration actually occurs.

Table 2-12 summarizes estimates of the helpfulness of both further formal education courses and job-related informal learning for doing one's job better. Doctors and lawyers are most likely to consider their further education courses as very helpful (62 per cent) and less likely to find their informal learning as helpful (50 per cent). This pattern is consistent with the earlier findings that they are most likely to pay for their own further education and least likely to rely on colleagues for informal workplace learning. Nurses are the only other professional occupation in which a majority find their further education very helpful (57 per cent) and informal learning less so (46 per cent). In this case, the more positive estimate of course helpfulness is likely related to substantial recent increases in certification requirements for nurses and the imperative for many experienced nurses to meet these new requirements through such courses. Most other professionals who have taken further education, as well as most others in the labour force, tend to find their informal job-related informal learning to be at least marginally more helpful than courses. In spite of the fact that teachers are somewhat more likely than most to pay for their own further education, they are more likely to rate their job-related informal learning as more helpful.

So, we can now see that teachers are among the professionals most frequently required to take formal upgrading courses (Table 2-9), but they are among the least likely to evaluate such courses as their most important source of professional knowledge (Table 2-4). They are also less likely to rate further education as very helpful as compared to their job-related informal learning (Table 2-12). These findings are consistent with the increasingly frequent suggestion in the literature that there are chronic problems in integrating informal job-related learning with formal PD for the teaching profession.

Table 2-12. Helpfulness of further education and job-related informal learning to do job better by professional occupation, 2004

Occupation	Further education "very helpful" (%)	Informal learning "very helpful" (%)	Further education- informal learning difference (%)
Doctor/lawyer	62	50	+12
Teacher	47	52	-5
Nurse	57	46	+11
Programmer	41	58	-17
Engineer	27	46	-19
Other professional	46	53	-7
Other labour force	40	49	-9
Total labour force	42	50	-8

CONCLUDING REMARKS

Professionals are found to rely primarily on informal learning attained with aid of colleagues and on their own much more than on further formal education to remain competent in their jobs. In this respect, they are no different than others in the labour force. This finding should come as no revelation since the pervasiveness of informal learning has been documented for many years (Tough 1978). Professionals are more dependent than most others on formal educational qualifications for entrance into their jobs. So it should be little surprise to find that they also tend to participate more highly than most others in further education to maintain these qualifications. However, the "arms race" for educational credentials has become increasingly intense (Livingstone 2009). Among the consequences are a narrowing gap between the formal educational attainments of professionals and the rest of the labour force, and growing underemployment of formal education in relation to job requirements. There may be a diminishing reverence for the special character of many professionals' knowledge, not so much because of "deprofessionalization" *per se* but the relative increase of the formal educational attainments of others and their greater accessibility to particular forms of knowledge.

There are some substantial differences in the educational attainments and further education of particular professions, differences that should be understood in terms of the differential power of specific professional occupations and class positions of professionals. Doctors and lawyers have attained much higher levels of completion of post-bachelor degrees than the other professional occupations we have examined. They also maintain participation rates in further education that are as high as any other profession. The high rates of advanced degrees are intimately connected with similarly high memberships in self-regulating professional associations. We have further argued that this high level of self-regulation is grounded in the predominantly proprietorial class position of doctors and lawyers which has served to ensure direct control over sale of their services as well as training requirements for entry into their professions. Their proprietorial position also means that they are most likely to fund their own further education and to take only courses highly relevant to their particular needs.

Proprietorial classes generally have managerial prerogative over the working conditions and further education requirements of their employees. For example, doctors have retained considerable influence over the working conditions and further education requirements of nurses, whether as direct employers or as advisory authorities. Most of the professional occupations we have examined are mainly in the class position of professional employees whose working conditions and formal educational provisions are subject to negotiation with their employers. While a university degree has become a nearly universal criterion for entry into most professional occupations, variations in further education appear to be more related to differences in collective negotiating power with employers than to previous educational attainments. For example, nurses have relatively low completion of post-bachelor degrees. Their relatively high rates of participation in further education correspond more closely with their high rates of union membership. The relatively high further education rates of teachers also appear to be more closely related to their high unionization than to their level of post-bachelor degree completion.

Delegated power to professional employees, in terms of recognized discretionary choice in performing their own jobs or in designated participation in organizational decision-making roles, is also associated with and apparently enables somewhat greater rates of participation in further education. But it should be kept in mind that professional employees' greater general level of further education participation than working class employees is also influenced by employers' relatively high financial support for it. In any event, variations in further education related to delegated organizational power seem to be minor compared to those related to differences in collective negotiating power (compare Livingstone & Raykov 2009).

Differences in the negotiating power and organizational decision-making power of professional occupations have rarely been considered in prior research on professional learning. The current findings suggest that this has been a serious oversight.

Perhaps the most striking finding in terms of professional development programs is the very low importance accorded by most professionals to further education courses in relation to on-the-job informal learning. While many professionals who take further education consider such courses to be helpful, they tend to see their job-related informal learning as much more important and recognize it as far more extensive. There is clearly a challenge in many professions to more effectively integrate formal professional development with informal learning. The evidence from this comparative analysis suggests that further genuine empowerment of professional employees may be one of the most likely ways to narrow this gap. Teachers may be particularly notable in this regard in terms of the large discrepancy between their high classroom autonomy and lower involvement in organizational level decision-making. Their greater involvement in decision-making beyond the classroom, especially in the design and delivery of professional development programs, might aid considerably in bringing informal and formal learning experiences closer together. More generally, a clear implication of these findings is the necessity for job-related further education programs, not only for professional groups but all workers, to give greater recognition to prior learning as it relates to everyday work practices.

SECTION B: TEACHERS' WORK AND LEARNING

HARRY SMALLER

3. OVERVIEW OF TEACHERS' WORK AND LEARNING

INTRODUCTION

A number of conceptual issues, themes and questions ground this study. Multiple meanings of 'work' and 'learning' topped this list, but many more also pertained – 'informal' and 'formal' learning, teacher knowledge, professional/ism, 'professional development,' and teacher induction. All of these concepts clearly warranted further historical, theoretical and/or sociological exploration, and it was on this basis that we undertook our examination of some of the relevant literature – academic, professional and general; Canadian and international. These concepts also form the basis on which this chapter is structured. Clearly, given the number of themes covered here, providing a completely comprehensive literature review for each would take up much more space than is possible to allocate here. However, it is hoped that at least some of the basic studies covering each of these themes have been included in this chapter. In addition, each of the ensuing chapters will also cite literature pertinent to the themes covered.

It is important to note – as suggested already by the focus of the first two chapters – that underlying all of these themes is our sharp interest in examining and analysing the ways in which they are fundamentally influenced and shaped, in one way or another, by the social relations of the school as a workplace and the role played by teachers themselves, as they wrestle – knowingly or otherwise, overtly or otherwise – with the issues of power, control and autonomy.

TEACHERS' WORK

Given the historical importance of schooling across much of the world, it is not surprising that teachers have been the subject of much formal academic research over the years. Willard Waller's study published in 1932 (The Sociology of Teaching) and G.W. Hughes thesis of the following year ("The social and economic status of the elementary school teacher in England") marked the beginning of a series of classic explorations of teachers, their lives and their work – very much reflecting a functionalist and arm's-length approach to observing and attempting to understand teachers. In many cases as well, these studies were motivated by an interest in seeing teachers and schools become more instrumental in promoting "proper" cultural values, and becoming more "professionalized." This mode of inquiry continued well into the post-war period, as exemplified by H.S. Becker's 1952 article, "The career of the Chicago public school teacher." This "distancing" pertained into the 1960s, at which time teachers remained in the research literature as "shadowy figures on the educational landscape mainly known, or unknown, through large scale surveys, or historical analyses of their position in society, the key concept in approaching the practice of the teaching was that of role" (Ball & Goodson 1985, p. 6). Similarly, in relation to the underlying motivations for much of this research, Dan Lortie (1975, p. vii) noted that "books and articles instructing teachers on how they should behave are legion." By contrast, "empirical studies of teaching work – and the outlook of those who staff the schools – remain rare."

By the mid-1970s, however, research approaches to understanding teachers and their work took on new methodological directions, advanced by Lortie's 1975 monograph, *Schoolteacher: A sociological study*. While still being concerned with what he saw as schools and teachers needing "improvement," he criticized earlier approaches which were mainly "detached" and overly prescriptive in nature. Lortie's own work drew on symbolic interactionism (SI) as a methodology to explore themes relating to how teachers themselves took up their identity and status. At the same time, this methodological approach was also subject to critique – particularly by those more concerned with the structures of schools and schooling and who noted that SI overly emphasized individual perspectives and issues, and ignored the larger issues of power, control and change in schools (see, e.g., Troyna 1994). However, others, like Sandra Acker (1994), observed that, in spite of the emphasis on individual teachers, many of these researchers were still "squarely concerned with the disjuncture between modernist efforts to reform schooling through controlling teachers' work and the reality of schooling in a post-modern society" (p. 4).

In addition to symbolic interactionism, other researchers located their examination of teachers within the context of school cultures – an approach which certainly assisted in providing an important framework for understanding schooling and teachers' work. This approach progressed through a series of phases over the ensuing decades, during which teachers themselves were taken up in different lights. Early studies, concerned mainly about the outcomes of working-class and minority students in the system, often saw teachers as "villains" in the process (see, e.g., Kohl 1967, 1974; Kozol 1967). By the late 1970s, as Ball and Goodson (1985, p. 7) point out, "attention began to be directed to the constraints within which teachers work." In this process, however, teachers "were transformed from villains to 'victims' and in some cases, 'dupes' of the system within which they were required to operate" (see also, e.g., Goodlad 1984). Researchers often found themselves on one side or the other in regards to their philosophical approaches to the issue. As Acker (1994) points out:

> Erring in one direction leaves teachers as interchangeable cardboard figures, buffeted about by forces – proletarianization, bureaucracy, social reproduction – beyond their knowledge or control; in the other, teachers suffer or prosper according to their skills in life planning. (p. 13)

By the 1990s, the dominant intent of teacher research shifted from interest (or concern) about teachers' work in general, to focus more directly on what was seen as the need for the "improvement" of the individual teacher, often embedded in a renewed interest in "professionalism" – but which continued to ignore the larger issues of power, control and change in schools. In this context, widely circulated studies included such titles as "Who teaches and why: Dilemmas of building a profession for twenty-first century schools" (Darling-Hammond & Sclan 1996) and "The new professionalism: The synthesis of professional and institutional development" (Hargreaves 1994). As a number of researchers have pointed out, this prescriptive turn was related to the increasing promotion of neo-liberal approaches to the restructuring of the public sector, including schooling (see, e.g., Goodson 1994, p. 30; Lawn 1996). Certainly, judging from the terrain of schooling policy change in many Canadian and American jurisdictions starting in that decade, these prescriptive studies have served to develop and steer programs requiring teachers to engage increasingly in officially prescribed further training programs relating to their "professional development" (Elmore 1995; Ashton 1996), to their teaching methods (Corrie 1995; Hargreaves & Dawe 1990) and to procedures for evaluating their work (DfEE 1998).

On the other hand, there has also been a more recent blossoming of research which critically examines these neo-liberal forces at work. A number of researchers have explored the ideological foundations of professionalism and its effects on teachers and teachers' work (for an earlier example, see Densmore 1987). Much more recently, Stevenson et al. (2007) have drawn on the recent 'remodelling' and 'restructuring' of teachers' work by government in England and Wales – new regulations which have been enacted with the agreement of some (but not all) of the teacher unions there, and which have been underpinned through the development of an official "discourse of new professionalism." While this plan has the appearance of reducing teachers' involvement in areas such as pastoral care, administration, and so on, in fact the authors argue that the overall workload for most teachers has actually increased, through the imposition of other duties and responsibilities. Others, such as Easthope and Easthope (2000), have more directly examined the ways in which workload has intensified and complicated the lives of teachers in recent years. Similarly, Gillian Forrester (2005) has published an ethnographic study of teachers' work in England and the ways in which "the education policies of successive Conservative and New Labour administrations in Britain have tightened central control over education undermining teacher discretion and directly impacting upon the labour process of the professionals concerned" (p. 133).

Perhaps most poignantly, Stephen Ball (2003) has drawn on Foucaudian methods to explore the concept of "performativity" as it relates to the effects of these external forces on teachers and their work. It is, he argues,

> a new mode of state regulation which makes it possible to govern in an "advanced liberal" way. It requires individual practitioners to organize themselves as a response to targets, indicators and evaluations. To set aside personal beliefs and commitments and live an existence of calculation. (p. 215)

Finally, a number of researchers over the past several decades have focused their investigations explicitly on the nature of teachers' work itself, and the ways which it intersects with both the material and ideological structures of their workplaces (Connell 1982; Lawn 1987; Reid 2003). As we note in Chapter 1, some of these studies, including our own work over the past decade, have also explored issues of teachers' control of their collective work – in relation to their own instructional practice, their own further learning, and input into larger school-based policy and procedures. Literature pertaining more specifically to these aspects will be discussed below.

PROFESSIONAL/ISM: AUTONOMY, POWER AND CONTROL OF TEACHERS' WORK

The chapters in Part I of this book have dealt with general issues of professionalization and deprofessionalization – the various and contested meanings of these terms, and an analysis of the differing conditions among various worker groups which have been associated with claims of professional status. A number of factors have been identified in this regard: enterprise ownership, managerial authority, and the extent of subordinated employees' participation in decision-making – most of which have typically been ignored in terms of their implications for the control of specialized knowledge, which is the standard criterion for achieving professional status. In comparing levels of power and authority of various occupational groups, historical contingencies also play a strong role, intertwined with issues such as the gender composition of each group, its political and economic leverage in various jurisdictions, and so on.

Professionalization is a complex concept – with strong historical, ideological and material connections. Viewed through the eyes of social stratification theorists such as Larsen (1980) and Derber et al. (1990), professionalization has been, and remains, an ongoing historic process, in both concrete and ideological terms. The status and authority of particular middle-class, historically male-dominated, occupational groups have been enhanced through state intervention, in exchange for their social and self-regulatory work. A recent example in Ontario relating to the fluidity of these historical contingencies involves a battle between the Ontario Medical Association (OMA) and the provincial government – including public billboards, etc. – over the latter's policy/program initiative to enhance and support the expanding role of nurse practitioners and their new government-funded centres. Professional status for even the most established professions remains subject to continuing negotiation.

Like doctors and lawyers, teachers as well have struggled with the issue of professional status over the years. But teachers have never been part of the "inner circle" of most-favoured occupational groups, in spite of an official rhetoric of their purported "professional status" and importance to society. As a number of educational historians have noted for some time now, because of teachers' importance as "proper" role models for future citizens, in most western nations the control over their selection, training, certification and practice has generally remained very much in the hands of government and/or monitoring government agencies (see, e.g., Duman 1979; Gorelick 1982; Lawn 1996; Labaree 1992; Atkins & Lury 1999).

Over the years, classroom teachers have debated the advantages and disadvantages of more "professional autonomy." In Canada, classroom teachers have nominally belonged to legislated "professions" under each provinces' Teaching Profession Act. However, they have had little to no autonomy, partly because of the very limited powers granted under these acts, and also because of their status as employed workers of school boards (Smaller 1998, 2004). From the outset of plans by two Canadian provinces (British Columbia and Ontario) to legislate "colleges of teachers," teachers' union officials in both jurisdictions strongly (but ultimately unsuccessfully) opposed these changes, partly or mainly because they saw this move as part of a larger government agenda of neo-liberal schooling reforms and/or as an attempt to reduce the influence and effectiveness of unions (Smaller 1996). These concerns were certainly not unrealistic; for the past decade tensions continue between the union and College of Teachers over the ways in which "professionalism" is understood and governed – for the benefit or otherwise of teachers, individually and collectively.[1]

In any event, even though each of these "professional" colleges has been actively in place for well over a decade, they have not occasioned any more workplace autonomy and control than that experienced by teachers in other provinces, as our own findings, to be described in Chapter 4, demonstrate. Nor has classroom teachers' status necessarily been enhanced by the advent of these new quasi-autonomous regulatory bodies – either in the eyes of school board officials, parents, students or the public at large. In fact, there seems to be reluctance on the part of officials of these professional bodies even to recognize the growing tensions between the "autonomous professional" and the organizational managerial cultures in which teachers work. For example, the Registrar of newly formed Ontario College of Teachers (OCT) announced in the College's initial publication, that the College saw itself as ensuring "accountability to students, parents and the public" (OCT 1997, p. 30). Clearly absent from this mandate overview was any recognition of the fact that, as employees of school boards, teachers were very much caught in the middle of sometimes conflicting agendas held by their employers. Similarly, none of the five main themes identified in the College's "Standards of Practice"[2] recognize these ongoing managerial tensions.

The role which these new colleges play in Canada in regard to tensions between teachers' professional autonomy and managerial control is not unusual. For example, the Code of Ethics incorporated by the Australian College of Education includes a statement recommending that "Where, in serious issues, a disagreement cannot be resolved, or a teacher is unable to accept a direction properly given, she or he should consider resigning rather than acting against personal convictions or sense of personal integrity" (Australian College of Education cited in Campbell 2000, p. 208).

This contradictory nature of professionalism among those who are hired employees has certainly been demonstrated in the recent context of neo-liberal schooling reform initiatives being promoted in many western jurisdictions. While the rhetoric of professionalism is often used in these contexts, the general import is usually that of the "need" for the "upgrading" or "retraining" of teachers. Given these strong ideological messages, it is not surprising that an Ontario survey found a significant percentage of parents (75 per cent) in favour of requiring teachers to submit accounts of their learning activities to their principals (rather than being allowed to use their own professional judgements about their own in-service learning), and an even higher percentage (83 per cent) in favour of principals being required to use provincial guidelines and methods to evaluate their teachers (Livingstone et al. 2001, p. 32).[3]

In the context of teacher education, very few teachers, and certainly none of their unions, are opposed to provision of opportunity for further education and training. However, many are very concerned about the control of these programs being taken out of the hands of local teachers at the school and community level – leaving others with the power to determine unilaterally what shall be learned, how much, when, and in what manner. In Ontario, the College of Teachers (2008) has worked continuously to (re-) construct new regimes of teacher pre-service and in-service programs. While this college works diligently to proclaim that it is ultimately controlled by members themselves, judging from the anecdotal comments of classroom teachers/members over the past few years, there is little indication that they have a meaningful say in determining what the structure, process or content of these regimes might be, and whether these regimes would be designed to build on existing teacher knowledge or be oblivious or in opposition to it.

SCHOOLING REFORM

Schooling reform is a ubiquitous theme across all aspects of the educational literature – not to mention being omnipresent in the real world of schooling, teaching and learning. (Plugging "school" and "reform" into Google in June 2011 produced over 38 million hits.) Sessions involving almost 400 papers given at the 2011 annual conference of the American Education Research Association (AERA) were listed specifically under the category "School Reform" (AERA 2011). In some respects, one might argue that virtually all of the global research undertaken on schooling could be construed as being motivated by concerns about the efficacies of state schooling systems as we know them, and the "need" for reform.

Demands (whether popular, political or academic) for schooling reform have been in place almost from the inception of state schooling itself, as critical educational historians on several continents have long noted (Katz 2001; Prentice 1977; Curtis 1988; Gardner 1984; Spaull 1997). These pressures for change have historically been based (at least by dominant voices) on the "need" for schooling to be linked more closely to the economic "wants" and "needs" of the nation (e.g., Althouse 1929; Ontario Royal Commission on Education 1950; Goodman 1995), a call which has certainly not diminished in the past decade. In fact, many argue that schooling reform is now linked even more closely to transformations in the larger political economy of provinces and nations – a movement consistent with globalizing, neo-liberal economic trends, including tighter control over, but less funding for, public sector social institutions (Ranson 2003; Carnoy & Rhoten 2002; Dale & Robertson 2002). Students and school systems alike are increasingly being pressured to be more "competitive" in the global (education) market. These pressures intensify in spite of increasing evidence that such connections between education, employment opportunities, and national advantage are not necessarily empirically valid (see, e.g., Herbert 2004; Livingstone 2004).

This unease with public schooling is not a recent syndrome; even the birth and early years of our centralized, compulsory public schooling were fraught with doubt, animosity and wide opposition (Curtis 1988; Katz 2001). Throughout the decades since then, these differences have continued unabated. Even today, concerns expressed about a particular school or teacher's approach are often embedded (knowingly or otherwise) in fundamental differences of opinion about the basic aims of schooling – for example, development of the individual versus societal cohesion versus economic "progress." In other cases, concerns and complaints focus on what are perceived as weaknesses in relation to specific aspects of schooling – school structure, curriculum, pedagogy, "discipline," differential treatment of students based on gender/race/ethnicity, streaming, individual teacher effectiveness, and so on.

However, in the context of widely disseminated claims of unease with the state of public schooling, it is worth noting the seeming discrepancy of the "distance from schooling" phenomenon often evidenced in surveys of school satisfaction. As compared to adults with no children in school, a vast majority of parents of elementary school students find their local school to be highly satisfactory.[4] Interestingly however, even those same parents, highly satisfied with their own school, are much less likely to express positive views about schooling in general (Hart & Livingstone 2010). This phenomena has led researchers to question how these more generalized negative opinions have come to be (even though everyone, everywhere, seems relatively satisfied with their own local school), and in the process some have examined the role of the dominant media and its corporate connections in supporting these more negative beliefs (see, e.g., Bushaw & McNee 2009).

To be sure, judging from the nature of many of the reports and addresses of the economic and political elite across the twentieth century (certainly those which seem to garner considerable media attention), deep concerns have always been expressed about the effectiveness of schools and schooling – and the need for reform (see, e.g., Lieberman 1993). One could also argue that these concerns, although emanating from the elite, are often expressed in ways calculated to find favour among at least two different groupings of parents in North America and beyond – working-class and minority parents concerned about their children's relative lack of schooling success (not to mention their treatment generally in schools), and middle-class parents concerned about what they believe to be falling "standards" in schools.

In any event, calls for schooling reform have not fallen on deaf ears over the years, and tens of millions of dollars are expended annually in attempts to change various aspects of the system – schooling governance and administration, financing, structures of schools, school syllabi, school year/timetable, curriculum, textbooks, pedagogy, measurement and evaluation, student attendance regulation, parent/community relations, and so on (see, e.g., Ravitch 2010). These reforms have been accompanied (before, during and after) by much debate as to their usefulness, and overall we are left with considerable argument that their effect has been slight.[5]

Where are teachers, in all of this? While recent calls for reforms in education continue to range across the many dimensions of schooling – funding, governance, curriculum, resources, facilities, etc. – teachers themselves seem to have been singled out for special attention, in unprecedented ways. Historically, teachers have been addressed very much as an entity, and improvements to education have often been associated with the need to improve conditions for teachers collectively – class sizes, resources, salaries, benefits, pensions and job security. Even where teachers were seen to be in need of further education themselves, governments at various levels often moved to expand and improve teacher education programs and/or to offer generic incentives for all teachers to engage in further study, whether in pre-service or in-service models (Hopkins 1969; Robinson 1971; Fleming 1972).

In the past two decades however, there has been a dramatic shift from this more collective approach to one of focus on the individual teacher. This theme dominates the ways in which teachers' work is being restructured and controlled (see, e.g., Gleeson & Husbands 2003; Mahony et al. 2003). Moreover, individualization is also dominant in the ways in which teachers are increasingly being educated, trained, evaluated and tested. (Holmes Group 1990; Labaree 1992; Darling-Hammond 1998; OECD 1998; Ontario Government 2000). In many areas of the United States, for example, salaries, promotion, and even basic job tenure for individual teachers are increasingly being determined by teacher testing regimes, increased external evaluation of teacher practice, and/or by student "scores" on standardized examinations (see, e.g., Medina 2008). While these measures have yet to gain a foothold in Canada, in at least one province (Ontario), student results from external examinations now appear in the public press, displayed on a school-by-school basis. The implications for individual teachers in these schools seem clear, particularly for those working in schools with lower test scores. While many other causes may be at issue here, beginning with schooling structures, curriculum mandates, and so forth, it is typically teachers themselves who are saddled with the blame.

One major schooling reform approach in this regard has been what Andy Hargreaves (2003) refers to as the imposition of "Performance-Training Sects" – "large scale initiatives" consisting of top-down programs that focus on the work of individual teachers, and which involve "a strong insistence on performance standards and prescribed classroom techniques" (p. 176). He argues that, while some of these programs may have evidenced short-term success, few have demonstrated any effective sustainability of results. Teachers, he suggests, "dislike losing their classroom discretion by being locked into an instructional straightjacket. They feel less satisfied, less professional, less motivated to teach overall … [M]andating instructional change by force is undesirable because it can damage teachers' long-term commitments to their work" (pp. 179–180). The findings in Chapter 2 mentioned above suggest that teachers' sense of discretionary control within their immediate workplaces has been higher than most other professionals, and perhaps most sensitive to challenge.

As noted in the previous section, reform initiatives are often being promoted through a rhetoric of a "need" for increased professionalism. As noted earlier in this chapter, in some jurisdictions government initiated and controlled "colleges of teachers" have been established, with a mandate to control the training, certification and practice of teachers. In addition to these new controls over teachers' classroom practice, there have also been increasing calls from education think tanks and politicians to introduce compulsory "professional development" programs for teachers, and also the closely-related phenomenon of regular, and compulsory, teacher recertification programs. While such programs have been successfully resisted to date in Canada and seem not to exist in most other OECD countries (OECD 2005), they are widespread in the United States (see, e.g., Illinois State Board of Education 2010). While few teachers, and none of their unions and associations, argue against the need for, and benefits of, ongoing professional development, questions are rightfully posed about the intentions behind and practices of such state-initiated and controlled interventions. Judging from professional development regimes in the United States, teachers understandably might ask who might be involved in the development and implementation of these programs. Importantly in this regard, one might also ask what assumptions underpin the identification of this necessary or important knowledge and whether these assumptions are based and build upon existing teacher knowledge rather than the contrived beliefs and demands of state education officials.

These are pivotal questions in terms of teachers' quest for professional status and autonomy, and the literature suggests that they are being asked by teachers in many jurisdictions (see, e.g., Glassford & Salinitri 2007). In addition, a number of researchers have suggested that alternatives to this top-down control over schooling change are possible – one in which teachers' own authority and autonomy can be not only respected but sought out. These changes in policy can be seen, for example, in the context of the findings of Hargreaves and Shirley (2009), as a change from the typical market-driven, testing-driven policies still prevalent in the United States today, to the more democratic, evidence-driven 'Fourth Way' which the authors advocate as more effective for true educational improvement.[6]

TEACHER KNOWLEDGE

There is increasing interest among educational researchers about the concept of 'teacher knowledge.' This research has taken a number of directions in recent years, including explorations about what it is, what it should be, how it is acquired and/or enhanced, and the nature of its relation to student and school success. Although there is large and increasing volume of literature covering these themes, to date there has been much less attention paid to how teachers themselves see these matters personally – what they think is important to know and to learn, how they would like to engage in this learning process, and what they are already doing in this regard. These questions have borne directly on the purpose and methodology of this study.

Interest in this field of inquiry accelerated during the 1990s in the context of the increased pressures for schooling reform, and "increased professionalism" everywhere (see, e.g., Briscoe and Peters 1997; Klein 1996; Gibson & Olberg 1998). As a practical example, it is not surprising that the newly established Ontario College of Teachers (1999) listed "Professional Knowledge" as one of the five "principles" for their "Standards of Practice" to which all teachers were/are required to adhere. By the mid-1990s however, there were also strong critiques being raised against instrumental ways of presenting (and promoting) adherence to "proper" teacher knowledge.

For example, Robert Donmoyer (1995) provocatively challenged the common belief that:

> teaching does have a distinctive knowledge base, that the knowledge is expressed in articulated understandings, skills and judgements which are professional in character and which distinguish more productive teachers from less productive ones. (p. 2)

He recognized that this insistence on a specific knowledge base came in part from historical struggles to "provide the basis for professional rather than political control of education." The persistent political power tension between aspirations for professional status/control and state managerial control is clearly evident here.

As he notes, many scholars have argued and shown "that no knowledge is objective and that all knowledge is inevitably political" (1995, p. 2); "Professionalism which is grounded in a knowledge of empirical research is not really an alternative to political control of education; it is simply a different kind of political control" (p. 15). This, he explained, was particularly true in relation to the attempts during previous decades to promote particular teacher education routines on the basis of a belief in "process-product forms of analysis ... identifying teacher behaviours which correlated with and presumably caused greater amounts of student learning." As he noted, numerous studies made it very clear that this approach to schooling improvement was highly problematic, and that results were "quite varied from setting to setting – most effective interventions were not effective in [other] places, and vice-versa." In fact, as he found in his extensive meta-analysis, "[a]pproaches which aggregate data certified as relatively ineffective were, in certain settings, among the most effective of all the strategies studied." In short, rather than promoting concepts of universality of teacher knowledge, he concluded that the peculiarities of individual teachers, schools, neighbourhoods, and homes influence pupil "achievement far more than whatever is captured by labels such as basic skills or affective education" (p. 6).

This more critical examination of the complex issues relating to the nature of teacher knowledge and its relation to further learning continues. Scribner (2003), for example, found that the general nature of teachers' knowledge and understandings varied greatly, "partly depending upon the degree to which a subject area is perceived as a well defined discipline (e.g., mathematics) or a more loosely defined set of knowledge and concepts (e.g., social studies or language arts)" – factors which also influence how teachers engage in their own learning. "Teachers in the core academic areas tended to have broader notions of professional learning than their career and technical education colleagues." The latter, Scribner found, had little interest in learning about "issues of pedagogical theory and skill, education reform, or content area knowledge. The focus of these teachers was squarely on developing concrete, 'real world' skills to pass on to their students." By comparison, although the academic teachers participating in his focus group discussions also initially expressed interest in these areas, they

> described a process in which they banked knowledge gained. That is, while they expressed a desire to focus their learning on practical and immediately relevant knowledge, they actually sought a wide array of knowledge that often was used over a much longer time frame. (2003, p. 8)

This bifurcation of knowledge and knowledge sources for teachers was also explored by Jensen et al. (2011) in their study comparing knowledge themes among a number of professional occupations in Norway. In this study, however, they critique teachers for their purported excesses in favouring localism of knowledge over a more abstract, extra-local knowledge culture. As proof of this, they cite a national teacher union's efforts "to promote and enhance the distribution of experiences and reflections of individual teachers to the group as a whole by way of a major project called Professional Awareness," comparing it unfavourably to "the Norwegian Nurses Association [which] has established development of nursing science and the organization of common knowledge resources as a central professionalising strategy" (p. 18). Again however, what is unfortunately missing from their analysis is any clear understanding or exploration of the tensions evident between the professional aspirations of teachers, individually and collectively, and the effects of managerial control over teachers' work.

The following three chapters will explore more fully our findings in relation to the differences in these aspirations, tensions and managerial control, as experienced by teachers occupying different positions within the school system – full-time permanent teachers as compared to beginning teachers and those who are employed only on a contingent, non-permanent basis. As will be demonstrated, signficances exist, both in relation to their existing knowledge, and to their interests in further engagement in job-related learning, both formal and informal.

FORMAL AND INFORMAL LEARNING

To begin, some argue that these two concepts should not differentiated, that the ways we learn are complex and inter-related (see, e.g., Billett 2004). However, for the purposes of exploring the ways (planned and otherwise) in which teachers engage in their own learning, we have found this broad distinction useful.

Formal learning can be described simply as intentional learning which takes place in formal settings established for that purpose (e.g., classrooms, lecture halls, seminar spaces, etc.), usually institutionally sponsored and formally structured (lectures, courses of study, curriculum, teachers, etc.). In the context of teacher learning, it can be associated with workshops, lectures, courses, "professional development day" activities, and so on.

Informal learning, by comparison, is somewhat more challenging to define or describe. What is it, actually? When does it happen? How can you tell? How is it differentiated from other kinds of learning? To be sure, these are complex questions, and this complexity is certainly reflected in the existent and ongoing research and literature. Livingstone suggested that informal learning is:

> any activity involving the pursuit of understanding, knowledge or skill which occurs outside the curricula of institutions providing educational programs, courses or workshops ... Explicit informal learning is distinguished from everyday perceptions, general socialization and more tacit informal learning by peoples' own conscious identification of the activity as significant learning. The important criteria that distinguish explicitly informal learning are the retrospective recognition of both a new significant form of knowledge, understanding or skill acquired on your own initiative and also recognition of the process of acquisition. (Livingstone 1999b, pp. 3–4)

Another similar definition is offered by Watkins and Marsick:

> Informal and incidental learning is learning from experience that takes place outside formally structured, institutionally sponsored, class-room based activities. Informal learning is a broad term that includes any such learning; incidental learning is a subset that is defined as a by-product of some other activity. Informal learning can be planned or unplanned, but is usually involves some degree of conscious awareness that learning is taking place. Incidental learning, on the other hand, is largely unintentional, unexamined, and embedded in people's closely held belief systems. (1992, p. 288)

In both cases, these definitions suggest that informal learning occurs apart from formal courses or institutions, but at the same time they carefully designate "explicitly" informal learning as that learning which is intentioned and/or identified by the learner, as compared to "incidental" learning which is unintended (Watkins and Marsick, 1992) and/or unidentified (Livingstone, 1999b) by the learner. As written, they certainly summarize concisely much of the discussion and debate, at least concerning definitions of the term informal learning. At the same time, however, implicit in concise definitional statements like these are a multitude of nuances and complexities. Some of these will become apparent in later chapters, as we attempt to "operationalize" these definitions in order to assess reports from respondents – to determine or confirm in some way that informal learning had indeed, taken place in each instance.[7]

Over the past two decades an increasing number of researchers have been examining issues relating to teachers' informal learning in their workplaces. Retallick (1999) for example, in his case study of one school in Australia, found that the "connections between the culture of the school and the nature of workplace learning appear to be fundamentally important. Some of the features of school culture which seem to have high salience for workplace learning relate to beliefs and values, while others relate to organizational structures and functions" (p. 40). However, while he did recognize agencies at work relating to values and structures ("Of crucial importance is the role of the principal" [p. 39]), little detail was provided about the ways in which these relations of power and control operated within the school.

By comparison, the work of Marks and Seashore Louis (1999) explicitly deals with the ways in which teachers' power and autonomy influence the ways in which they engage in their own and in collective faculty informal learning. In their comparative study of 24 schools (elementary, middle and secondary levels), they found "a strong and consistent relationship between organizational learning and teacher empowerment, measured both as a school organizational characteristic and as an experience of individual teachers" (p. 707). For the purposes of their study, "teacher empowerment" was examined in relation to teacher influence or control over four specific and separate domains: school policy, teacher work life, student experiences, and classroom control. While the level of teachers' engagement in learning corresponded positively to their level of control in all four domains, it was particularly strong when they experienced autonomy and control in the areas of their own work life and in their influence over their students' school experience.[8]

Finally, Cochrane-Smith and Lytle (1999) conducted a lengthy analysis of the ways in which teachers understand and take up their own workplace learning activity in relation to their own levels of experience as well as the social contexts in which they work and learn. As they conclude,

> When groups of teachers and others come together to learn, there are issues related to negotiating the agenda, sharing power and decision making, representing the work of the group, and dealing with the inevitable tensions of individual and collective purposes and viewpoints. These issues are seldom self-evident but always present. How and whether they are surfaced and dealt with indelibly shape the group and either circumscribe or open up its possibilities for productive work over time. (1999, p. 295)

PROFESSIONAL DEVELOPMENT

Many states in the United States require teachers to engage in professional development (PD) programs, and to "document ... hours of professional development annually in order to renew and maintain their standard teaching licence."[9] Although most jurisdictions in Canada do not explicitly require this engagement in order to maintain licensure, formal PD programs are widespread and offered by a multitude of agencies – provincial governments, local school boards, teachers' unions, universities, private organizations and companies, and so on. As suggested by findings in Chapter 2 and as will be described more explicitly in Chapter 4, we found that virtually all Canadian teachers engage in some form of work-related formal professional learning each year.

Not surprisingly, given both the extensive nature of this engagement in continuing teacher education, and the overriding debates about schooling reform more generally, much discussion continues about the governance, objectives, contexts, methods and outcomes of teachers' engagement in PD. For example, should these programs focus narrowly on achieving immediate improved results for students on standardized tests, and if so, should they concentrate on subject content or improved pedagogy? Alternatively, should PD take a broader approach to improving the teaching and learning process, in the hopes of broadening and deepening teachers' knowledge and understandings about schooling more generally? Or, to what extent should PD even explore issues only indirectly related to specific student academic success – themes such as student welfare, communicating with parents, bullying, workplace health and safety, and so forth?

In this regard, Thompson and Zeuli (1999) argued strongly that more traditional PD programs implemented in the wake of standards-based reforms have largely failed. "Tinkering with the social and structural arrangements of teacher learning is insufficient;" rather, teachers must be allowed to develop "their own ideas and connections among the materials that students are to learn, understanding the various ways students experience a given content area, and learn ... how to foster student engagement with the material" (quoted in Scribner 2003, p. 5). Thompson and Zeuli (1999) contended that teacher learning activities, to be meaningful, must provide cognitive dissonance-creating and dissonance-resolving opportunities related to teachers' classroom experiences. This reflexive approach to professional learning should be designed to develop "new conceptual knowledge (understanding), rather than, say, new habits of practice" (p. 356). It is through new conceptual knowledge that new practices develop. Similarly, Scribner (2003) draws on the same "tinkering" metaphor to emphasize the importance of teachers "experienc[ing] their own learning." As compared to those who believe "that teachers are merely tinkerers who favour improving around the margins of their expertise," he pointed to the possibility of "transformative learning ... [becoming] the goal of professional development" (p. 6).

A number of other significant factors intersect with these more philosophical debates about the aims and objectives of PD programs. For example, governance questions often arise – who should make these decisions, and how should PD initiatives be planned and controlled? To what extent should PD objectives be determined centrally (at the board level, or higher) based on "system needs," as compared to being determined at the school or department (or even individual teacher) level based on perceived local interests and needs? (See, e.g., Sykes 1999; Hawley & Valli 1999.) In his study of teacher learning in one school district in the American mid-west, Scribner (2003) describes what is probably a very widespread phenomenon, one which was certainly echoed in the frustrations of the teachers in our study (and as explored in Chapter 4 below):

> In order to stretch resources and achieve economies of scale, the districts often held district-wide professional development events. While some teachers benefited from the workshops and speakers, most teachers interviewed found the events to be ineffective. For example, because most teachers in the district represented primary and middle school grades, teachers in this study often found the activities to be irrelevant to their needs. These teachers believed that by casting a wide net to accommodate all teachers, learning became superficial. Generally, teachers were frustrated by the waste of time spent at district professional development activities. (p. 15)

One could suggest that this bureaucratic, top-down approach to teacher engagement in learning probably does little to encourage the development of a professional culture of collaborative engagement in pursuit of knowledge within these schools. In fact, there seems to be relatively little in the overall PD research literature which draws directly on the issue of teachers' own autonomy and authority in relation to their engagement in PD programs, either as co-planners or participants. At best, there is only lip-service provided. For example, as an alternative to traditional PD Days and programs, there has recently been considerable attention given to the development of teachers' "professional learning communities" – efforts undertaken to encourage groups of teachers within individual schools to work together on their own learning agendas (Buffum & Hinman 2006; Dufour 2004; Hord & Sommers 2008; Brown Easton 2009). While much is being made of the purported success of this movement (see, e.g., King 2002), critiques also are fairly widespread. On the one hand, some researchers suggest that traditional notions of individual teacher learning persist, along with a resistance to "deprivatize" their own practice (Louis, Kruse & Marks 1996). On the other hand, as Hargreaves and Dawe (1990) note, many teachers raise concerns about and resist what they see as the top-down "contrived collegiality" of these programs. One empirical study which did involve a direct examination of teachers' authority and autonomy in relation to their willingness to engage in professional development was carried out by Scribner (2003). In his study of three high schools in the western United States, he did find that teacher take-up of these more collaborative approaches was highly influenced by the role taken by school principals and that significant activity resulted where teachers were actively supported in their efforts to engage in their own self-learning, thus enhancing an empowerment-learning nexus.

Recently, terminology has become important for researchers into teacher knowledge and teacher learning. Instead of 'professional development,' which implies top-down and externally determined programs frequently aimed at training teachers in new policy initiatives, researchers advocate a shift towards a focus on 'professional learning,' which implies self-directed, ongoing, and job-embedded learning (Broad & Evans 2006; Fullan, Hill & Crevola 2006; Easton 2008; Hannay, Wideman & Sellar 2006). While "the kind of high-intensity, job-embedded collaborative learning that is most effective is not a common feature of professional development across most states, districts, and schools in the United States" (Darling-Hammond et al. 2009), the landscape is changing with the new terminology, as teachers in progressive jurisdictions described in Chapter 7 of this book are being given more power over their own professional knowledge acquisition.

In summary, perhaps this debate about professional development in the context of "new conceptual knowledge" is best enunciated by Cochrane-Smith and Lytle (1999) in their analysis of their findings examining the ways in which teachers take up their own learning. As a grounding, they suggest that there are three basic models of learning, models that are closely related to the number of years which individual teachers have spent on the job. Relatively new teachers, they claim, engage mainly in seeking "knowledge for practice," a conception which "hinges on the idea that knowing more (e.g., more subject matter, more educational theory, more pedagogy, more instructional strategies) leads more or less directly to more effective practice" (p. 254).

By comparison, those with some experience shift to a "knowledge *of* practice" mode of learning. Here,

> the emphasis is on knowledge in action ... A basic assumption here is that teaching is, to a great extent, an uncertain and spontaneous craft situated and constructed in response to the particularities of everyday life in schools and classrooms. The knowledge teachers use to teach well under these conditions is manifested in their actions and in the decisions and judgments they make in an ongoing way. This knowledge is acquired through experience and through considered and deliberative reflection about or inquiry into experience. (p. 262)

However, the authors claim that, given proper conditions, it is possible for teachers to move to a third mode of learning – "knowledge *in* practice."

> Unlike the first two, this third conception cannot be understood in terms of a universe of knowledge that divides formal knowledge, on the one hand, from practical knowledge, on the other. Rather, it is assumed that the knowledge teachers need to teach well is generated when teachers treat their own classrooms and schools as sites for intentional investigation at the same time that they treat the knowledge and theory produced by others as generative material for interrogation and interpretation. In this sense, teachers learn when they generate local knowledge of practice by working within the contexts of inquiry communities to theorize and construct their work and to connect it to larger social, cultural, and political issues. (p. 250)

It seems clear that this particular context for teacher learning places front and centre issues of autonomy and professional control, both over teachers' own learning as well as their teaching practice. This emphasis on inquiry – "inquiry as stance" – positions teachers very differently than the ways in which they have traditionally been subjugated, within standardized, top-down PD programs and activities. Rather, the

> idea of *inquiry as stance* is intended to emphasize that teacher learning for the next century needs to be understood not primarily as individual professional accomplishment but as a long-term collective project with a democratic agenda. (p. 296)

In summary, it would appear that considerable steps have been taken – at least in the realm of critical praxis – towards the realization that issues relating to teachers' own authority and autonomy underlie their engagement in effective workplace learning. Whether this recognition will be evidenced in the continuing attempts by schooling authorities in North America and beyond to support more effective forms of professional development remains to be seen.

NEW TEACHER INDUCTION

Along with the recent influx of new teachers into schooling systems, and the concomitant concerns about their ability to survive their inaugural years, a number of research studies have pointed out the purported inadequacies of more traditional modes of support. As Dymoke and Harrison (2006) note from their empirical study of new teachers in the United Kingdom:

> For our sample of second year teachers, our analysis indicates that the support systems in school do not encourage the new teachers to become self-monitoring or critically reflective practitioners. Their professional development seems to be largely rooted in performance-led school managerial systems that may leave them unsupported in relation to their career aspirations and personal and professional targets. (p. 71)

Similarly, Spindler and Biott (2000) note that there are different and somewhat conflicting cultures at work in these more traditional approaches. On the one hand, there is a strong emphasis on managing teacher practice and "and providing training so that deficits can be rectified." Alternatively, there is a "practice-setting discourse" that is somewhat more embedded in the school culture in order to promote new teachers' feeling of belonging and encourage them to focus on supporting this school culture through their own efforts. Regardless of these approaches, a number of studies have indicated the high levels of professional and personal isolation experienced by teachers during their first years in the classroom (see, e.g., Tickle 1991; Weiss & Weiss 1999; Harrison 2002).

Given these concerns about the limitations of traditional approaches to supporting new teachers, the concept of "induction" and the development of proactive plans have become frequent additions to the PD field (Moir 2005; Fulton et al. 2005). While the implementation of these programs has involved a variety of activities, including special workshops, observation sessions in other classrooms and specially developed formative assessments, a major component in many jurisdictions has involved a mentoring program. These programs have taken many forms, but are all based on the concept of a more experienced teacher establishing a personal developmental relationship with a less experienced one.

Like other methods designed to promote teacher learning, mentoring has experienced various levels of success. Williams et al. (2001), for example, found that even where these particular practices were found to be successful, it was largely due to local factors related to their conception and implementation. As they noted, such practices were "by their nature, not amenable to statute or external mandate" (p. 265). As the British Department for Education and Skills (DfES) admitted in its own report on teacher induction (DfES 2003), strong local commitment is needed from the school administration and the larger school community in order to provide success for new teacher induction programs. Similarly, in examining the reasons for a 2007 cut back in New York City's new teacher mentorship program, Bess Keller found that "the program had not won over principals as it had in districts elsewhere," quoting a city official that only "about half the principals would give new-teacher mentoring their best thought and planning" (Keller 2007, n.p.).

In summary, the literature seems to make clear that neither the traditional non-interventionist "sink or swim" approach to new teacher induction nor the "one size fits all" provision of top-down, standardized formal professional development lectures and workshops provide much in relation to supporting or enhancing new teachers' learning. By comparison, more recent studies have suggested that effective induction programs are often based on individualizing approaches to new teachers – through mentoring and/or programs that allow teachers to engage in activities based on their own perceived needs and learning styles.

CONCLUSION

The purpose of this chapter has been to identify and explore a number of themes and issues related to teachers' work and learning: the nature of teachers' work itself, 'informal' and 'formal' learning, teacher knowledge, schooling reform, professional/ism, 'professional development,' and teacher induction. The historical analysis provided has suggested that public school systems, virtually since their inception, have been under attack from all sides – understandably, given that the various "stakeholders" have always occupied a variety of positions in our stratified societies, each with their own interests in the *raison d'être* of state schooling. Given these tensions, it is no surprise that most, if not all, of the major initiatives over time, related either to continuity or change in school systems, have also reflected these tensions. It is also no surprise that few of these initiatives have served to satisfy even a minority of these stakeholders, let alone achieve sustainable "success" in the eyes of the majority.

Often caught in the middle of these tensions are teachers themselves.

Chapters 7 and 8 of this book will provide more specific details about policy alternatives and successful programs.

PAUL TARC

4. FULL-TIME TEACHERS' LEARNING

Engagements and Challenges

INTRODUCTION

Mary is an elementary school teacher with twenty years experience teaching in urban settings. She is critical of what she calls "data-driven" reform that moves the focus from supporting students' learning in the classroom towards tasks which are more peripheral and wasteful of teachers' time and energy. Accordingly, she reports that her work is intensifying in multiple ways because of increasing bureaucratic demands with diminishing resources available. Although a seasoned practitioner, she feels she still struggles to complete her responsibilities without working beyond a "nine hour" day. While she continues to want to take formal courses she is also more selective and quite critical of the lack of flexibility she encounters in professional development options. Mary finds that collaborations with a few close colleagues represent her main mode of learning.

Cindy is also an elementary teacher in the same urban centre but with only eight years of teaching experience. She has moved rapidly through the phases of beginning teacher to curriculum leader and now is being trained to become a vice-principal; she is heavily engaged in both formal and informal modes of learning. Cindy too is aware of the data-driven reform pressures, but understands that it is not only top-down. She is aware that parents, including teachers, buy into accountability logics in the increasingly competitive school environment. She recognizes that much of her learning and approach to learning is shaped by these pressures and the need to respond to change.

Arif is a secondary school teacher, also in the same urban centre. He has only been teaching for a few years and has thus far been transferred from school to school and been required to teach a range of subjects in each of his early years of full-time contract teaching. He has come into the profession of teaching relatively late in his life. Arif might be seen as a kind of idealized 'lifelong learner' and less securely employed. He has multiple degrees and courses in education, including a doctorate and extensive computer training. Given his more transitive employment he moves from one steep learning curve to another; in each setting he seeks out and values greatly collaboration with his colleagues. While also reflective of the changing working conditions, he is much more deeply affected by these changed realities.

R. Clark et al. (eds.), Teacher Learning and Power in the Knowledge Society, 87–108.
© 2012 *Sense Publishers. All rights reserved.*

The purpose of this chapter is to describe *full-time* teachers' engagements in their formal and informal modes of learning and to examine how both the more explicit top-down professional development initiatives and the implicit day-to-day demands of teaching shape teachers' engagements in learning. By drawing upon the WALL empirical research on Canadian teachers' work and learning, the complex inter-relations of full-time teachers' workload (and stress), professional learning practices and current and prospective autonomy are also discussed. Most explicitly, teachers' professional learning is shaped by the requirements of (re-) certification and professional development (PD) programs initiated from the multiple levels of government, school board, and school administration. Generally, and more traditionally, this learning is conceived as taking place *formally* through the use of courses and workshops. More implicitly, teachers' learning is structured by the day-to-day demands of classroom teaching and shaped by teachers' internalized conceptions of what it means to be "professional."[1] Most often these day-to-day demands influence teachers' ongoing *informal* modes of learning. Informal modes of learning represent learning that is more self-directed, without the presence of a formal teacher or prescribed curriculum.

The chapter begins with the above composite accounts of three full-time Ontario teachers who participated in focus group interviews. By no means do these three profiles represent the diversity of perspectives or identities encountered in our research on Canadian teachers' work and learning. They do, however, begin to construct a basic pattern of the analysis presented. This suggests that while these teachers are substantively engaged and invested in formal and particularly informal learning, their engagements are influenced by their (shifting) working conditions and career trajectories. The reader will note that these three profiles also suggest somewhat different levels of perceptions of increasing work intensification, based partly on the seniority of the teachers interviewed.[2]

I tentatively suggest that veteran teachers maintain more traditional conceptions of workplace 'autonomy,' which align these teachers' critique of workplace intensification with the 'deprofessionalization' thesis of the 'deskilling' of teachers introduced in Chapter One. By comparison, newer teachers, who are constructing their teacher identities more recently, may perceive working conditions in more contradictory ways. The question of whether teachers' professional autonomy has been losing or gaining ground in the past decade will be taken up in the later discussion section, but I suggest in this introduction that the newer generation of teachers may find, and even be seduced by, new and contradictory forms of (neo-liberal) autonomy whereby teachers have a sense of greater local freedoms to achieve objectives that are increasingly regulated centrally ('steering from a distance' regimes[3]). This 'governmentality' analytic is discussed in the concluding discussion.

Following this introduction, the first section of this chapter presents teachers' self-reports on how they are engaging in formal and informal learning. Before turning to consider how teachers conceive of the challenges or obstacles to their learning, the next section explains how teachers understand their shifting working conditions. Teachers' workload and stress obviously will have impacts upon their learning practices. The final section turns to consider teachers' autonomy in their professional learning. Autonomy in teachers' work and learning is an elusive concept and needs to be unpacked a bit before leaving this introduction.

Where Chapters 1 and 2 lay out a larger frame for understanding ways of conceiving of teachers' class positioning, workplace control and power, and autonomy in learning, this chapter will mine the WALL teachers' data set[4] to both illustrate and test certain elements of these conceptions, particularly along the register of teachers' autonomy in their professional learning. Although 'power' in the vernacular sense represents something that is held and can be wielded to demand adherence to obey on the part of those with less 'power,' Foucault (1980) argues that power is dispersed and works at the most micro levels of human action. Power is productive, enabling as well as policing. Power is employed to do the work mandated from above and generated from below. In this sense, teachers employ power ubiquitously in their day-to-day practices (as do students, irrespective of their low positioning in the authority relations of schooling). For the purposes of attempting to understand teachers' control over their professional learning (in a larger institutional and social context), the discussion in this chapter will employ the term 'autonomy' as opposed to 'power.' Further, as an entry point we might hold on to a kind of structure–agency relation between the top-down control of teachers through governmental or institutional structures and the control by teachers exercised in their individual work practices, as in Anthony Giddens' structuration theory (Forrester 2005, pp. 137–138). Forrester emphasizes the key intention of structuration theory:

> Structuration theory attempts to link structure and action theories in a "duality" and explore the unclear relationship between the constraints placed on individuals by the (reconceptualised) structure of society and the choices and decisions individuals make. (p. 137)

Autonomy, then, is enabled and constrained but not determined by structures. The introductory chapters in this book present a similar conception.

In Chapter 1, Livingstone and Antonelli make important distinctions between the authority to "negotiate terms of provision of service or labour," the authority to make organizational change, and the "individual discretion and autonomy in conducting one's own labour tasks." As noted, it is the latter level in which teachers claim to have the greatest autonomy.[5] Although these three levels are conceptually distinct, in practice they do blur to a degree, because 'individual discretion' is not completely independent from the larger contexts. That is, organizational (infra-) structures and social relations, largely outside of the teacher's control, influence how the teacher conceives of his or her range of feasible options in terms of their local practice. Further, although personal 'teacher empowerment' shows promise (Boglera & Somech 2004), it remains tied to larger, socio-historical constructions of the 'good teacher.'[6] Thus the personal is always already embedded in the social. And also, for better and worse, 'teacher empowerment' is not immune from becoming a technique of self-regulation, whereby the teacher 'chooses for him or herself' practices that align with the needs of the organization. A later section in the chapter returns to this discussion.

CANADIAN TEACHERS' ENGAGEMENT WITH LEARNING

The NALL and WALL Teacher Projects confirm that during the 1998–2010 period most teachers have been significantly engaged and invested in their learning. This section considers both the quantitative teachers' survey data and the focus group interviews to summarize how teachers perceive their engagement with learning.[7] The first part focuses on teachers' formal modes of learning and explicit pressures to participate in PD. The second part centres on teachers' informal modes of learning.

Formal Learning

According to the 2004 WALL teacher survey, 90 per cent of all teachers reported participating in formal courses and workshops in the past year,[8] with a median of four courses/workshops (see Table 4-1). On average, full-time teachers reported an average of about seven one-half hours of work-related formal learning per week. The most engaged in formal learning activities were teachers with less than ten years of experience, who reported almost nine hours of formal learning activities per week. This finding is consistent with the demands made on new teachers for participation in additional qualifications courses. The finding from the WALL teacher survey that more experienced teachers generally participate less in further education courses is also consistent with the findings of the general WALL study for the general labour force.[9]

Table 4-1. Average weekly hours spent on courses/workshops, by seniority

Teaching experience	Mean	N
1–10 years	8.8	189
11–20 years	6.6	229
21+ years	4.3	290
Total	6.3	708

There was also variation in teachers' reporting of their weekly hours of formal learning across regions. As Table 4-2 illustrates, Ontario teachers reported significantly more hours of formal learning per week than their colleagues in other provinces. To attempt to account for this difference, we present the reasons teachers indicated for taking courses and note the different professional development regimes instituted across the differing regions.

There have been significant differences between the professional development programs mandated by the provinces of Alberta, Ontario and Nova Scotia (Clark et al. 2007, pp. 36–37). Ontario's previously enacted (2001–04) "Professional Learning Program" (PLP) was the most prescriptive, requiring Ontario teachers to complete 14 compulsory courses in a five-year period in order to maintain their license to teach. Nova Scotia was enacting a less rigid "Professional Development Profile" (PDP) requiring 100 hours of learning to be completed and documented within five years. In Alberta, teachers participated in the even less prescriptive, union-supported "Teacher Growth, Supervision and Evaluation" (TGSE) policy, whereby each teacher submits an annual growth plan to the principal detailing learning plans for the year.

Table 4-2. Average weekly hours spent on courses/workshops, by region

	Atlantic	Ontario	West	Total
Mean hours per week	5.8	7.0	5.2	6.2
N	100	369	245	714

The national teacher survey of 2004 asked teachers to identify the reasons for taking courses and which level of authority, if any, was requiring the course(s) taken. Almost a fifth of respondents (18 per cent) indicated that they took a course that was part of a degree, diploma or certificate. A fifth also reported that they took a course to be used as additional certification. And, just over a third reported taking a course because some authority required it. Table 4-3 below compares respondents' reasons for taking courses across three regions in Canada.

Table 4-3. Reasons for taking courses and workshops, by region

	Atlantic (%)	Ontario (%)	West (%)	Total (% and N)
Part of a degree, diploma, certificate	17	19	18	18 (N=117)
Additional certification	17	23	16	20 (N=124)
"Course was required"	32	37	35	35 (N=195)

Given the relatively small N values, the table shows no significant differences across regions; it does illustrate, however, that roughly one-third of courses taken by all teachers are required by external authorities. It is worth noting that, as discussed in Chapter Two, teachers (along with nurses, doctors and lawyers) have the highest level among professionals of further education participation and the table suggests that most of this PD is required by external authorities.

Where courses were required, Table 4-4 shows how the different levels of authority requiring courses vary between regions. Employers, likely the school boards, were the most cited level of authority requiring that courses be taken; about 60 per cent of Canadian teachers who stated that they were required to take courses identified their employer as the reason. Professional bodies were the next most common authority cited (at about 20 per cent). Again differences are small between regions. One significant difference is that about twice as many teachers (proportionately speaking) in Ontario have reported that the courses they took were required by a professional body. However, this five per cent difference might be explained by the fact that only Ontario and British Columbia have professional

Colleges of Teachers to enact such requirements and Ontario also has professional teacher certification bodies requiring certain courses for various salary levels. The fact that there is no real difference in courses required by government suggests that the more heavy-handed mandated PD regime in Ontario (discussed above) led to few discernable differences in teachers' engagement in formal PD compared with the regimes operating in Alberta or Nova Scotia.

Table 4-4. Authority requiring courses and workshops, by region

	Atlantic	Ontario	West	Total	N
Required by employer	27%	25%	30%	27%	543
Required by professional body	5%	10%	5%	8%	543
Required by government regulation	5%	4%	4%	4%	543
Required by other organizations	4%	6%	5.5%	5.5%	541

If there were Ontario teachers who were primarily compelled to take courses because of the PLP, this rationale was not corroborated in our interviews with them. Teachers unanimously felt that the program was professionally demeaning and not flexible enough to meet their actual professional learning needs. A number explicitly stated that they had taken some formal workshops but had not submitted them to the College of Teachers, suggesting that the PLP mandate was largely ignored by teachers as was recommended (and supported) by their unions. A couple short statements from two teachers are illustrative:

I participated as best I could [in courses] and did not submit any of my signed forms because it was trying to mandate something which is counter [to] learning.

Thankfully for myself and many of my colleagues, we haven't been involved in any of the PLP courses and we made sure that we stayed clear of them. Thanks to the wonderful support through our union and our Local that made it very clear to us what we should do.

By contrast, based on the focus group interviews, the professional learning program in Alberta did not seem to be overly controversial to teachers; additionally, they seemed to be inconsistently enacted across schools or school boards. A few teachers spoke about their professional growth plans primarily as ways of making explicit and tracking their professional learning needs. For some teachers the follow-up stage with their supervisors took place and for others it was deferred. For example, one Alberta teacher commented that the Teacher Professional Growth Plan (TPGP), within the TGSE policy framework, was not fully supported:

Teacher: *I did not complete half of my plan this year because my time was taken up doing other things ...*

Interviewer: *Did you process [the plan]?*

Teacher: *We did not this year, but for two years previous we have had a review at the end of the year. I do not think that it was very much observed. I am not sure it was even looked at, the review. This year we did not even have it. But we did have to write it, and turn it in; it is on file.*

In the case of Nova Scotia, teachers, unions and government officials collaborated to produce the PDP. Based on comments from teachers of a large urban board in this province, it appeared that the program was losing institutional priority as it basically confirmed that teachers were already engaging in as much or more hours of professional learning as had been mandated. It was suggested that the tracking of all these activities seemed somewhat of an unnecessary activity, although a few individual teachers in our Nova Scotia focus groups reported that they continued to track their PD hours. As to the value of the PD courses taken, across all the provinces represented, there were varied perceptions.

In the focus group interviews teachers did speak positively of a number of formal courses with diverse content and forms of delivery. Most indicated that they would likely continue to take courses to support their ongoing development. One of the few common themes, where teachers spoke positively on their formal learning, was the preference for courses that were directly applicable to their classrooms. The criticisms that teachers had of their respective professional development programs, however, were more unified.

In general teachers often spoke critically of prescribed professional development activities that had a "one size fits all" approach. Teachers, who felt that they already had the expertise or felt that the particular professional development focus was not relevant to their particular teaching assignment, spoke very negatively of such mandated experiences. Professional development "trends" (as fashions) were also spoken about a number of times. While some teachers felt that formal workshops stressing "literacy" (as one example of a trend) were directly helpful to their work as teachers, others saw these trends as diminishing their own professional development interests and autonomy as learners. Some teachers with many years in the classroom reported that trends tend to repeat themselves over time, invoking the metaphor of the "swinging pendulum." From their historical perspective, these trends seemed to diminish the autonomy of teachers who had to constantly adapt to the latest 'new' development making its way down to them regardless of its usefulness. It was also noted that these trends were often politically rather than educationally motivated. Two comments exemplify teachers' concerns with formal professional development.

[A]nd the major obstacle I see to this kind of PD is that they tell you what you have to do and they do not rely on you to trust your own instincts and know what you have to do yourself. It is being challenged by the [teachers' union] for that very reason: that it is rigid, it is top-down and it is unprofessional because it does not allow the teacher to choose the direction that Professional Development needs to go.

Well, every year is different. Five years ago we had a push on math in-servicing. Then we had a couple of new superintendents who wanted to be more accountable so we had this battery of reading tests and PD based on those results ... the same thing over and over again. They say, "Well, that is the way it has to be done because it is cost effective, and there are new teachers" ... which sounds great, except you have teachers who have had the PD already.

This critique of mandated formal PD is a clear example of the negative impacts of how teachers' constrained autonomy in organizing their professional learning impact negatively upon the usefulness, or even 'buy in,' to the PD on offer.

Informal Learning

Although teachers were more ambivalent in their accounting of their experiences with formal modes of learning, virtually all teachers reported on the necessity and value of informal modes of learning. In the 2004 teacher survey almost all full-time teachers reported that informal learning was either "very helpful" (51 per cent) or "somewhat helpful" (46 per cent). As Table 4-5 illustrates, teachers reported engaging, on average, in four hours of informal job-related learning per week. In addition to job-related informal learning, respondents averaged 6.5 hours per week on community work, household work, or other general interest related informal learning. A large proportion (78 per cent) also indicated that the informal learning they reported in these other domains was helpful in their work as teachers.

The 2004 survey results also provided interesting information on the content of teachers' informal learning. The content area reported most by teachers, at 80 per cent, was learning knowledge and skills of computer usage. Table 4-6 reports on a number of other areas in which many teachers indicated informally learning.[10] One can see that the full range of domains – teaching content, teaching methods, fostering student and staff relations – are areas in which teachers focus their informal learning.

Teachers also reported engaging informally on a number of wider job-related issues as presented in Table 4-7. The table illustrates the range of relevant learning beyond teachers' engagement with students in the classroom.

Table 4-5. Time spent on all informal learning, by geographic region

	Work-related avg. hours/wk	Total informal learning avg. hours/wk	N
All full-time teachers	4.2	10.7	776
Alberta	4.6	10.8	86
Ontario	3.9	10.0	358
Nova Scotia	4.8	9.4	33
other provinces	4.0	10.0	216

Table 4-6. Content themes for teachers' informal learning

Content area	% of teachers engaging (N=714)
Computers	80
Teaching subject	70
Keep up with new knowledge	63
Curriculum policy	62
Classroom strategies/management	61
Learn about student problems	51
Team/communicating skills	50

Table 4-7. Wider job-related issues

Content area	% of teachers engaging (N=714)
Curriculum	63
Teacher Ed	47
Employee rights	44
Health & safety	39
Environment issues related to work	26
equity issues	19

When asked how this work-place informal learning took place, respondents indicated that significant amounts took place collaboratively with colleagues (70 per cent), students (10 per cent), administrators (eight per cent) and parents (four per cent). Almost half of respondents (48 per cent) indicated that they also engage in informal work-place learning on their own. When considering their informal learning generally across multiple domains of their lives, *collaboration with others* remains a dominant approach to learning. This finding links up with the finding presented in Chapter Two that, compared to other professions, teachers place high import on informal collaborative learning. Table 4-8 specifies how teachers generally go about learning. Note that multiple responses were allowed.

In the *focus group interviews*, teachers typically began by discussing their learning in courses and workshops, but as the discussion probed deeper into the day-to-day dynamics of teachers' work, the importance of informal learning emerged as dominant. Collaboration with colleagues was the most often cited example of teachers' informal learning. The following two quotes are reflective of the teachers interviewed:

> Okay, well I was in great need of professional development this year. And actually my greatest source was another teacher who became a partner to me …

> I think the best professional development I have ever had that I had gotten the most from is talking to people in my own school, and having the time to do that …

Table 4-8. Favoured modes of informal learning

	% Response
Consult friend/peer/family	53
Consult text or guide book	45
Look on the internet	34
Work it out on my own	35
Consult expert or professional	28
Co-operate with group, network of friends, or family members	20
Other (several listed)	2
Do not usually plan	1
	N=714

Even in the context of discussing formal learning in conferences or workshops, teachers often highlighted the importance of meeting and talking with other teachers in the in-between times (e.g., during coffee break). While a few teachers spoke of enjoying or valuing contact with teachers across different contexts – for example, elementary with secondary teachers – the majority of teachers consistently privileged "teacher talk" or collaboration with colleagues having similar teaching assignments (whether by grade level or subject discipline). Use of terms like "relevance," "usefulness," "hands-on," and "things to take in the class tomorrow" signified the importance of sharing ideas around one's immediate context of learning under the demands of teaching. Similarly, a number of teachers spoke of the enhanced learning in collaborating around shared tasks, such as evaluating a common set of exams or building curricular units.[11] However, a few teachers spoke very negatively where collaboration was mandated by authorities around some particular educational theme bringing teachers together in (prescribed) groups. Again, these teachers' comments reinforce the positive value of teachers having control over the processes of collaboration and professional learning. And again, we see that, even for informal learning, there are linkages between organizational decision-making power and the teacher's individual discretion over their 'own labour tasks.'

When teachers were pressed to speak about the most salient contexts for learning from collaboration, a number of specific recommendations surfaced. Several teachers spoke highly of the chance to observe their colleagues teaching. They valued both the chance to see other ways of approaching a lesson or a class, as well as the shared context to discuss teaching methods and ideas. This opportunity was occasionally made available by a teacher's individual request or suggested by a supportive administrator. Consider the following response on the opportunity to observe:

> sometimes principals will free up teachers to go visit another teacher and see what they are doing. Just to sit in their classrooms for the day, not to read with kids, not to do anything else, just to sit and see what they have done on their walls, to see how they interact with kids, and to get a totally different perspective because at the five or four year point, I think that is really good learning. I am still okay, but sometimes when I see other people doing things

I think "That is brilliant, I did not know about that." And even to just have a day once a year to say I am going over to K's class for the day.

Another common suggestion for supporting informal learning, especially in the context of beginning teachers, was mentoring. Many interviewees described an increase or decrease in mentoring over the years, or from one school to another, but typically all spoke of its positive value. Some of the less experienced teachers spoke of a mentor-colleague as the single most valuable support for their informal learning. Some more experienced teachers expressed the view that the mentoring role also provided a context for their own further learning.

Reading and surfing the internet were also commonly mentioned modes of informal learning. While internet use was not emphasized by all teachers, those who did report utilizing the internet stated that they did so extensively and found it very helpful. A number of teachers echoed the following comment:

I do not know how I taught before the internet. I take so much material off of there, especially because I have had such a turnover in the subjects that I taught.

Similarly, some teachers talked about their use of books, magazines and journals, television and videos as a way to keep up with pop culture or world events and in order to make connections between students, the world and the curriculum. As one teacher commented:

I was trying to explain how Shakespearean ... fiction and all this and you can just kind of [see that] this is going nowhere, so I said, "Okay, write to me in MSN chat language. Try and write me a letter that I cannot understand and I am really good at language" ... [It went] right over my head, I had no idea ... and they loved it. It was a mutual lesson, and I really wouldn't have thought about it unless I read it in the focus section of The Globe *[newspaper].*

Some teachers also reported increased use of e-mail for collaborating with colleagues across distances. For a few teachers working in more remote areas or in smaller schools, e-mail was an essential way of getting help. Some teachers spoke of e-mail as a way of continuing conversations started in conferences or meetings:

Our school district has a monthly Counsellor/Facilitator meeting. Our district is huge ... and we all meet together once to see what is going on and that has been awesome for making connections [with] other people doing the same job I am doing, and we communicate through e-mail all the time. I think internet and e-mail have been huge for where I learn things.

TEACHER PERCEPTIONS OF CHANGES IN WORKING CONDITIONS

Perceived Changes in Workload Levels

In our 2004 national teachers' survey, respondents were also asked about changes, if any, that they had noted in their workload over the previous five years (or less, if they were new teachers). About four-fifths (78 per cent) reported experiencing increases over the preceding five years. Table 4-9 below also shows that the more experienced the teacher, the greater the perception that workloads had increased over previous years. Given that more experienced teachers generally have already learned how to "do the job" – or do it more efficiently through their years of endogenous workplace learning and continuing education – this difference is likely even more an indication that changing policy and curricular reforms are increasing workload. There were no significant differences reported between elementary and secondary school teachers in terms of workload.

Table 4-9. Teachers' perceived changes in workload over previous five years

Years of teaching	Significant increase %	Increase %	About the same %	Decrease %	N
0–5	24	31	37	8	62
6–10	32	36	29	3	119
11–15	50	32	16	3	97
16+	49	36	14	1	372
Total	44	35	19	3	650

There were differences by gender with a greater percentage of women reporting a significant increase in workload (see Table 4-10). It is pertinent to note here that, although teaching is a predominantly female profession, the WALL teacher survey found male teachers to be twice as likely to have official administrative positions (21 per cent versus ten per cent). Male teachers were also more likely to indicate a great deal of choice in their jobs (71 per cent versus 56 per cent). Furthermore, male teachers were more likely than women to have employer financial support for their further education (56 per cent versus 38 per cent). Women teachers may be more vulnerable to workload increases because of relatively less workplace power. They may also be less enabled by employers in seeking further formal qualifications to cope with workplace changes.

What were the specific reasons for these perceived increases in workload? From the teachers' survey questionnaires, the two highest increases reported were "Dealing with administrative requests for information, forms, data, student attendance, etc." (81 per cent) and "Time/effort required for assessing and reporting on student progress" (80 per cent). These perceived increases in work had much to do with increased bureaucratic requirements, taking time and energy away from supporting students' learning.

Table 4-10. Overall workload change in past five years, by gender

Stress levels	Significant increase %	Increase %	About the same %	Decrease %	N
Female	47	34	17	2	465
Male	38	35	24	3	184
Total	44	34	19	3	649

Certainly, the information gathered from the more in-depth teacher interviews emphasized these concerns. When asked to describe how their work lives had changed over the previous five years, a majority of teachers spoke about increased timetabled hours, increased class sizes, increased supervision tasks, and so on. "Accountability" was a term mentioned innumerable times by focus group participants. It was raised, not in the context of teachers' obvious and accepted professional responsibility, but in relation to new or increased requirements to meet bureaucratic dicta with very little, if any, connection to useful evaluation of their work as teachers. Common concerns to teachers in all four provinces selected for in-depth interviewing were the periodic impositions by their provincial governments of new course curricula and new student assessment, evaluation and reporting procedures often with insufficient in-service support to implement these changes. These government policies and related paperwork, forms and "individual education plans" were frequently cited as causes of the increased workload.

A perceived "lack of time" appeared as a common denominator across most interviews and focus groups, whether it related to the inability of schools or school departments to find common time in their busy schedules or to the many ways in which individual teachers saw the increase in workload affecting their own capacity to engage in more overview activities in their programs. The simple lack of availability of time in the day seemed to be a major consideration for many. One teacher accounted:

I don't know how to say that, like when you are in the classroom all the extra things that you are being asked to do and I know it's just one piece of paper here, and one piece of paper there and two pieces of paper here, but they all add up. And the amount of anything from supervision time, I mean they are all little tiny things but they are building up to being a lot of time. And that's the time you might have spent planning your ... program that you just learned in wherever [workshop].

Yet another teacher made it very clear how her working routines both at home and at her school strongly influenced her ability to consider engaging in any kind of non-teaching activities, even in talking with colleagues during recesses or after school.

I think one other thing I would like to add to my list is energy. I think sometimes I run out of energy to do the next thing. And it is real hard to learn how to have enough energy before school because I do a lot of things before I even walk into the classroom. I have two children to get ready to go to school, and my own things that have to be done and then you make it through the whole day. I do not think in a year I have three lunch hours to myself, and we have no recess in our school. And then I go right home to being a mom and getting dinner ready and finding out who has homework.

Teacher Stress

Over 80 per cent of all respondents on the 2004 national survey reported that the "overall level of stress" in their work had "increased" or "significantly increased." Similar to the workload statistics, there were clear differences in levels of stress based on years of teaching experience and gender (see Table 4-11). Once again, in spite of their greater experience, more senior teachers were found to be facing increasing stress levels as great as or greater than newer teachers, indicating that recent workplace changes have had widespread and deep effect on all teachers. Once again, women teachers indicate greater increases in stress levels, indicative of relatively less workplace power to mediate such changes.

Table 4-11. Overall stress-level change in past five years, by gender and seniority

Stress levels	Signif. increase	Increase %	About the same %	Decrease %	Signif. decrease %	N
Female	50	32	14	3.4	0.5	443
Male	35	41	22	1.7	0.6	178
Total	46	35	16	2.9	0.5	621
0–5*	26	34	25	15	0	61
6–10*	33	31	32	4.5	0	111
11–15*	40	44	12	2.2	1.1	90
16+*	54	34	11	0.8	0.6	361

* Years of teaching experience

The general link between increased workload and increasing stress levels is illustrated in Table 4-12. With about 80 per cent of teachers reporting both greater workload and stress levels, increased workload and increasing stress are closely corresponding variables. Increased levels of stress certainly must impact upon the quality of teachers' engagement in their informal and formal learning – whether at school or outside of school.

Two different levels of distress are presented here, by two different teachers. The second teacher's comment marked a very emotional moment during one of our focus groups.

I used to direct plays, the good creative stuff we used to do. Our kids are more challenging, our classes are bigger. I teach English; I have more marking that ever before. I went to bed at two o'clock last night. We have more mechanical tasks. I have three e-mails [i.e., addresses], so I must now check three e-mails. I have now three phone message machines I have to now check. Parents can access any one of these, and thus more communication that's happening, that's the problem. And that takes more time and that creates more stress ...

We've had all kinds of things and this was the first time in my 25-year career that I applied for stress leave, twice. Twice that I felt heart palpitations, shortness of breath, constant crying and feeling like I was never good enough [voice starts breaking as she tears up]. And I left the school ...

Table 4-12. Overall workload change by overall stress level change

Overall workload change (past five years)	Signif. increase %	Increase %	About the same %	Decrease %	Signif. decrease %	Total N
Signif. Increase	72	23	5	< 1	< 1	279
Increase	32	53	13	2	< 1	219
About same	11	31	50	8	0	123
Decrease	13	7	40	27	13	15
Total N	45	34	17	3	< 1	636

These quotes do not refer directly to teachers' learning, but if teachers are to engage in learning activities in proactive and mindful ways, having the time, (emotional) energy and organizational support are crucial for doing so.

INHIBITORS AND REACTIVE MODES OF LEARNING

Beyond the teachers' survey results already reported, workload intensification was also a dominant theme in the focus group interviews, explicated with reference to, for example, the downloading of administrative duties onto teachers, increased paper work, increased reporting on students and increased supervision. In turn, several teachers reported that this intensification impacted negatively upon their time (and energy) to engage in learning, both formally and informally. The 2004 survey results show a small but significant increase of 1.3 hours per week of work-related activities since 1998 (Clark et al. 2007, pp. 36, 48). The significant numbers of respondents indicating workload increase on an independent question may also be suggestive of a compression of activities, or more diversions from what they conceive as their central tasks (i.e., curricular objectives). Again, as already presented, the focus group interviews provided some illustrative examples of "compression" and increased tasks, accompanying stress levels and their negative impacts upon teachers' health or wellness.[12]

Lack of time was consistently reported in teacher interviews as the primary obstacle to informal learning (and one of the most emphasized constraints for participating in formal learning as well). This finding is consistent with Lohman's

(2000) research on inhibitors to teachers' informal learning, where lack of time was found to be the predominant inhibitor.[13] And as in the Lohman study, the problem of insufficient time was typically explained in the context of work intensification, as related above.[14] For example, the time pressure created by the increase in workload, for some, seemed to directly impact upon the quantity and quality of collaboration with colleagues. In addition, some teachers spoke about other impediments, such as work schedules which did not include common planning times or the lack of a common meeting area. An anecdote often repeated was of the teacher working alone while eating his/her lunch rather than going to the staff room. Another was administrative downloading, with multiple manifestations, diminishing both time and infrastructural supports for learning. A couple of quotes for illustration will suffice here:

The paperwork. It impacts on the time that you might do some of that informal learning after school or at lunch because you are busy filling out forms in triplicate or putting together yet another referral package for an assessment.

... unfortunately our latest contract allowed that cap to be pierced ... so some classes do get very large, which then again affects the whole workload issue, which allows for less time for formal learning. That has affected me because I am in a small school, so there is a large amount of supervision time which perhaps high school teachers do not have to deal with, but my planning time now is less than my supervision time. So I do 160 minutes of supervision and I only have 120 minutes of preparation time [per week]. So that is where it cuts down on my informal learning, and it cuts down on that informal congeniality thing because you are always on duty. So you do not have a chance.

Also, in the context of workload intensification, teachers sometimes spoke of informal learning almost as a survival mechanism – learning how to manage amidst all the challenges – rather than as a more autonomous activity directed proactively by the teacher in an area of pedagogical interest. For example the following teacher quotes illustrate the "survival" side of informal learning:

And I think because the working conditions have changed so much, the formal learning has decreased and the informal learning has skyrocketed because you are constantly learning. You have to learn that new curriculum, you are just moving along, moving along, so it's never ending.

I think we learn to do whatever we can to be successful at whatever our success is: whether it is success for our students or success in your personal life or success in getting through the day. Expedience is the word.

This "on the go" and "getting by" informal learning, if considered within the definitional bounds of informal learning, also leans toward 'reactive' rather than 'deliberative' learning, categories in Eraut et al.'s (2000) typology of "non-formal" learning. While some teachers clearly recognized the existence and pervasiveness of this "survival" mode of learning in response to intensified workload with insufficient supports (lack of timely training, learning new software in the process of doing report cards electronically, teaching new courses before textbooks have arrived, repairing photocopiers, etc.), many teachers emphasized the more proactive meanings and uses of informal learning in their work. For example, the teachers interviewed did not typically associate their "learning" (and their desires for learning) with the technical or administrative demands impacting their workload to which they clearly were responding. Even when the interviewer drew out this connection for some of the groups, in the context of exploring possible obstacles to the teachers' learning the teachers downplayed the "survival" aspect of learning across the wider dimensions of their work, quickly refocusing their discussion on what they perceived as the needs of the classroom.

In a sense, then, there were two conceptions of learning emerging from teacher discussions in the focus group interviews. Where responding most directly to the interviewer's set question, teachers explained their learning practices and preferences in relation to improving their teaching practice in the classroom. However, in more spontaneous and engaged conversation about the day-to-day challenges of teaching, teachers' more reactive modes of learning became very prevalent once the interviewer drew attention to these modes of learning. This prevalence resonates with the findings of Hoekstra and colleagues (2007) that a significant proportion of teachers' learning occurs in the reactive or tacit modes. Stress and workload then represent variables relevant to how and how proactively teachers are engaging in learning. The next section turns to a consideration of teachers' autonomy in their professional learning.

TEACHERS' LEARNING AND 'AUTONOMY'

The 2004 national teacher survey did ask teachers whether or not, over the previous five years (or less, if newer to teaching), they had perceived any change in the "level of autonomy" afforded them in their workplace. As indicated in Table 4-13 below, while about half of respondents believed that the level of their autonomy had not changed over this time, over one-third (35 per cent) stated that it had diminished, as compared to only 14 per cent who indicated an increase. As the WALL general survey findings in Chapter One suggest, teachers express the highest sense of personal autonomy of all professionals in their immediate workplaces. The teacher survey and case study findings suggest that teachers are trying tenaciously to hang on to a sense of autonomy within their classrooms in a context of extensive organizational restructuring and relatively little organizational decision-making power.

There were some differences in perceptions of changing autonomy, based on the years of teaching experience of respondents. While just under a quarter of relatively new teachers (0–5 years) believed that they are already experiencing a decrease in their autonomy in their work, 40 per cent of senior teachers report a similar conviction in this regard. As with perceptions of changing workload, veteran teachers may have a better sense of shifting contexts in their workplace environment.

Table 4-13. Perceptions of change in teacher autonomy, by seniority

Years teaching	Signif. increase %	Increase %	About same %	Decrease %	Signif. decrease %	N
0–5	2	18	56	21	3	61
6–10	5	11	58	21	6	107
11–15	2	19	47	28	4	90
16+	3	9	49	30	10	354
Total	3	11	51	27	8	612

The introductory chapters have quantitatively compared teachers' sense of organizational decision-making control and sense of autonomy at the classroom level to workplace power in other professions. In addition, we can track explicit demands placed on teachers' professional learning – ranging from compulsory PD regimes to forms of "steering from a distance" through the centralized control of curricula or assessment. Further, as also emphasized above, we can illustrate how learning becomes reactive in a context of work intensification.

But it is much more challenging to illuminate the structure-agency relation in the context of teachers work and learning. In Chapter 1 (p. 45, above), it was emphasized that:

> Teachers hold distinctive control within their own classrooms in relation to their students. But such control is continually in jeopardy because of organizational decisions made outside the influence of classroom teachers. Educational practices like standardized curricula, testing and reporting, ballooning classroom sizes, and increased administrative duties, just to name a few, have an enormous impact upon the immediate workspace of teachers.

On the one hand, teachers recognize that they have little control of the organization as professional employees largely responding to the demands placed upon them legally and contractually. On the other hand, teachers' generally understand themselves as retaining considerable autonomy at the micro level of classroom pedagogy. Complicating a top-down control versus bottom-up autonomy/creativity dichotomy (see, e.g., Forrester's use of structuration theory)[15] are the multiple and complex relations between social ideologies embedded in discourses of professional development, professionalism, and more general social values and norms, with the individual teacher's own sense of acting with agency. For example, more recent proposals to accentuate professional learning by teachers against the prior dominance of compulsory, top-down professional development regimes have been advocated as a concrete improvement for teachers (e.g., Hargreaves 2000). However, these new discourses of teacher reflection and empowerment also represent new regimes of *self*-regulation. Thus (teacher) autonomy is a very elusive and complex concept to theorize. Not only is there no "outside of" control in the context of work, it remains unlikely that "autonomy" (as with "freedom") can ever be defined in wholly positive terms. Rather, it is only possible to consider shifts in relative autonomy given changing conditions of work.

Clearly, there are very real constraints, such as time and material supports, that can limit how creatively, reflectively, and deliberatively teachers can practice. Nevertheless, changing contexts present both new possibilities and new dynamics of control – even under new initiatives promoting informal modes of teacher learning. Accordingly, we turn to a governmentality[16] lens to further elaborate upon the complexities of autonomy and control in relation to teachers' workplace learning.

Given the ubiquity and growing recognition of the value of informal modes of work-place or professional learning (Tuschling & Engemann 2006), informal modes present new possibilities and challenges for teacher autonomy. In discourses of professional development, there is growing interest in supporting informal modes of teachers' growth and learning, as with the following approaches: building 'learning communities;' building 'capacity for 'organizational learning;' teacher leadership; action research; reflective practice; and teacher mentoring (Darling-Hammond & Sykes 1999; Fullan 1995; Hoekstra, Beijaard, Brekelmans & Korthagen 2006; Katzenmeyer & Moller 1996; Marks & Seashore Louis 1999; Williams 2003). Most of these recommended practices rest on the assumption that greater teacher autonomy leads to improved working conditions and improved student learning. Autonomy, however, can be envisioned more as means than as ends.[17] For example, under (neo-) human capital paradigms, worker autonomy or 'empowerment' can be a tool for shaping workers subjectivities to correspond with organizational goals (Garrick & Usher 2000). Governmentality theorists and other critical theorists who analyse 'lifelong learning' and 'worker empowerment' warn that these approaches can effectively work more as subtle forms of control rather than liberating or democratizing initiatives (Garrick & Usher 2000; Smyth 1991; Tuschling & Engemann 2006). A related critique by Marks and Seashore Louis (1999) emphasizes that without organization learning founded on democratic decision-making processes, 'teacher empowerment' remains nominal. Such empowerment may reduce to merely retaining some control over one's classroom.

Based on our focus group interviews, there is a definite institutional impediment to optimizing teachers' collaboration and 'flexible mobilization' to build and sustain 'learning communities.' In spite of the interest in promoting and supporting teaching as the "learning profession" (Darling-Hammond & Sykes 1999), the limited material support and sometimes limited social or administrative support for teachers' informal learning suggests that schools do not necessarily represent a "knowledge intensive work context" for teachers, as it is described by Belanger and Larivière (2005, p. 20): "There is a direct relationship between knowledge intensive work context and organizational support of informal learning activities." For example, while many teachers spoke of the value of mentoring and of observing colleagues teaching, these valued learning activities came with obstacles that militated against their take-up. A number of times teachers cited the difficulty of leaving one's "own" classroom or students. A few teachers explained that one of their colleagues could "lose" their planning period where they took the initiative to observe a colleague teach. Other teachers explained the difficulties of finding common planning times in complex and full schedules and of extensive supervision time that interfered with the possibilities for collaboration. Further, teachers noted that in more recent years department heads and administrators had diminishing time to support or engage in peer observation.

Teachers' anecdotal reporting suggests that while collaborative modes of learning are possible and even sometimes promoted by administration, the rigidity of the timetable, the teacher's traditional role (that each teacher needs to be sovereign over his or her class or classes for the duration of the year or semester), and the curriculum and testing regimes, among other factors, limit teachers' participation. In some sense, the interviews revealed the contradictory space teachers have to negotiate – for example, jumping on-board as team players in accord with the latest professional development trend but with limited material supports – and sometimes limited administrative supports.[18] Teachers have to negotiate the devolving of accountability in the contradictory spaces of educational reform (Dehli & Fumia 2002). On the one hand, they are invited to initiate learning activities as peer coaching but understand that their absences ought not affect their day-to-day routines and supervision, nor how "their" students perform.[19]

Based on our focus-group interviews with full-time teachers, teachers generally are not the optimally flexible (Tuschling & Engemann 2006) knowledge workers of the post-modern learning organization (Garrick & Usher 2000). Veteran teachers, while "stressed out" with work intensification and obviously adapting to change, generally resisted envisioning themselves as 'adaptable' or 'flexible.' Clearly, teachers with more years of professional and institutional work experience are positioned to more clearly perceive changing workload and stress levels. They articulated more established notions of themselves as professionals and learners. These teachers were quite aware of the educational restructuring taking place in their provinces and criticized aspects of neo-liberal reform and rhetoric. In their critique, teachers employed terms such as: "accountability;" "data-driven" reform; "compressed" working schedules; "expediency" as an operating principle; and "conservative ideology-driven" reform. Remarks from two teachers are illustrative:

> *[Administrators] are very much data-driven. Most boards today are data-driven. That's the big word these days – data-driven, which means your EQAO [Education Quality and Accountability Office mandated test] scores mean an awful lot. And so they are helping teachers and pushing teachers, encouraging teachers, signing them up for every course under the sun ... You know what's the newest coin, what's the newest word that we are using, what's the newest program; therefore, you get on board because we have to bump up those scores. And every school now of course is mandated to have a school improvement plan. So teachers and administrators are gearing their educational style according to their improvement plan. But again, what is driving that again is data.*

> *[L]earning has become ideologically driven. We've always had ideologies involved in education somewhere because after all we are part of an ideological system ... but when it comes overtly ideological, it's ideologically driven by the masters, like Mike Harris in Ontario and Margaret Thatcher in England. When you take learning and you overtly drive it ideologically, with*

an ideological agenda, then it takes away from us as educators what we've been doing for decades.

Nevertheless, more nuanced analysis of the survey data offers some correspondences with premises emerging from the governmentality theorists who suggest workers are taking on, "for themselves," learner dispositions, such as "flexibility," conducive to the larger goals of the organization.[20] In a previous paper (Tarc et al. 2006), we compared teachers who reported more than ten hours of informal learning weekly ("high informal learners") against teachers who reported one hour or less. High informal learners also reported higher levels of formal learning, higher levels of working hours, and higher stress. This result, although tentative, does connect with Garrick and Usher's (2000) description of the "'seduction' at work and by work – a seduction through empowerment" (p. 12). In other words, being empowered as a "life-long learner" and more productive employee is "seductive" in the sense that teachers take on more opportunities for professional learning and 'self-improvement' even as these produce greater levels of work intensification and stress.

Moreover, a few teachers interviewed *do* seem to be taking on some of the characteristics of the flexible, enterprising self, especially teachers with little seniority or teachers who are un(der)employed. Arif, the teacher profiled at the outset, exemplified the subject-position of the flexible, lifelong learner; he was highly engaged in both formal and informal learning and able to respond to his frequently changing assignments. Arif also described himself as "very flexible," being repeatedly shifted ("pink-slipped") from one school to the next and from one teaching assignment to the next. Had we interviewed more teachers with little seniority, we might have heard similar narratives about the need to stay current and be permanently updating.[21] We also hear these narratives from the contingent workers (occasional and internationally-trained teachers), to be discussed in Chapter 5.

Informal learning has traditionally been primarily the responsibility of workers themselves. However, a hallmark of our times is that workers' informal learning is increasingly prone to managerial surveillance and hortatory appeals for workers to do more of it for the greater good of the learning organization. At the extreme, informal learning becomes a form of ongoing, unpaid overtime exerting pressure on contract teachers who try and maintain reasonable work–home boundaries and even more centrally for occasional teachers who are trying to secure full-time contracts (as discussed in Chapter Five). Even for teachers with job security, the following comments are illuminating in terms of the blurring of boundaries between paid work and home, heightened in an age of interconnectivity and competitiveness. One teacher remarked:

So we are constantly on call in terms of ... last night I got an e-mail telling me that I better review something that I had taught yesterday because this woman felt that her child didn't learn it properly, and she and her husband struggled to teach him, and the e-mail was sent at 9:30 last night. I had a phone call from a parent this year; she left the message at 3:40 a.m.

And now that's just so common place. I mean now with the e-mail we have teachers that are going berserk because there are parents e-mailing and saying we want a report every week on how their kid is doing in high school – every week! And they feel entitlement to that, and it's like, where are our boundaries.

These examples, among others, illustrate the changing working conditions with the blurring of job–home boundaries and pressures for continuous communication and responsiveness to the stakeholders in schooling. These changing conditions, in turn, shape what and how teachers are learning, and can further diffuse the focus of teachers' learning from the domain of classroom pedagogy.

CONCLUSIONS

We can track the explicit control of teachers through formalized certification and PD regimes. Teachers generally maintain great investment in their ongoing learning regardless of top-down professional development programs. Yet, control of teacher learning is even more complex, being influenced by a whole set of factors from school architecture to (internalized) norms of professionalism and self-conduct. Our teacher interviews suggest that, for Canadian full-time contract teachers, at least some of teachers' informal learning is reactive in a context of work intensification and thus can be seen as working against teacher autonomy, as in conceptions of deskilling. Even where teachers are encouraged to be self-directed autonomous learners through more recent discourses of professional learning, such a mandate can be seen as a technique of governmentality which presses for teachers' self-directed and life-long learning as new modes of self-regulation through updating, self-recording and acting "professionally." Prospects for teacher's autonomy in learning are diminished when teachers' lack the very resource which can most influence how the mandate to be a life-long learner unfolds – time for thinking, reflection, and engaging in more deliberative modes of learning. On a positive note, Chapters 7 and 8 present a few examples of where the resource of "time" and supports are worked into mentoring and other professional learning programs. The degree of success of these more recent initiatives needs further study in order to inform policy.

This chapter has illuminated the inter-relations of full-time teachers work, learning and prospects for autonomy to some degree. Yet it seems that there is much conceptual (and empirical) work that remains to be done to better understand the structure–agency inter-relation for teachers' practices in the contemporary moment. 'Autonomy' in the work of teaching and learning remains complex and elusive. Even if we were to employ a less foundational term such as 'creativity' (Storey 2007), the problem of how it (creativity) is conceived by teachers and how these conceptions are informed by external forces (explicit mandates or techniques of self-regulation) needs further illumination before we can use the concept robustly as a category for empirical research.

KATINA POLLOCK

5. OCCASIONAL TEACHERS' JOB-RELATED LEARNING

INTRODUCTION

Publicly funded schools are hierarchical institutions with many different levels or divisions of power. Each level of authority has a role to play, and each level is situated between those with more authority and those with less. Substitute teachers are treated poorly because they can be. They exist at the lowest level of a hierarchy and are governed by others with more power ... It is important to understand that the inherently hierarchical nature of the school system prevents [occasional] teachers from ever becoming full members of the teaching profession. (Duggleby & Badali 2007, p. 31)

In Chapter 1, Livingstone and Antonelli argue that professionals in class positions with ownership prerogatives have more power than those who are part of the professional employee class, like teachers. However, we also need to acknowledge that there are differences among professional employees. Not all professional employees have equal power. This is particularly the case for teachers. Teachers' power is associated with their positioning within the hierarchy constituting the teacher workforce. This means that certain groups of teachers, and in particular those who are employed in non-permanent arrangements, will have less access to power than do permanent full-time teachers. These arrangements will influence how they do their job and how they learn about their job. This chapter explores how non-permanent job arrangements for teachers – occasional teaching – influence their professional ability to control their job, work environment, and professional learning.

OCCASIONAL TEACHERS

In Canada, one-fifth of the teacher workforce in the public education system work as non-permanent teachers (Livingstone 2011; Work and Lifelong Learning Network, 2005). Non-permanent teachers are a growing contingent professional workforce, reflecting present global employment trends. Contingent work, as defined by Bjorkquist and Kleinhesselink (1999, p. 3), "is any job in which an individual does not have an explicit or implicit contract for long-term employment;" such work can include casual employment, temporary employment, and/or short-term contract work. In Ontario, as elsewhere, non-permanent teachers occupy the lower levels in the professional hierarchy described in Chapter 1. Moreover, non-permanent teachers have the least delegated power – in organizational decision-making participation and perceived choice in planning

R. Clark et al. (eds.), *Teacher Learning and Power in the Knowledge Society*, 109–125.
© 2012 *Sense Publishers. All rights reserved.*

one's own work – of any teacher group. Because they are often sent in at the last minute to replace sick colleagues or colleagues engaged in formal professional learning outside the classroom, they cannot control who they teach, where they teach, or what they teach. One way non-permanent teachers cope with limited delegated power, particularly in planning their own work, is to develop particular strategies that help them deal with the unpredictable teaching situations that they find themselves in. They do this by engaging in job-related learning that specifically prepares them for their job arrangement. This chapter describes a qualitative study that was comprised of eighteen semi-structured interviews; fifteen with occasional teachers from the southern Ontario region and three others who had knowledge of occasional teacher and teaching (Kelly,[1] a union representative who bargained on behalf of occasional teachers, Daniel, an employee from the Toronto District School Board and Katherine, a past staff member of a bridging program for internationally trained teachers seeking work in Ontario and a past principal). Specifically, this chapter explores how fifteen non-permanent teachers in Ontario attempted to control and access job through their job-related learning, both formal and informal.

The terms 'substitute teacher' and 'supply teacher' dominate the literature that refers to non-permanent teachers who are hired to 'cover' "when the regular (timetabled) teacher is not able to teach a scheduled class, and another adult is called on to teach or supervise these pupils" (Galloway & Morrison 1994, p. 1). They are identified by a number of different labels which are used interchangeably, such as occasional, temporary, floater, emergency cover, short-term supply, substitute, recruitment agency teacher, relief teacher and teacher on-call, to name a few. Because this chapter focuses on Ontario as a case, terminology from the Ontario context and legislation is used. Thus,

> A teacher is an occasional teacher if he or she is employed by a board to teach as a substitute for a teacher or temporary teacher who is or was employed by the board in a position that is part of its regular teaching staff including continuing education teachers. (Education Act 1990, S1 (1.1))

Like any Ontario teacher, occasional teachers must undergo the Ontario teacher accreditation process and become a member of the Ontario College of Teachers (OCT). But unlike full-time permanent teachers, they are employed on a temporary basis: "They may work in one school or many. Some are able to work almost full-time in this way, yet do not have a regular contract with any employer or institutions; others work only infrequently" (Galloway & Morrison 1994, p. 1). In Ontario, an occasional teacher may also work in more than one school district and be "a member of more than one teachers' bargaining unit" (Education Act 1997, S122 (277.5)). Occasional teachers can work on a day-by-day (known as daily) basis or in Long Term Occasional (LTO) positions, but neither job arrangement includes long-term employment. The average LTO position is between five to six months (Ontario Ministry of Education 2007). This study specifically focused on occasional teachers who worked on a daily basis.

This sort of contingent work is "practiced in all fields of work and at all occupational levels of private and public sector employment" (Bjorkquist &

Kleinhesselink 1999, p. 3), but most research (Connelly & Gallagher 2004; DiNatalie 2001; Gariety & Shaffer 2001; Golden 2001; Hipple 2001; Redpath, Hurst & Devine 2009; Osterman 2010) does not include teachers' work in alternative employment arrangements (such as occasional teaching) as part of the contingent workforce. Professional, technical and managerial temporary workforces are developing in areas such as information technology, nursing and medicine (Allan & Sienko 1998), so it is not surprising that such a workforce would develop in the teaching profession. In the United Kingdom, Grimshaw, Earnshaw and Hebson (2003) have gone so far as to contemplate whether 'supply' teachers working with teacher recruitment agencies in England can consider themselves as working on a self-employed basis.

GROWTH IN THE CONTINGENT TEACHER WORKFORCE

Expansion of the occasional teacher workforce has been stimulated by a number of influences, including changing student enrolment, the teaching supply and demand cycle, changes in labour practices and the changing nature of work. Similar to other jurisdictions worldwide, the Ontario teacher population has experienced large fluctuations in supply and demand. Teacher retirement hit record highs in the English-speaking public system with approximately 7,000 retirements annually from 1998 to 2002. Ontario teacher education programs increased their intake in response to the resultant teacher shortage. Teachers were also recruited from US border colleges with programs designed for the Ontario market and from the increasing pool of internationally educated teachers (McIntyre 2007). These strategies proved to be successful in meeting the immediate teacher demand. However, the rate of teacher retirement has since decreased to less than 4,600 annually during 2005–09 (Ontario College of Teachers 2011, p. 2) and the success of these strategies has subsequently created a surplus of qualified teachers. Two out of five English-language teachers have had to wait up to four years to be employed, if indeed they are fortunate enough to find full-time employment at all (Ontario College of Teachers 2011, p. 57). In 2010, 11,800 teachers entered the English-speaking teacher workforce (Ontario College of Teachers 2011, p. 2), many of whom joined the growing number of teachers already certified to teach in Ontario and increased the already large number who had not been able to secure a full-time permanent teaching position. Of these new graduates in 2009–10, two out of three were involved only in occasional work or could find no job in teaching of any description (McIntyre 2011).

In 2011, the job queue continued to grow; the Ontario College of Teachers' annual *Transition to teaching* report noted that:

> The involuntary unemployment rate for first-year teachers has increased every year for the past five years. What was a three per cent unemployment rate in 2006 is now 24 per cent. For those who did some teaching in their first year, the underemployment rate[2] also rose from 27 per cent in 2006 to 43 per cent in 2010. (McIntyre 2011, p. 33)

Some new teachers will wait as long as five years to receive a permanent teaching contract. In 2011, one out of five teachers who received certification five years previously was still unemployed or underemployed (McIntyre 2011). This means the occasional teacher pool will grow substantially, and in doing so, will intensify, expand and perpetuate hierarchies in the current teacher workforce.

TEACHER WORKFORCE HIERARCHY

A hierarchy is a system of ranking and organizing things or people, where each element of the system (except for the top element) is subordinate to a single other element. A hierarchy can link entities either directly or indirectly, and either vertically or horizontally. (Wikipedia n.d.)

The Wikipedia definition captures more concisely than most other definitions the key elements of the concept of a hierarchy. It also has its limitations, however. While it points to links among entities, it nevertheless fails to capture how the ordering of these entities revolves around power and control, as it occurs in professional organizations, for example. Hierarchies are implicit in many social processes (Corson 1986), particularly organizations such as governments, educational institutions, businesses, religious groups and political movements. Professions, including teaching, are no exception.

The expansion of the Ontario occasional teacher workforce mirrors differentiated hierarchical workforces in other work sectors and professions, including teaching in other jurisdictions (Harvey 2000; Reich 1992; Soucek 1994). Soucek (1994) describes a three-tier, differentially-skilled, hierarchical teacher workforce as "highly skilled professional workers, specifically skilled peripheral full-time workers, and generically-skilled peripheral part time or casual workers" (p. 55). According to Soucek, the highly skilled professionals in education are core teachers (teachers who teach 'core' subject areas such as math, science and English – usually subject areas tested in state-wide standardized tests), senior management, senior staff and expert teachers (teachers that have been identified as having [or supported in developing] expert skills and knowledge in specific key education areas such as special education, assessment, etc., and are targeted for eventual promotion to school district positions). They enjoy job security, promotion opportunities, professional development, and pension and other benefits. Of the limited power that teachers hold, this highly skilled group of teachers has the most negotiating and delegated power of all three worker-groups. Peripheral workers are teachers who are generally permanent and specifically skilled teachers who have less access to career opportunities and exhibit a higher labour turnover, such as core French teachers (Richards 2002) and English as a Second Language (ESL) teachers (Bascia & Jacka 2001). Teachers identified as peripheral workers generally experience less power, while generically-skilled peripheral teachers hold little power. The generically-skilled peripheral workers are the part-time, casual or contract staff who work in arrangements such as occasional teaching (Morrison 1999a, 1999b), under enterprise bargaining arrangements, recruitment agency teaching (Barlin & Hallgarten 2001; Grimshaw et al. 2003; Johnson 2001), and part-time teaching (Young 2002; Young & Grieve 1996). This group has even less job security or access to professional development, benefits and pension than the first peripheral group. Livingstone and Antonelli (2004) point out that (within particular limits) teachers' sense of autonomy is among the highest of all professionals. But not all teachers experience the same degree of classroom autonomy. Because of their job arrangements, daily occasional teachers have the least sense of classroom autonomy.

OCCASIONAL TEACHING, AUTHORITY AND LEARNING

Occasional teachers' inferior positioning within the teacher workforce hierarchy influences both their power and learning. Daily occasional teachers find themselves in a unique situation. While permanent teachers may struggle with professional authority and control over their work, their struggles pale in comparison with the struggles of many daily occasional teachers. For example, occasional teachers in this study explained that because they worked intermittently within the school system, they had a very different type of relationship with students than do full-time teachers. Nicole, a career occasional teacher maintained that:

As a regular teacher you have time to get to know your kids, you've got established routines, you're there all the time with them [students] and so that sets the whole tone, within the classroom, in the school, with the parents, with the administrators, with whomever you come in contact with in the school. As an occasional teacher you're there for the day ... you're parachuted in, you're there for the seven hours and then you're gone. You might never be back in there.

Because the job arrangement of daily occasional teachers was such that there was no long-term, on-going consistency with a particular group of students, occasional teachers did not have the opportunity to build rapport with students nor were they able to develop routines or implement classroom management strategies that had consequences that extended further than the immediate day of teaching. For this reason, students did not perceive daily occasional teachers as having any sense of authority in the classroom, whether or not they are qualified to teach. When describing the occasional teachers' lack of authority in the teaching profession, Andrew, who also taught in the teacher pre-service program, explained, "As an occasional teacher you have no credibility; nobody knows you." As Sonia put it, "You don't have the opportunity to build that rapport with the student."

All the occasional teachers in this study described how students treated them differently from full-time teachers. Students treated occasional teachers with a lack of respect. For instance, Ping commented, "The day the regular teacher is not there, they think it's a long break. So sometimes they stop at nothing to drive you crazy." Consistent with the literature (Lawrence 1988; Shillings 1991), all participants described occasions when students demonstrated little respect for the occasional teacher in the classroom. As one union representative, Kelly, commented, "The students don't treat them like a real teacher. They're considered by many students to be a babysitter." Thomas conveyed this lack of respect when students engaged in such acts as "changing the time on the clocks ... changing their name, or sitting in other people's desks or their favourite thing was everyone goes into fits of coughing." Participants in this study believed that unless a teacher was a 'regular' teacher – someone who teaches on an on-going consistent basis with repeated interaction with a particular group of students – students did not feel that the teacher held any legitimacy. Because of occasional teachers' job arrangement, students were disrespectful to them because there were no consequences; there was no means for meaningful recourse or follow-up.

Even though daily occasional teachers are subject to the same credentialing requirements as their permanent colleagues and are formally considered professionals according to traditional notions of professional qualifications, their job arrangements and hierarchical positioning eroded their professional authority and control over their work. Daily occasional teachers do not have the same kind of legitimate authority that full-time permanent teachers have because they do not hold an official position (Clifton & Rambaran 1987). This leaves daily occasional teachers with little to no control over the frequency or type of teaching they do in the classroom. It also creates difficulty in accessing appropriate learning for their job arrangement.

Daily occasional teachers' learning for their job could best be described as job-related learning rather than professional development. Professional development has been described as the "formal and informal provisions for the improvement of educators ... in terms of the competency to carry out their assigned roles" (Joyce, Howey & Yarger 1976, p. 2); as "efforts to improve teachers' capacity to function as effective professionals by having them learn new knowledge, attitudes and skills" (Gall & Renchler 1985, p. 6); and the "natural learning experiences ... those conscious and planned activities which are intended to be of direct or indirect benefit to the individual, group or school, which constitute, through these, to the quality of education in the classroom" (Day 1999, p. 7). In the field of education, the dominant conception of professional development tends to focus specifically on the expert knowledge and skills required for classroom teaching (Furlong, Barton & Whitty 2000; Clarke & Newman 1997). Thus, present notions of professional development do not include all the other informal learning crucial to occasional teaching, such as understanding how schools are organized, how to work with colleagues, how to network with other teachers, how to develop marketing skills, or how to come to understand the culture and social processes within different school sites. Conventional notions of professional development are often not appropriate for daily occasional teachers because they typically assume that teachers return to the same established workplace each day.

The concept of job-related learning better suits the experiences and needs of daily occasional teaching than professional development or learning (Fullan, Hill & Crevola 2006) because it includes these other facets of learning central to occasional teachers, such as gaining access to daily teaching and navigating the education system. As professionals, both full-time permanent and daily occasional teachers actively engage in job-related learning. Every day they informally learn about such things as pedagogy, relationships with members of the school community, classroom management and so on. They need to engage in this learning in order to do their jobs. But full-time and daily occasional teachers do not always (opt to) learn about the same kinds of things because they are positioned differently within the educational system and have different needs. Daily occasional teachers are compelled to develop different skills than their full-time colleagues, and as such, they also opt for different learning experiences. The job of full-time teachers is ongoing and consistent with consecutive days of employment, whereas an occasional teacher's job is contingent on the absence of a full-time teacher – it is not ongoing and continuous nor is there any guarantee of any employment.

How occasional teachers' work was arranged influenced how they engaged in their work and job-related learning. For example, occasional teachers in this study were interested in either modifications of classroom management strategies or different kinds of classroom strategies. Substitute teachers in this study generally did not use classroom management strategies that required continuous, on-going contact with students (i.e., behaviour contracts) because they were not useful in their daily work arrangement. Ping, for example, related how one method that she learned in teachers college would not work. She was taught that when faced with student(s) who are chatting and not paying attention, she was to walk closer to the student without stopping the lesson. This tactic was designed to encourage the student(s) to refocus. If they persisted, she was supposed to say the student(s)' name(s) and continue with the lesson. She pointed out, though,

that doesn't work as a substitute teacher. You could say 28 names and there would still be talking ... many of the classroom management strategies that I learned in teachers college work if you're the classroom teacher and if you have authority in the room. But, I don't think they really work if you're just walking in [as a substitute teacher].

Ping went on to say that she tries to find other classroom strategies in occasional teacher resources that are more applicable to her job arrangement. Ping went on to explain how it is all about being proactive and setting the classroom expectations at the beginning of the day/class. For example, she mentioned having students at the primary level choose various types of birds or animals to represent themselves and then setting up a reward system where individuals and groups were rewarded for appropriate behaviours throughout the day. If students did need to be addressed, it did not matter if she knew their name; she could refer to them by the animal they represent, and peer pressure to receive the end-of-day-reward would help to keep other children in line. Daily occasional teachers not only opted for different learning experiences when it came to their classroom practices but also spent more time learning about unique aspects of their job, such as how to increase the frequency of their daily employment or secure a full-time teaching position (Pollock 2010).

TYPES OF OCCASIONAL TEACHERS

Just as Acker (1999) argues, "In its search for generalities about teaching and the teaching occupation, the literature on teachers has been guilty of creating a category of 'teacher' that does no justice to the diversity contained within the term" (p. 19), occasional teachers as a group were not homogenous, but rather diverse. For 2006, the Ontario Ministry of Education reported that the occasional teacher workforce was composed of approximately 20 per cent retirees, 40 per cent career occasionals, and 40 per cent new entrants (Ontario Ministry of Education 2007). The Ontario College of Teachers further sub-divided the occasional teacher workforce by reporting that the large "new entrant group" could be further divided into four groups: Internationally Educated Teachers (IETs) representing just under one-half of the occasional teacher workforce, compared to approximately one in five new Ontario graduates, one in four teachers educated in other provinces; the remainder are teachers educated at American border-colleges that allowed Ontario residents to take education degrees and do their practice teaching in Ontario classrooms (McIntyre 2007).

The fifteen occasional teacher participants interviewed in this study of occasional teachers' learning were part of the Ontario English-speaking public school system (for details, see the Appendix). All of these occasional teachers participated in the teacher workforce through daily teaching. In fact, participants were selected only if they had taught just as a daily occasional teacher within the previous 12 months. The participants represent three of the types of occasional teachers identified above: internationally educated teachers (which is a sub-group of the new entrant category), career occasional teachers and retirees. The groups were not always completely distinct from one another; that is, the characteristics of particular individuals sometimes overlapped with those in other groups. For instance, some career occasional teachers who previously held a full-time, permanent teaching position began their teaching career as occasional teachers until they secured a more permanent job. Even though there were general characteristics shared across all groups of occasional teachers, such as their non-permanent job arrangement and relative powerlessness, each group nevertheless displayed some unique tendencies.

Internationally Educated Teachers (IETs)

The internationally educated teachers sought full-time, permanent work. These teachers were not necessarily new to the teaching profession – some had more than ten years of teaching experience elsewhere – but they were new to the Ontario context. According to 2001 and 2006 Canada census data, IETs made up 5.4 per cent and 6.9 per cent of the teacher population, respectively. More importantly, however, the increase in this proportion is less than the increase in the proportion of visible minority citizens in the general population, which increased from 13.4 per cent to 16.2 per cent (Ryan, Pollock & Antonelli 2009, p. 597). Four IETs were interviewed from this group: three women and one man. The women are referred to by the pseudonyms Ping, Zahra, and Sonia; the one male is referred to as Ogus.

In addition to receiving certification outside of Canada, each teacher also possessed additional certification or higher education, such as master's degrees in areas such as education, mathematics and physics, some before coming to Canada and some after immigrating to Canada.

Career Occasionals

Career occasional teachers in this study had either held a previous permanent teaching position within the Ontario English-speaking public school system before taking up their occasional positions, or had been teaching as an occasional teacher for more than five years. Members in this group did not intend to seek full-time, permanent teaching jobs within the next five years. Six of the seven teachers in the study had held full-time permanent teaching job previously, but because of other commitments and responsibilities, they chose to teach as daily occasional teachers. Only one teacher indicated that she began her teacher education with the intention of doing daily occasional jobs. She reasoned that she was going to have children immediately and that occasional work fit well with her life on a farm where she helps her husband during harvesting season. Five of the seven career occasionals were women. The women all indicated that their motives for occasional work centred on balancing parenting responsibilities while still working at a job that they enjoyed. The five career occasional women are referred to, using pseudonyms, as Emily, Helen, Claire, Nicole, and Heather; the two men are Andrew and Paul. All these respondents were in a mid-career stage, each having taught for a number of years in the teacher profession.

Retirees

This group of occasional teachers, four in total, consisted of three women (pseudonyms: Andrea, Melissa, and Pam) and one man (pseudonym: Thomas). These teachers were retired from permanent teaching and were collecting an Ontario teacher's pension, whose rules allow a limited numbers of days of continued teaching after retirement. All were transitioning out of the teacher workforce and anticipated eventually leaving teaching entirely.

OCCASIONAL TEACHERS' JOB-RELATED LEARNING: FORMAL AND INFORMAL

Occasional teachers engage in both formal and informal job-related learning. A more meaningful way to consider occasional teachers' engagement in job-related learning than merely recording which groups engage in what kinds of formal learning is to consider their motivations. Participants in this study had already navigated through the accreditation system and were certified teachers. The following sections discuss the level of, and motivations for, both formal and informal learning.

Formal Learning

In this case, formal learning is the institutional learning required for certification and the formal professional development opportunities offered by the school district, teacher federations and provincial ministry of education. Daily occasional teachers in this study engaged in various kinds of formal learning. The teachers identified formal learning with organized formal professional development programs such as professional activity (PA) and professional development (PD) days. Other forms of formal learning included Additional Qualification (AQ) courses, Additional Basic Qualification (ABQ) courses, General Equivalency Diploma (GED) night courses, and bridging programs (programs for teachers who had recently immigrated to Canada and were working towards their Ontario certification and or trying to secure a teaching position), such as the *TeachinOntario*[3] program. Findings indicated that participants, who had little control over their job arrangements and were struggling in the classroom, were motivated to participate in more formal learning. For example, during her interview, Sonia declared that she was at "total odds with the Ontario education system," and it appeared from her responses that she participated in more formal professional learning than other participants. Those who perceived they had sufficient expert knowledge and had considerable access to daily teaching jobs participated less in formal learning. For example, new entrants as an entire group participated more in formal professional development than career occasionals and retirees (Pollock 2010). Indeed retirees participated in next to no formal learning. Andrea, a retiree, commented,

> *I just didn't feel the need for it. And the professional development that I did do over my years [32 years] as a teacher, I ended up finding not the least bit helpful. A lot of the workshop leaders were people that had been around for 20 or 30 years and it was the same thing over, and over, and it was, as far as many of us [full-time, permanent teachers] were concerned, a waste of time.*

Unlike the internationally educated teachers in this study, retirees were not seeking full-time teaching employment and therefore did not perceive a need for additional formal education as a means of providing better employment opportunities or learning new things. Retirees in this study felt that there was no real need for more formal professional learning. This is consistent with Livingstone's (2007) survey finding that adults in their mid-50s substantially reduced their participation in job-related formal training because of declining employment-incentives as they approached retirement. Retirees in this study also believed their previous formal professional learning and on-the-job experience as full-time, permanent teachers provided them with the necessary skills and knowledge to continue teaching as daily occasional teachers. In fact, according to the retirees, many administrators employed retirees because they believed that retirees held 'expert knowledge' about classroom management and teaching – they already had experience as full-time, permanent teachers. Daniel, also a former principal, commented that principals looked for experienced teachers:

because the principal is counting on having somebody very reliable. If you can get a retired teacher to come back to your school, someone who knew your community, your community knew them, knew the culture of the school, knew the students, and if your board allows you to request people, and many school boards do, yes, that person [retiree] is going to get the job.

This passage reflects what many occasional teachers believed were the ideal knowledge and skills that administrators were looking for in a daily occasional teacher; that is, the kind of contextual knowledge most needed to be effective in different classrooms in that particular community/school/board. Daniel believed that utilizing recently retired teachers could be beneficial to a school if the retiree continued to do daily occasional jobs at the school from which he/she retired. Retirees continued to carry some of the prestige, power, and respect associated with a full-time, permanent teaching position. Initially, they had more classroom control and were given more authority for classroom decision-making. However, this power and level of authority existed only for a limited time after the retirement – a honeymoon period. After the honeymoon period, the retiree goes from

being part of a community, to being isolated, 'cause they've spent 25, 30 years as part of a community no matter which school they've been in for however long in their careers, all of a sudden they're a non-entity ... (Kelly, local union representative)

As some participants in the study reported, this position of privilege was only temporary. The teacher's identity shifted as students, who at one time identified the individual as a full-time teacher, progressed through the grades. New students entering the school site identified the retiree as a daily occasional teacher who was lower on the hierarchy than a full-time teacher. The retiree, originally considered an ideal occasional teacher, became just another occasional teacher as student attitudes towards the teacher changed. This in turn left the retired occasional teacher with less power and authority in the classroom. A number of retirees mentioned that when working non-permanently for more than five years, they began to intentionally seek out more informal professional learning (Pollock 2010) as a way to deal with their shifting authority.

Both career occasional teachers and internationally educated teachers in this study participated in formal professional learning, but to different degrees and for different reasons. For instance, career occasional teachers engaged in formal learning more out of personal interest than for resumé-building, although the latter did occur to some degree. When asked why she attended workshops, Emily, a career occasional, commented:

I would say it's my own incentive ... you get a certificate to put in our portfolio when you're done, but I would say for the most part it's my own initiative. What things are going to help me?

Some felt that they had completed enough formal schooling and did not need additional training for their job. When asked if she would like to be involved in any type of formal learning, Helen, another career occasional, stated:

> ... not really ... I've done so many courses and extra-curricular this and AQ that, like I've done enough. I've done my masters. I'm finished ... I'm done ...

Heather, also a career occasional teacher, commented that she took a few additional AQ courses and attended professional development events at the school level, "more out of interest" than anything else. A career occasional for a few years, she had established herself in a number of schools and was receiving fairly consistent work, and therefore did not view further formal education as a means of securing more work. She also did not feel that there was any financial gain to doing additional formal training because in her local collective agreement, daily occasional teachers received a flat rate of pay.

The internationally educated teachers in this study, however, appeared to participate in substantial amounts of formal learning, motivated by the desire to secure more occasional teaching days or a full-time, permanent teaching position. One respondent stated that he took "an ABQ course in English to get [an] interview [to be put on the occasional teaching list]." Another engaged in formal learning despite the fact that she already had considerable credentials and experience. Even though Zahra taught for more than ten years in her home country, has undergraduate and master's degrees in math and physics, and a teaching degree, she was still having difficulty securing teaching work, so she attended a Grade 12 mathematics class at a night school. She argued that it gave her a better pedagogical understanding of the Ontario context, and expressed the hope that it would indicate to others that she had formal understanding of it.

Ping, another new entrant, was certified and had taught in Hong Kong for over ten years. In Canada, she received her Ontario certification but found little work. She then completed a bachelor of arts in linguistics at an Ontario university and began occasional teaching. After her interview, she was short-listed for an LTO position. She then "joined five courses during the summer to equip myself to teach math" at the elementary level.

In this study, most IETs participated in additional professional development. At the time of the study, this professional development included bridging programs such as *TeachinOntario*. *TeachinOntario* supported IETs through an informative web site, individual and group counselling, assistance in obtaining documents, language assessment and training, teacher orientation sessions and help with job search strategies.[4] It also assisted IETs in gaining access to the teaching profession. Ogus pointed out that during the program "speakers from a local school board were invited to talk to us about how to apply for work, how to write a proper resumé, and so on." Ping mentioned that in her bridging program they were guaranteed an interview (but not necessarily a job) with one of the local school boards if they completed the program. These programs also help IETs in gaining the cultural capital that they need to navigate the Ontario education system. For instance, *TeachinOntario* not only provided IETs with information on provincial curriculum and legislation such as the Safe Schools Act, interview training, resumé writing, classroom management, and understanding of the current educational terminology, but also addressed cultural differences that centre on issues of respect, dress code, and customs. For example, in terms of classroom management and discipline, Zarha, described how in her bridging program she shadowed a few teachers in different schools to learn how "different teachers demonstrated different strategies in front of us and these [were] very effective."

Programs like *TeachinOntario* can assist IETs in receiving certification and gaining access to the 'eligible to hire" list, but this does not guarantee that the occasional teacher will secure any days of work. The program did not offer ongoing support that enabled occasional teachers to move up the workforce hierarchy. The Ontario government has recognized the importance of this sort of support for new teachers in permanent teaching positions and has introduced the New Teacher Induction Program (NTIP),[5] discussed more thoroughly in Chapters 6 and 7, which has recently included new occasional teachers who hold long-term teaching contracts (Ontario College of Teachers 2008a). Yet, little on-going support exists for daily occasional teachers who do not have a long-term contract, particularly IETs.

Informal Learning

Just as full-time teachers engage in a great deal of job-related informal learning (Smaller 2005), so too do daily occasional teachers. However, this engagement differs. One of the key differences revolves around the focus of the informal learning. Participants indicated that most of their learning occurred through some type of informal learning. This is due, in part, to the fact that most formal learning opportunities do not help them with their work (Pollock 2009). As Retallick (1999) points out, even full-time teachers struggle with ownership and meaningfulness of ideas presented at formal professional learning opportunities. Success of formal professional learning appears to come once full-time teachers have an opportunity to try and test ideas out in their own classroom practice; only then do they report the professional learning as possibly useful. Occasional teachers are even more removed from this process of meaning-making and ownership of ideas because they do not have the luxury of testing out ideas in their 'own' classroom. The situation is compounded by the fact that the content of formal professional learning opportunities is often not relevant to what they actually do (Pollock 2009).

Occasional teachers may attend formal professional development sessions because the subject or activity being presented is a board priority and not because it is helpful for their immediate work situation (Pollock 2009). They may use the formal professional learning opportunities to build a resume in hopes of securing either more frequent work or more permanent work, not because it will help them with their immediate teaching practice (Pollock 2009). For example, a professional development session that involves new reporting procedures in Ontario would not be helpful to occasional teachers because they are not required to evaluate students or track their progress. However, knowledge of the new reporting procedures could be helpful for future teacher interviews. Unfortunately, few formal learning opportunities meet the needs of teachers working in non-permanent teaching positions because many of these activities are designed for full-time permanent teachers whose work differs from that of occasional teachers (Betts 2006;

Damianos 1998; Duggleby 2007; Duggleby & Badali 2007). So, occasional teachers have little choice but to rely heavily upon in informal learning.

In this study, internationally educated teachers reported participating more in informal learning, as well as more formal learning, than career-occasionals and retirees. That is not to say that career occasionals and retirees did not engage in informal learning. But they engaged in informal learning more frequently when there was a substantial change in work arrangement such as location (different school, board, province, country). For daily occasional teachers in this study, much of the informal learning occurred at the job-site, as Emily, a career-occasional indicated.

> It's all perpetual ... development. You go into hundreds of teacher classrooms and you see the way they do it, you have access to their lesson plan, you have access to their daybook, probably you see more about how a teacher runs the classroom in a day than the principal sees doing an evaluation cause you're there so you massively accumulate ideas. For people who are hoping to go into a full-time position it really does give you professional exposure to a wide range of pedagogical styles, classroom set-ups, means of planning ...

Daily occasional teachers generally often found themselves in unique learning situations. They had little professional autonomy as they were expected to follow instructions from the absent teacher as well as the provincial curriculum guidelines. Occasional teachers' professional autonomy came into play when they had to decide whether they had the subject knowledge to carry out the assigned lessons, and/or if the lesson plans left for the students were appropriate for the immediate context of occasional teaching. Occasional teachers encountered many different lesson plans that included different pedagogical strategies for a broad range of curricula. This breadth and depth can be a good source for ideas of practice. Livingstone (2005) points out, "Most adults probably engage in multiple forms of learning on an ongoing basis, with varying emphases and tendencies" (p. 5). According to Livingstone, the physical classroom offers up numerous opportunities for simultaneous learning. Some daily occasional teachers may go about their teaching day engaging in "tacit forms of learning and other everyday activities" (Livingstone 2005, p. 5) without a purposeful agenda of consciously learning from the regular teacher's classroom. Other daily occasional teachers may explicitly go into new teaching environments with intentions of gaining new knowledge, understanding, and skill. The type of learning depends on one's social and cultural context. This was certainly the case for IETs who want to learn the general culture and climate of Ontario schools.

Church, Bascia and Shragge's (2008) definition of informal learning reflects the learning IETs engage in when attempting to access their profession and effectively teach in the classroom:

> *Informal learning is both voluntary and involuntary, sometimes simultaneously. It blurs the boundaries between intellectual, technical,*

social, political and emotional forms of knowledge. It is embedded in the processes of daily life as a means for coping, survival and change. (p. 3)

IETs in this study explicitly engaged in more intentional informal learning than career occasional teachers and retirees. The main purpose of their engagement was to gain a better understanding of the Ontario public education system. These understandings included knowledge of the structure of the provincial and local education system, pedagogy, knowledge, skill, and cultural differences. One way in which IETs engaged in informal learning was through classroom volunteering. Classroom volunteering in this case was reported as actual assistance with, and observation of, teaching in a classroom, not necessarily extracurricular activities such as coaching sports teams that full-time teachers report participating in, for example. As Ogus stated,

Volunteering ... Volunteering, I would say, ninety per cent of it was to my benefit, ten per cent to the benefit of the school ... I learned what the school was about, the people who work [there], the principal, vice-principal, department heads, schools are not that big in my country ... I am not accustomed to the department thing, because I taught in university, but not in a school like this. And the volume of the job is really a lot ...

Besides volunteering at a school site to network with staff, building resumés, securing a reference, and gaining 'experience,' Sonia, Ping, Zahra and Ogus commented that volunteering in a school site that included volunteering within a classroom was *the* way of consciously learning about the Ontario public school system. Daniel, a school board employee, and Katherine, who was also a past principal, encouraged the practice of classroom volunteering as a way to understand the education system. In general, IETs were advised by school administrators to do classroom volunteer work as a way of learning about the Ontario public school system. No retirees or career occasional teachers in this study engaged in classroom volunteering as part of their professional learning nor were they encouraged to do so by others such as school principals.

The learning in which IETs engaged was different from the everyday perceptions, general socialization and more tacit informal learning of Ontario-raised teachers because the Ontario public education system is part of the latter's culture. Specific knowledge, beliefs, attitudes, behaviours and practices associated with the education system were largely taken for granted by those who grew up in Ontario's school system. For individuals not familiar with the Ontario public system, however, these unconscious behaviours and practices were new and unfamiliar and were judged against the individuals' prior knowledge and learning from some other context. As Zahra said:

You work here as a volunteer and observe. You watch the teacher; what she is doing, how she prepares the lesson plan, how she delivers the lesson, what electronic resources she uses here, how she accommodates the diversity in the classroom, how she accommodates the student with different learning styles and how she facilitate the students with his or her instructional technology and all of the multiple intelligences ...

Therefore, what one person considered tacit knowledge, another made a conscious effort to acquire in his/her informal learning practices. Perhaps more significantly, volunteering at school sites appears to be one of the few ways that occasional teachers can receive effective mentoring from other teachers.

TEACHER WORKFORCE HIERARCHY AND LEARNING

The findings from this study illustrate that the degree of professional authority and control over work influences learning. While many teachers higher up the workforce hierarchy engage in both substantial job-related informal learning and in formal professional learning, those occasional teachers at the bottom of the hierarchy, particularly internationally educated teachers, appeared to be more preoccupied with job-related intentional informal learning. Some of the latter learning had little to do with actual teaching in a class. Given their marginal position, occasional teachers were also concerned with learning that which allowed them to gain access to increased or more secure teacher employment. The higher up an occasional teacher was in the hierarchy, the more opportunity he/she had to engage in formal professional development. Conversely, the further down the hierarchy, the less opportunity one had for formal learning and the more one engaged in additional informal job-related learning. This also applied to differences among occasional teachers.

In the study, daily occasional teachers said that they participated in less formal professional learning than full-time teachers and for a number of reasons. One reason for this is that some were asked to cover for full-time teachers who themselves are attending formal professional learning. Daily occasional teachers' professional decision-making in this case centred on either working for the day or attending a professional development session. The way their work was arranged means that some occasional teachers tended by default to have less access to formal professional learning opportunities because they choose work over formal professional learning. Occasional teachers who hired into long-term occasional teaching positions (and are higher up the hierarchy), on the other hand, had more access to formal professional learning opportunities. Take, for example, an occasional teacher employed in a long-term teaching contract for four months. If the teacher's employment coincides with some type of formal professional learning for teachers in that school or board (such as a professional development/activity day), the occasional teacher is usually expected to participate. A sample collective agreement stipulates:

> F.11.1 A long-term occasional teacher who is scheduled to work when there is a Professional Activity Day will be paid for the day and will be required to participate in the scheduled professional activity. (York Region District School Board 2004, p. 13)

This participation is considered part of their employment, and therefore they are paid to attend. This is not the case for occasional teachers who are working on a daily basis at the time of the scheduled professional activity day. In most cases they are neither required to participate in the professional learning opportunity, nor paid if they choose to attend, as shown by this collective agreement provision:

> 11.02 A Short Term Occasional Teacher may attend, without pay, scheduled Professional Activity Days arranged by the Board subject to space availability. (Renfrew County District School Board 2004, p. 9)

In some cases daily occasional teachers require approval of the school's superintendent of education or designate (York Region District School Board 2004).

Daily occasional teachers' motivation for participating in different kinds of professional learning varied in the study. For example, teachers educated internationally found themselves positioned low on the hierarchy. Motivated to secure more teaching work and better understand the local education context, many IETs engaged in substantial amounts of informal learning. By classroom volunteering, IETs informally acquired not just information about pedagogy and curricula, but knowledge of school cultures and the school system in general. This knowledge in turn made it possible for them to acquire more days of teaching and more formal professional learning opportunities. In terms of professional autonomy and decision-making, IETs often found themselves at the lowest level of the workforce hierarchy, especially when volunteering, which provided little to no professional autonomy or decision-making power. In these subordinate positions, they were at the mercy of other professionals who control their time and work.

CONCLUSION

Learning is an integral part of occasional teaching. The type of learning which occasional teachers undertook depended on the motivations for engaging in occasional teaching and the stage these teachers were at in their teaching careers. Retirees and career occasional teachers engaged less in formal learning than did IETs who needed to acquire learning to enhance their job prospects and status. While the majority of IETs and career occasionals wanted to participate in continued formal learning, they also recognized that not all professional development sessions covered areas of concern to them. Occasional teachers also engaged in informal learning. Internationally educated teachers were more consciously involved in intentional informal learning than the other occasional teachers as they attempted to acquire not only knowledge about the organizations in which they worked but gain the necessary cultural capital to navigate the current education system. In other words, in this study, the least powerful group of Ontario teachers were perhaps the most engaged in conscious intentional informal learning.

HARRY SMALLER

6. BEGINNING TEACHERS

INTRODUCTION

How to teach to so many different learning levels ... how to assess the different learning levels and how to report on the very low students. I just did my first report cards and I felt very lost. I've gone through a difficult process of throwing away the book and starting to try and teach to the "real" needs of my students.

Our school district has monthly Counsellor/Facilitator meetings. Our district is huge ... and we all meet together once to see what is going on. That has been awesome for making connections [with] other people doing the same job as I am doing, and we communicate through e-mail all the time. I think internet and e-mail have been huge for where I learn things.[1]

If occasional teachers have the least power and control of any group of teachers, a close second may go to beginning teachers – those in their first years on-the-job following teacher education and certification. As compared to the former group, however, new teachers have been the subject of much more attention, and concern, particularly over the past decade. Boards of education, government departments, teacher unions and faculties of education across the United States and Canada have all increased resources towards enhancing beginning teachers' "induction" into the profession. Many of these additional resources have been devoted to developing and implementing professional development programs which might better meet new teachers' interests and needs.

There seemed to be a number of reasons for this increased attention. On the one hand, there has been expressed concern in a number of quarters about the purported high drop-out rate of new teachers in their first years of teaching.[2] At the same time there was also increasing appreciation that, like in many occupations, neophyte teachers could benefit from particular teaching/learning supports to assist them at the outset in building a strong foundation for their developing new knowledge, skills and understandings. Accompanying this rationale were wider contexts of change – from increased pressures for accountability and diminishing enrolments in schools, to the increasing diversity of their student populations. New teachers are embedded in these changed contexts – indeed, for many, the school one entered as teacher has dramatically changed from the school one experienced as a student. The new teachers who participated in our study spoke often about these changed contexts.

More recent research literature has also been much attuned to the issue of new teachers – including the ways in which they take up their own learning, both informal and formal – as they struggle to understand the interests and needs of their increasingly diverse students and to develop effective ways of meeting these professional obligations within the context of school systems which have become increasingly bureaucratic. One common approach is that taken by Knight (2002), among others, who argues that "continuing professional development should [no longer] be dominated by courses, workshops and suchlike events," and that "communities of practice" based within school departments should be utilized as prime source for more successful professional development (p. 229).

Another exploratory approach, taken up by McNally et al. (2009) among others, uses ethnographic methods to investigate the ways in which new teachers "draw on their tacit, experiential knowledge in practice" and the challenge this raises for those wishing to support these neophyte professionals. How might learning support systems be arranged, they ask, "to accommodate notions of the emotional as well as the cognitive, the ontological as well as the epistemological, as intrinsic to the complex, personal nature of new teacher development" (p. 330).

As reported in Chapter 4, our national surveys indicated that teachers everywhere are significantly engaged in their own learning. Overall, newer teachers' basic motives were no different in this regard than their more senior colleagues. As indicated by their comments on the surveys and in our follow-up interviews and focus groups, the reasons for their engagement in professional learning seemed relatively straightforward – both intrinsic and instrumental. Many beginning teachers talked about the challenges of being new in the classroom, and thus their interest in seeking out answers and support in order to enhance their practice. In addition, a number also commented on the potential material advantage from engaging in this further education and certification – ranging from concerns about keeping their positions in what was perceived as a time of declining enrolments and an increasingly tight job market, to the possibility of better remuneration and/or opportunity for promotion. There were, however, some differences in their engagement in various forms of learning activity, as compared to their more senior colleagues. These similarities and differences, based on seniority, are explored in the following sections.

Our own studies also revealed significant differences between newer and more senior teachers in regards to the ways in which their lives and life styles intersected with the capacity to engage in their work and in their further learning practices. While more recently the hiring of new teachers has dropped off considerably (Ontario College of Teachers 2011), in the six-year interval between our two national surveys (1998 and 2004) there was a definite surge in new hiring, mainly from the ranks of newly certified teachers (Grimmet & Echols 2000). Using data both from our study and from other sources, this chapter will examine the ways in which beginning teachers are both similar to, and different than, their more senior colleagues. This comparison will focus on two dimensions. First, we examine the specific learning interests of new teachers and the ways in which they have sought out and engaged in their own further learning. Second, we examine the underlying contexts which shape this interest and engagement – the specific material conditions of their work, their own personal/family circumstances, and the complex nature of the social/authority relations which new teachers face within their schools and classrooms.

NEW TEACHER ENGAGEMENT IN FORMAL LEARNING

As shown in Tables 6-1 and 6-2 below, the engagement of new teachers (0–5 years experience) in formal learning activities is comparable to that of their more senior colleagues overall – whether measured in terms of participation rates or in terms of numbers of hours per week spent on this formal learning. In contrast to many other studies of adult learning that have found that younger people participate in greater numbers, it appears that new teachers may tend to have slightly less engagement than that undertaken by their next more senior colleagues (6–10 years). There are a number of reasons why this might be so. As will be explored more fully later in the chapter, we found that new teachers were particularly burdened by what they perceived as the demands of their work. As many of their interview comments noted, this workload burden left many with lack of time and energy to engage in formal learning programs (in spite of their relatively young age).

Another main reason may lie in the perceptions which some new teachers expressed to us about the usefulness of engaging in yet more traditional formal learning. As recent graduates of teacher education, now immersed in (and driven by) the minutia of successfully managing and teaching new groups of young students, there was less interest in seeking out time-consuming programs which were often seen as not meeting their immediate classroom needs.

Table 6-1. Taken at least one course in past 12 months, by seniority

Years teaching	% taken one or more courses	N
0–5 years	90	62
6–10 years	96	114
11–15 years	92	101
More than 15 years	88	349
Total	91	626

Table 6-2. Average hours per week of job-related formal learning, by seniority

Years teaching	Mean hours	N
0–5 Years	7.5	64
6–10 Years	9.8	116
11–15 Years	5.9	100
More than 15 Years	4.9	389
Total	6.1	669

Another section of our national teachers' survey explored the kinds of courses which teachers engaged in. While there was little difference between more and less senior respondents in relation to academic, recreation/leisure-related or work-related courses, as indicated in Table 6-3 there were sharp differences in regards to two other course content areas. New teachers were much more inclined to engage in language-related courses, while their more senior colleagues were much more heavily involved in computer-related programs. While there were no specific details provided as to the types of language courses taken, or the reasons for engaging in them, one possibility for this interest may relate to new teachers' interests in pursuing further specialization in a specific teaching area. In many school districts in Canada and the United States there is increasing interest on the part of parents and students to engage in second and third language learning (see, e.g., Murphy et al. 2003) and an increased demand for teachers in this area. Thus, newer teachers in particular, often concerned about job security, may well see this extra training as being helpful in regards to their continued employment. By comparison, increased engagement in computer-related courses by more senior (older) teachers undoubtedly reflects their perceived need to acquire knowledge and skills in this ever-expanding field – to access resources for teaching, and to meet increasing demands from school administration for computer-based reporting on student progress, and so on.

Table 6-3. Teachers' engagement in types of formal courses, by seniority

Seniority	Academic (%)	Recreation/ leisure (%)	Work related (%)	Language (%)	Computer (%)	N
0–5 years	45	27	86	23	16	62
6–10 years	46	22	77	10	28	116
11–15 years	43	23	86	10	32	102
16+ years	36	27	86	9	32	357
Total	40	25	84	10	30	637

Seniority certainly seemed to be a factor when teachers were asked if they were planning on taking any additional courses "in the next few years." As shown in Table 6-4, interest in further formal learning tapered off as teachers gained seniority. Well over three-quarters (77 per cent) of all new teacher respondents (0–5 years) indicated commitment to further formal learning, while their more senior colleagues expressed proportionately less interest as they aged. Interestingly however, when it came to providing reasons for taking further courses, there were no significant seniority differences reported in relation to the need to do so "in order to maintain your certification or employment." Whether new or long-standing in the classroom, less than 20 per cent of these respondents, including new teachers, indicated this requirement (Table 6-5). This finding is noteworthy in

BEGINNING TEACHERS

relation to the later discussion in this chapter concerning issues of teacher autonomy and power.

Table 6-4. Plan to take courses in next few years, by seniority

Seniority	Plan to take course in next few years			N
	Yes (%)	Maybe (%)	No (%)	
0–5 years	77	21	2	62
6–10 years	66	29	4	116
11–15 years	56	38	6	102
16+ years	45	34	21	355
Total	54	32	13	635

Table 6-5. Planned courses are required, by seniority

Seniority	% stating planned courses are required	N
0 to 5 Years	20	51
6 to 10 Years	19	97
11 to 15 Years	17	79
More than 15 Years	17	237
Total	18	464

Even though new teachers indicated strongest intention of engaging in further courses, it is interesting to note that this group also most strongly expressed concern about the possibility of doing so, based on financial costs. As indicated in Table 6-6, new teachers were over twice as likely as their most senior colleagues to indicate that the costs of these courses might well prevent them from further engagement.

Table 6-6. Costs of courses a factor in planning, by seniority

Seniority	% stating further courses may be "too expensive" to consider	N
0–5 Years	69	16
6–10 Years	61	41
11–15 Years	40	45
More than 15 Years	32	196
Total	39	298

NEW TEACHER ENGAGEMENT IN INFORMAL LEARNING

Similar to teachers' substantial engagement in formal learning activity, data from our 2004 survey suggests that virtually all teachers, whether new or senior, see themselves as engaged in a continuous process of engagement in new informal learning. In spite of the "steep learning curve" associated particularly with new teachers, given the relatively recent and widespread changes in schooling previously discussed which affect all teachers, it is perhaps understandable that all seniority groups in our study report similar high levels of engagement with informal learning in the workplace. As Table 6-7 summarizes, there are no significant differences indicated when comparing hours per week of engagement in job-related informal learning by teaching seniority.

Table 6-7. Average hours per week of job-related informal learning, by seniority

Years teaching	Mean hours	N
0–5 Years	4.3	64
6–10 Years	4.5	113
11–15 Years	3.9	97
16+ Years	4.0	376
Total	4.1	650

Seniority differences do pertain however, related to the reasons for engaging in informal on-the-job learning – at least as indicated by the specific content of these various learning activities (Table 6-8). Not surprisingly, new teachers reported much higher engagement in informal learning related to issues of classroom management, student extra-curricular activities, and special education/inclusion themes. By comparison, they were less involved than their more senior colleagues with themes less directly related to the day-to-day student/classroom routines – such as issues of occupational health and safety, curriculum policy and development, and work-related environmental issues.

Table 6-8. Teachers' engagement in informal learning, by seniority

Seniority	Classroom management (%)	Extra-curricular (%)	Special ed-inclusion (%)	Health-safety (%)	Work environment (%)	Curriculum policy (%)	N
0–5 years	78	64	47	22	20	41	64
6–10 years	68	48	38	40	30	63	119
11–15 years	58	51	45	45	17	71	105
16+ years	56	58	30	40	28	62	405
Total	61	54	35	39	26	62	696

Another systematic source for this "teacher voice" data arose in the context of the work of the author of Chapter 8 of this book, who has been responsible for provision of professional development services for all new teachers in the Toronto District School Board (TDSB). Over the course of three years (2005–08), all new teachers were asked to respond to a very brief, one question survey, administered both online and at formal professional learning sessions organized for them specifically. In total, 1,458 first and second year teachers responded to this open-ended question: "What issues are you encountering as a beginning teacher?" In responding, many teachers expanded on their comments, often citing more than one issue.

Perhaps not surprisingly, issues relating to "classroom management" topped the list of needs for this group (59 per cent of all respondents cited this theme). Responses reflected both a desire for proactive structures (e.g., building inclusion) as well as reactive strategies (e.g., dealing with conflict). As many respondents noted, the experience of inheriting an established classroom culture as a student teacher is very different than the experience of establishing a productive classroom environment for the very first time. In the words of one first year teacher:

Classroom management. Oh god, help! Is it my voice? Is it my language? ... Am I boring? Do I need a whistle? A bell? A door-bell? A cooler hand signal? An accent? A funny hat? A stun gun? Carpeted floors/walls/ceiling? ... What will get their attention, and sustain it?

Next to classroom management, issues relating to "student assessment and evaluation" also rated highly among new teachers (45 per cent of all respondents).[3] Many teachers noted their inexperience and difficulties in determining how to assess and evaluate student learning in a meaningful manner using of a range of strategies and tools. Related to this was their concern about ways in which they could communicate progress (or lack thereof) to both students and parents in meaningful but supportive ways. As one new teacher reported, "*It wasn't until I really had to put number marks into categories and crunch the numbers that I felt very uncertain of how to do it properly.*"

A third issue, which over one third of all respondents noted, was the challenge of meeting all "the needs of a diversity of learning levels and learning needs" among the students in their classrooms, and the realization that a "one size fits all" approach simply does not. Responses reflected a desire to implement differentiated instruction but an uncertainty about to actually implement it. In the words of one teacher, the issue was simply "*how to teach to so many different learning levels ... or how to assess the different learning levels and how to report on the very low students.*" This became abundantly clear when new teachers were required to evaluate diverse classes. "*I just did my first report cards and I felt very lost. I've gone through a difficult process of throwing away the book and starting to try and teach to the 'real' needs of my students.*"

In addition, a number of other issues concerned a variety of respondents. These included: writing report cards and completing Individual Education Plans for their students; communicating with colleagues, administrators and parents; navigating school culture; short and long range planning; paperwork and other administrative tasks; and preparing for their own teacher performance appraisal, which is required twice during their first year of teaching and on which their future career depends. The extent to which most of these same issues may also have been of concern to more senior teachers remains an open question, given they were not surveyed in this regard. Overall however, it would appear that the informal learning which engaged this particular group of new teachers was not dissimilar from that which engaged those teachers (new and seasoned) who responded to our national 2004 survey. In the following sections we will examine some of the accompanying factors which influenced the nature of new teachers' engagement in their own learning interests and practices.

NEW TEACHER WORKLOAD

The effects of workload particularly for new teachers became abundantly clear to us in a very non-intentional manner – during our attempts to arrange for new teachers to participate in our focus groups. As compared to others contacted, many informed us that they were unfortunately unable to participate, citing a variety of work-related reasons – department and school faculty meetings deemed important, supervision of student sports and other extra-curricular activities, engaging in often-mandatory upgrading courses and workshops, and most importantly, claims of lack of time just to undertake ongoing class preparation and marking of student assignments. As another clue about the extra pressure experienced by neophytes, it appeared to us that the numbers of survey responses received from new teachers may not have reflected their overall numbers proportionately in the schools – perhaps for the same reasons.[4] Given this relatively lower response rate, some of our more quantitative data on new teachers does lack the robustness achieved for more senior teachers, and in some cases, it was necessary to group together those with zero to five years of experience in order to make quantitatively justifiable claims. Based on our overall findings however, we can reliably conclude that those in just their first and second year of teaching were at least as pressured by work as those three to five year teachers who formed the other part of the overall zero to five year statistical cohort which reported the greatest workloads.

As noted in Table 6-9, teachers in their first five years report a significantly longer work week than their more senior colleagues – approximately five hours more. Some of this extra work seems to be taken up with increased timetabled duties (classroom teaching, assigned supervision hours, etc.). However, these newer teachers also reported more work time spent at school outside of formally assigned duties, and work at home/elsewhere, than any of the other more senior groups of colleagues. One can assume that this increased time can be attributed to the fact that they are learning intensively on the job and require more time to accomplish these tasks as compared to their more senior, experienced colleagues. In addition, the finding (discussed below) that this new teacher group was less burdened than more senior colleagues by family responsibilities, suggests that they had more time to devote to these new learning requirements.

Table 6-9. Average weekly hours of work, by seniority

Seniority	Total timetabled duties	Extra hours at school	Prep work at home/ elsewhere	Total work week	N
0–5 Years	34	11	10	55	64
6–10 Years	31	10	9	50	116
11–15 Years	32	10	10	51	100
16+ Years	31	10	9	50	389
Total	31	10	9	50	669

Mean number of hours of work

In addition to reporting on their actual hours of work during the year of the survey, teachers were also asked to report on perceived changes in their workload over the previous five years (or less, for newer teachers) (Table 6-10). A very high percentage of senior teachers (11+ years of teaching) reported an "increased" or "significantly increased" workload (83 per cent). However, it is interesting to note that they were joined as well in this perception by well over half (55 per cent) of their newest (0–5 years) colleagues and almost 70 per cent of teachers with six to ten years of experience. One might assume that, as new hires gained some experience, they might become more adept in their work, and thus report less overall hours required for carrying out their responsibilities. However, as noted in Chapter 4, this relatively high reporting of "increased workload" may pertain to all teachers, regardless of seniority. In this way, it is understandable why the common gap in learning time between new and experienced teachers has been narrowing, with these increased pressures on everyone to conform to increased dicta from authorities, relating to bureaucratic changes in student assessment and reporting, and added teacher evaluation requirements.

Table 6-10. Teachers' perceived workload change in past five years, by seniority

Seniority	Significantly increased (%)	Increased (%)	Unchanged (%)	Decreased (%)	N
0–5 Years	27	31	35	7	68
6–10 Years	33	36	29	3	135
11–15 Years	50	33	15	3	117
16+ Years	49	36	14	1	461
Total	44	35	19	2	781

NEW TEACHER STRESS AT WORK

As noted in Chapter 4, stress seems to be a major issue for many teachers, regardless of their age or years of teaching, and the phenomenon has certainly become an important theme for educational researchers across many nations (Wilhelm et al. 2000). In relation to potential causes of teacher stress, it is interesting to note that, in one major study which assessed future directions for research in this area, the first priority established for exploration was that of "monitoring the extent to which particular educational reforms are generating high levels of teacher stress" (Kyriacou 2001, p. 27).

Given this seemingly universal state of affairs, our national survey data clearly indicated as well that Canadian teachers of all ages reported increased stress on the job over the previous five years (Table 6-11). While older teachers reported very high increased levels of stress (83 per cent for those with 11–15 years experience; 87 per cent for 16+ years), even 63 per cent of relatively new (0–5 years) teachers reported a similar "increase" or "significant increase."

Table 6-11. Overall stress-level change in past 5 years, by seniority

Seniority	Significant increase (%)	Increase (%)	About same (%)	Decrease (%)	N
0–5 Years	28	35	21	16	57
6–10 Years	33	30	31	5	102
11–15 Years	39	45	13	3	87
16+ Years	53	34	12	2	340
Total	46	35	16	4	586

Our interviews and focus groups with new teachers suggested a range of reasons resulting in stress on the job. Dominant, understandably, were the causes which one would normally attribute to being "new on the job" – "classroom management," working with diverse students, student evaluation and reporting, administrative routines, understanding the "school culture," and so on. More recently, in the tightening job market, increased school transfers, "pink slips," and even layoffs have added a layer of concern, and some stress, for a number of respondents.

NEW TEACHERS: THEIR PERSONAL/FAMILY LIVES AND CAREER TRAJECTORIES

One further factor related to new teachers' engagement with learning and work became apparent to us as our research progressed. As noted at the beginning of this chapter, during the five-year interval between our two national surveys of teachers, we found a significant lowering of average ages of Canadian teachers and an increase in numbers who were raising children in their homes. As Table 6-12 shows, family responsibilities were a rapidly escalating concern after a few years in the profession. This was certainly reflected in our focus group discussions: in the context of inquiring about participants' engagement in formal/informal learning, "children" and "family" were often drawn into the mix. Similarly, a number of participants also referred to their perceptions about how they saw their work as teachers in the longer term, and the ways in which plans for engagement in further learning were influenced (or hampered) by these considerations.

Table 6-12. Family responsibilities, by seniority

Years teaching	% with family responsibilities	N
0–5 Years	6	16
6–10 Years	63	41
11–15 Years	53	45
16+ Years	38	196
Total	42	298

While these concerns seemed to be raised by teachers across the seniority spectrum, only six per cent of responding teachers with zero to five years of seniority indicated that they had family responsibilities at that time. By comparison, 63 per cent and 53 per cent of their colleagues in the next two respective seniority categories stated that they had family obligations. Interview transcripts for these more senior teachers provided clear evidence that parenting interfered with their ability to engage in learning (particularly formal), either at the workplace or elsewhere. As Judy explained:

In regard to formal learning I, like many people here, have done a number of AQ courses in the past, and especially after I first graduated I did French Immersion and then I did a Co-op Specialist which is three courses and a Guidance Specialist which is a three-course Specialist program, and Special Ed Gifted. So these were done in the evening during the school year or in the summer. I feel I was adding to my qualifications base and my diversity in order to stay in the system, and also be at most service to the students. So I felt they were very worthwhile, they were affordable at the time and I had time. I then had a little boy who is now just eight, and I have no time. I have my marking and whatever time I'm not marking I give to my child. And that leaves very little time left over for either formal learning or for exchanges with colleagues in a formal way.

Perhaps Danny's summary pinpoints the ambivalence which many teachers experience particularly around the capacity to engage in formal courses:

I would like to take more formal courses and pursue some education in terms of education courses and AQ courses. Whether that's going to happen in the next couple of years, I don't know, just because of my family.

The main point here, in regards to beginning teachers who are not yet as involved with family responsibility, is perhaps best enunciated by Mary. Reflecting on her family situation, she troubles the blurring boundaries between teachers' paid work and their personal lives:

I think that any learning we do should be in our work day. If you look at other fields of work, if there is training or new skills to be learned, people go during the work day, they are not working during their holidays, they are not working during the evening. And you know, teachers have personal lives. We have families that we have to look after, we have children that we are raising. We know as teachers what happens to students who are not given attention; to children who are not given attention by their families; and sometimes some of the expectations that are put on teachers.

She then makes a telling observation:

Some young teachers are putting off having families because they feel like they have to take this course and they have to do that when honestly they are hired to teach a certain grade. They have been hired to do this job but it seems like doing that job is not enough ...

Clearly even the more flexible modes of informal learning emphasized in Chapter 4 can have negative repercussions in terms of work intensification, as Mary highlights. Flexibility may help teachers juggling work and family, but also there are hard limits as the total number of hours of work rise. Young teachers, whether or not they have families, clearly have little choice but to continue to engage in learning. However, with work intensification, priorities and choices must be made which do impact upon the degree to which teachers can engage in formal and informal learning. More and more, these complex factors affecting all teachers seem to serve to narrow the gap between new and experienced teachers' participation rates and hours in both formal and informal job-related learning.

ISSUES OF AUTONOMY AND CONTROL FOR NEW TEACHERS

As discussed in detail in Chapter 1, we posit a clear difference between teachers' negotiating power based on professional/union organization strength as compared to delegated or assumed power within the workplace based on personal job autonomy and organizational decision-making.[5] These latter issues, in particular, are important aspects of the lives of new teachers. For example, one can certainly postulate that new teachers, coming with fresh ideas about innovative curriculum and other new ways of attempting to reach out to students, are bound to come up against the traditions and norms of the conventional school place. Interestingly, our national survey did include one question relating to this matter: "In the past five years (or less), to what extent, if any [was there change in the] level of autonomy which you have over your own work?" The results of this question, as shown in Table 6-13, indicated clearly that it was actually more senior teachers who most experienced a degradation of this autonomy – almost 40 per cent for the most senior group. However, it is worth noting that over a quarter (26 per cent) of new teachers also reported this same loss of power. Important to consider here is that the question refers to a *perception of change over time*. For newer teachers who claimed this decrease, we can only speculate as to the extent they were reflecting on actual change experienced during their relatively short time in the classroom; alternatively for some, it might have been the difference in their perceived situations compared to their (elevated) expectations for autonomy when entering the profession. Either way, it would appear that they were conscious of the overall issue of professional autonomy.

Certainly, other empirical studies involving new teachers which did explore issues of professional autonomy, power and managerial authority found that this was a significant issue. In their study of new teachers' learning, Wilson and Demetriou (2007) found a wide range of issues relating to their immersion into the social/authority relations in new workplaces. One teacher, for example, commented on how he saw power relations with his superiors in this regard:

> If you approach the Head ... too much, then you get a reputation as someone who has a problem with [grade] 10 or whatever. So I'm conscious of doing that. If it's a serious issue I will. But in the first instance I shouldn't have to, so I am dealing with things on my own that I shouldn't have to be. (p. 222)

Table 6-13. Perceived change in workplace autonomy, by seniority

Seniority	Increase (%)	About same (%)	Decrease (%)	N
0–5 years	19	55	26	62
6–10 years	15	58	27	114
11–15 years	23	45	32	97
16+ years	12	49	39	377
Total	15	51	35	650

By comparison, judging from another teacher's comments, one can speculate that authority relations in his school operated on a very different, much more intrusive, scale.

> Teaching is not about being micromanaged by your department head to the detriment of adopting your own teaching style, but should be to encourage you to adopt a range of teaching skills and therefore be able to plan your own lessons. (p. 223)

These issues of professional autonomy and control arise as well, even within the context of innovative induction projects developed with the intent of diminishing, or eliminating, the possibility of adversarial power relations between participants, such as with peer mentoring programs. For example, in their study of these programs, Achinstein and Bartlett (2004) noted tensions which sometimes existed between mentors and neophytes, where differing beliefs and/or perceptions collided.

As earlier chapters have suggested, tensions resulting from the intersections of managerial control and professional autonomy also afflict teachers regardless of their seniority, gender or status in the schooling system. As noted above, these tensions exist for new teachers as well, and in some cases affect the ways in which they are inducted into their careers and the possibilities for them being able to develop as successful teachers.

NEW TEACHERS: POSSIBILITIES FOR INNOVATIVE LEARNING INITIATIVES

Given the continuing concerns expressed by schooling officials everywhere about the efficacy of new teachers, along with the general lack of success of traditional formal, top-down, professional development programs for them, a variety of teacher-learning initiatives have been implemented in many jurisdictions. While these "induction" programs involve a wide variety of approaches – one-day workshops, special classes and courses, teacher "buddy" systems, and so on – by far the most common approach has been that of formalizing 'mentoring' programs for new teachers. The concept itself seems straightforward – pairing a new teacher with a more senior colleague. However, recent literature suggests that in reality it takes many forms, within many different contexts, and with differing results. In their comprehensive study of new teacher induction programs in three American states, Bartlett and Johnson (2010) found not only that those "districts able to mount effective induction programs benefit from decreased teacher turnover rates," but also speculated that this "increased teacher learning result[ed] in higher quality teachers ... and, by extension, to increased student learning" (p. 868). However, they also found that there were wide variations in the amount of direction and funding provided by state-level authorities and in the level of commitment shown by local schooling authorities. Among other discrepancies, they make strong mention of their findings that high poverty areas were much less successful in mounting induction programs. This is doubly problematic, given that new teachers in these schools might well benefit from the support of colleagues experienced in helping students from diverse backgrounds to succeed in school. This particular condition will be explored again in the context of the concluding chapter of this book.

A recent international comparative study of professional teacher learning undertaken for the National Staff Development Council (USA) by Darling-Hammond et al. (2009) also documents the recent rise of mentoring programs for new teachers. Among other findings, they concur that where such programs have been introduced, new teacher attrition rates have decreased, sometimes considerably. However, they seem more reticent to pronounce success in relation to other potential criteria for success, such as changes in teacher instructional practice and student achievement. Rather, they note that there are, to date, few studies reporting on these criteria; secondly, those which have been published report mixed findings in this regard. As they conclude, there is "need for more rigorous research into the impact of induction supports on instruction, teacher retention, and student achievement. As yet, such interventions remain promising but not proven" (p. 13).

The following chapter (Chapter 7) will examine policy implications in relation to developing and overseeing teachers' professional learning programs, along with describing the recent initiatives of one Canadian provincial government in this regard. Chapter 8 will then continue with a close case study of the implementation of a comprehensive new teacher induction program in one large urban school district in this province.

SECTION C: IMPLICATIONS AND APPLICATIONS

ROSEMARY CLARK

7. PROFESSIONAL CONTROL AND PROFESSIONAL LEARNING

Some Policy Implications

INTRODUCTION

When we get our PD days, half the time we are not allowed to do with them what we want to do. If they gave those days to us and let us plan what we want to do we would get so much done. But the board brings in these people who have not been in the classroom since God knows when, and we have to listen to these people that they paid thousands of dollars for ... [For example,] we spent the last in-service listening to ... Nancy Reagan. They brought her in to talk about being positive in life. 1,500 teachers sitting here with a million things to do, and she is telling us to be positive.

We just have to remember that we are professionals, and we have had our training, and when it comes to making decisions, you do what you think is appropriate and be proud of it. And a lot of professional development is not needed to do that. To some extent you can do it because you can see the need. You are the one with the children.[1]

The two teachers quoted above illustrate the classic dichotomy of not only educational policy, but also approaches to teacher professional learning, as government/school boards vie with classroom teachers over the best ways to improve student performance. To understand trends in professional development policy in Canada, it is critical to grasp the nature of the organizations to which Canadian teachers belong, the struggle for control of the profession which characterized the 1990s and early 2000s, and the emerging consensus over the value to both teachers and students of ongoing job-embedded professional learning. Two Ontario programs, the New Teacher Induction (NIP) program and the Teacher Learning and Leadership Program (TLLP), are described here to exemplify how recommendations from various experts around the world can be implemented, in an atmosphere of collaboration, not conflict, between government and teacher unions.

THE CANADIAN CONTEXT: A STRONG UNIONIZED, YET STRICTLY REGULATED, PROFESSION

Canadian teachers have long had a strong professional cohesion, since all Canadian teachers were required by provincial legislation to belong to province-wide teacher federations since at least the mid-twentieth century. This collective strength was evidenced by the emergence of powerful unions with advanced collective agreements who also devote considerable time to professional development, standards of practice and taking strong public stances on educational issues.

To try to counter and weaken the power of these unions, neo-liberal governments in two of the provinces – British Columbia (1987) and Ontario (1996) – created professional Colleges of Teachers. The history of both professional colleges has been one of sporadic political interference. For example, in 2003, the government of British Columbia amended the *Teaching Profession Act*, dismissed the democratically elected College Council, and named political appointees to carry out a government agenda. The British Columbia Teachers' Federation (BCTF) then launched a vigorous protest campaign, garnered public support, and forced the government to back down and restore an elected teacher majority to the college's governing council. In 2010, a "fact finder's" review of the BC College of Teachers (BCCT) has once again raised the potential for future government reversals on the matter.[2] Similarly in Ontario in 2006, a Liberal government amended the *Ontario College of Teachers Act* to grant slight majority control of the college's governing body to representatives of classroom teachers, with the effect that teacher federation opposition to the Ontario College has considerably decreased and the self-governing body can govern the profession in ways resembling other professions.

Teaching is governed by more laws than most other professions in Canada. Rigorous post-secondary educational and licensing requirements for teachers are enshrined in provincial legislation, and largely standardized across the country. In British Columbia and Ontario, the Colleges of Teachers administer these licensing requirements and accreditation of the faculties of education that train teachers. The colleges also have comprehensive Standards of Practice governing their members. In other provinces, the licensing requirements and standards of practice are legislated in *Teaching Profession* Acts or their equivalents. In addition, in all provinces teachers as employees are subject to detailed duties enforced by school board employers following comprehensive provisions in each province's *Education Act and Regulations*.

In Ontario since 2006 there has also been a legislated teacher performance appraisal regime. All Ontario teachers undergo a performance appraisal at least once every five years, in contrast to an average of about 20 per cent of experienced teachers in all OECD countries who are evaluated that often (OECD 2009). Further, the constitutions of the provincial teacher federations also include codes of conduct and professional standards of practice. The teaching profession in Canada, then, is strictly controlled, contributing to the lack of organizational decision-making power reported by teacher respondents in the national surveys in Chapter 1, but perhaps also contributing to the public's satisfaction with the work done by teachers (over 60 per cent satisfaction ratings over the past decade) – well ahead of their satisfaction with the education system in general (Hart & Livingstone 2007, p. 8).

As noted in Chapter 1, some other professions in Canada, most notably doctors and nurses, have similar strong professional associations. The highly unionized

SOME POLICY IMPLICATIONS

status of teachers and nurses has led to unified political action and negotiated salaries higher than those in many countries. But it is the history of government manipulation of the professional colleges of teachers, not found in most other professions, and election campaigns directly targeting teachers as part of a "reform" agenda, that sets teachers apart from other professions.

EDUCATION REFORM AGENDAS

Earlier chapters have documented that over the past several decades there has been a trend to less deference towards professions in general, and perhaps most especially towards teaching, a professional employee class which does not boast the recognized body of technical and specialized knowledge enjoyed by doctors, lawyers and engineers. The added factor of strong teacher unionism also encouraged targeting of teachers and the public grades K-12 education system by neo-liberal political campaigns. In the United States in 2010 and 2011, a number of Republican states, most notably Wisconsin, legislated curbs on teacher unions, salaries and benefits.[3]

In the past 15 years, it has become politically popular in right-of-centre election platforms to focus on "education reform" and "teacher accountability." In Alberta, for example, the Klein government of the 1990s led the way through the *Government Accountability Act* of 1995 which amalgamated local school boards, reduced educational funding and centralized control, followed by the Teaching Profession Act of 1996 highlighting stricter discipline of teachers.[4] The Harris government of Ontario enacted similar moves and went even further in direct attacks on teacher workload and teacher unions in 1997 through Bill 160, which led to a province-wide teacher walkout lasting two weeks. These and other provincial governments were elected on education reform and budget-cutting platforms and subsequently enacted these reform agendas. Included in the reform agendas was a greater emphasis on standardized test results as a leading measure of school accountability. For example, the *Alberta Accountability Pillar* report, issued annually, reports on results of provincial standardized tests by school board as its sole measure of student achievement.[5] In British Columbia, each school board must show progress as part of a "District Achievement Contract" which includes standardized test results as a major component of achievement.[6]

The education reform movement can also be seen through a sociological lens as part of labour process theory. Alan Reid (2003) argues that the state is constantly under pressure to reduce the cost of public sector activities, which can be achieved either by devaluing the work of teaching, or by asking its workers to do more (or both). The recent American attacks on teacher working conditions and benefits in Wisconsin and other states in 2011 are a perfect example. Attacks on teacher accountability and the decline in deference towards teaching as a profession fit in with this goal of the state. In addition, Reid argues that the state-generated curriculum functions as not only a critical vehicle of transmitting cultural norms to future workers, but also as the critical means of controlling the work of teachers. This theory serves to explain why education reform in recent decades has been such a critical policy piece for neo-liberal governments as they strive to assert their

147

hegemonic control over not only what constitutes the public interest, but also over strong teacher unions who may take a different view.

However, flaws have been exposed in these agendas. The most infamous is the Bush administration's *No Child Left Behind (NCLB) Act*, which received widespread bipartisan support when first enacted in 2002 and which is slated for re-authorization or amendment under the Obama administration. *No Child Left Behind* requires all students in grades 3 through 8, regardless of race, ethnicity, socio-economic status or special needs, to be proficient in math and reading by 2014. Such a goal, while it may have inspirational value, is simply not attainable. As Rothstein, Jacobsen and Wilder (2006) argue, "proficiency for all is an oxymoron," since proficiency represents the highest possible level. Diane Ravitch (2010) agrees, noting that applying this *NCLB* standard has meant that by 2007–08 more than 35 per cent of America's schools were labelled as failing.[7] Ravitch argues that:

> as a goal, it is utterly out of reach ... but if all students are not on track to be proficient by 2014, then schools will be closed, teachers will be fired, principals will lose their jobs, and some – perhaps many – public schools will be privatized. All because they were not able to achieve the impossible. (p. 103)

The *NCLB* system of punishing schools which "fail" has led to massive dropouts of minority students, and despite constant testing at the expense of other curriculum, improvements in test results have stalled under *NCLB*, with math increases slowing and reading on the decline (Darling-Hammond 2007).

No Child Left Behind was not the first unachievable national education policy for the United States:

> In the 1994 legislation, Goals 2000, a Congressionally mandated objective was that U.S. students should be first in the world in math and science by the year 2000. Many education reformers, even those who boasted of having the highest expectations, later acknowledged that this goal was absurd. (Rothstein, Jacobsen & Wilder 2006, p. 8)

Yet governments in the English-speaking world at both state/provincial and national levels since the mid-1990s have continued to set high, perhaps impossibly high, achievement targets for students to reach in terms of standardized test scores. Since such targets are not sustainable over time, they often have to be modified. Wales, for example, has now abolished all targets and England has abandoned many of its targets because of repeated failure to achieve them (Hargreaves and Levin 2008).

The proponents of neo-liberal education reforms often put the onus on teachers for student and school failures, (such as the *NCLB* provisions demanding "highly qualified teachers"). In Canada, various provincial governments in the 1990s and early 2000s pushed for stricter teacher licensing and mandatory professional learning schemes. For example, the Nova Scotia Professional Development Profile program, enacted as Reg. 138/2000, required each teacher to complete 100 hours of mandatory learning every five years. It was followed in 2001 by the Ontario amendments to the *Ontario College of Teachers Act* enacting the Professional Learning Program, which required each teacher to complete 14 mandatory formal courses over five years to maintain certification. As our 2004 WALL teacher survey found, these schemes were unpopular and not particularly effective. In fact, the three target provinces in our survey[8] showed no significant difference in overall hours spent in teacher learning compared to provinces without mandatory professional development programs (Clark et al. 2007, p. 40).

Eventually, in Ontario, many of the anti-teacher education reforms came to a halt with the election of the Liberal government in late 2003 and its subsequent re-election. Critical elements of state control – a centralized curriculum, funding formula, and province-wide testing – remain firmly in the hands of the Ontario government, bearing out Reid's labour process theory. However, governmental behaviour towards teachers changed. Public statements of respect for teacher professionalism and self-directed professional learning became the norm under this government's tenure (Levin, Glaze & Fullan 2008; Levin 2008).

TEACHER POWER IN THE FACE OF REFORM AGENDAS

As shown in Table 1-9 in this book, 89 per cent of teachers in the 2004 national survey reported a great deal of control over their own daily job, the highest among professional groups. However, in the larger teacher sample who participated in the 2004 WALL Teacher Survey, 35 per cent of teachers, and 40 per cent of those with high seniority, reported a decreased level of autonomy over the past five years, and only 14 per cent reported any increase in autonomy over that time period. In addition, when compared to other professions, our data (see Table 1-9) indicate that a relatively low number of teachers reported having any decision-making control in the organization they work for (i.e., the school or school board). These findings might indicate the fact that while teachers have been burdened with government initiatives imposing ever-increasing administrative tasks, province-wide testing and centralized curriculum, most believe that they are still able to "close the classroom door" and teach using their own lesson plans and evaluation schemes.

The power of an individual teacher inside the classroom remains strong. In fact, in analysing teacher responses to 1990s reforms in England, Day (2000, p. 127) found that "control over various aspects of their working lives had been ruthlessly relocated through legislation, but that almost all had found room to manoeuvre and thus to reassert autonomy, albeit within newly defined parameters."

Province-wide testing and standardized curricula remain popular with the public. For example, the biennial OISE/UT Survey of Public Attitudes Towards Education found 76 per cent support for province-wide testing in 1994, 74 per cent in 2007 (Hart & Livingstone 2007). Government policy change in these areas, therefore, is unlikely. However, the OISE/UT survey also finds increasing support for teacher control of students' final grades and promotion decisions. The ambivalence towards teacher autonomy evidenced by the conflicted opinions of teachers (reporting decreased autonomy in general but maintaining control over their own classroom) may thus be mirrored by the general public (supporting large-scale testing yet wanting to see teachers maintain control over each student's grading and promotion).

Teachers in Ontario maintained a strong confidence in their own work as they weathered an eight-year period of Conservative governments' education reforms, which included curriculum reforms, attacks on teacher professionalism, and increased standardized testing of students. The Ontario College of Teachers (OCT), created as part of this agenda to control teachers, surveys a significant number of its members annually. In 2001, in the midst of the Conservative government's tenure, teachers rated their confidence in the job they were personally doing and in the teaching profession as a whole very highly (4.4 and 4.0 respectively on a scale of 1 to 5, while the 2007 confidence ratings were slightly lower, 4.1 and 3.9 respectively) (Ontario College of Teachers 2001, 2007). Of course, the strong teacher unions in Canada have also been able to create unity and confidence in their campaigns fighting what they consider to be the most egregious reform agendas.

Similarly, in England, union campaigns against the heavy workload intensification brought on by years of reforms also led to a negotiated settlement in 2003 which featured support staff taking over a number of administrative tasks so that teachers could focus on their core task of classroom teaching (Stevenson 2007). In both these situations, teachers used their negotiating power, as explained in chapter 1, to maintain solidarity and effect changes in work and learning regimes for the profession.

One of the key side effects of the recent education reform agendas in Canada has been stress. Long and intensifying work hours,[9] including many hours spent after school and at home, plus lack of teacher involvement in organizational decisions about teaching and learning in classrooms and schools, has led to high levels of teacher stress. In the 2004 WALL teacher survey, 45 per cent reported job stress most of the time (see Chapter 4). Another contributing factor in increasing teacher stress is lack of time. The 2007 Ontario College of Teachers' survey also reported that time constraint was the most stressful aspect of teaching (Ontario College of Teachers 2007).

Why should policy makers pay attention to teacher stress? Kenneth Leithwood, in his book *Teacher working conditions that matter: Evidence for change* (2008), made observations and recommendations based on 26 reviews of research and 91 empirical studies. He argues that educational leaders and policy makers assume that the "change overload" which results in such high teacher stress is inevitable, while in actual fact there is typically an inverse relationship between the number of mandated educational changes and their benefits for students. Leithwood concludes that "teacher burnout seriously threatens the achievement of 20 per cent of the students" in Ontario. His advice for policy makers is thus "*Do less. Both students and teachers will be the better for it*" (Leithwood 2008, p. 81, emphasis in the original).

In Canada, the United States and most OECD countries, few political parties are likely to be elected on a platform of reducing either teacher work hours, curriculum intensification or programs of standardized testing. Changes are gradually coming, however, as evidenced by such recent events as the workforce remodelling agreement reached in England in 2003 (Stevenson 2007), the cancellation of national testing in Wales, and the slogan adopted by the education ministry in Singapore to "Teach Less, Learn More" (Hargreaves & Shirley 2009, p. 2). All three of these policies recognize teacher concerns over such issues as standardized testing and excessive workload to some degree. In addition, it is possible that stress may be relieved by empowering classroom teachers with respect to some or all of their professional learning choices, as outlined in the recommended policy changes presented here.

NECESSARY POLICY CHANGES TO FOSTER TEACHER PROFESSIONAL LEARNING

Throughout this book, we have documented relationships between teacher work and learning, and demonstrated the learning needs of particular groups such as occasional teachers (Chapter 5) and beginning teachers (Chapter 6). The analysis of professional learning and power relationships in Chapter 2 also suggests that the professional employee groups with the least organizational control will more actively participate in formal learning if a government deliberately delegates more power over their learning to these groups. If government education policy changes with respect to workload, curriculum and standardized testing are unlikely, improvements in teacher learning regimes can still be the focus of government policy changes that will eventually lead to improved student achievement. We suggest two necessary changes, therefore, to what has traditionally been government policy regarding teacher professional learning, suggestions which are supported by research and illustrated by some model programs in Ontario and elsewhere.

We Need to Rethink Our Traditional Approaches to Formal Learning

Overwhelmingly, teachers participate in formal learning. As our nation-wide surveys indicated, job-related formal learning activities occupy more than six hours per week. While less experienced teachers take more courses than their more senior colleagues (see Table 4-3), seeking to gain broader knowledge (and often higher pay and/or to enhance job security), teachers throughout their career continue to take part in PD workshops and conferences, courses, and other formal learning opportunities.[10]

Governments often seize opportunities to control the learning of teachers, implementing province-wide professional development programs related to the latest public policy initiative (such as, in Ontario recently, literacy and numeracy for elementary schools and student success initiatives for secondary schools).

However, as Chapter 4 of this book has shown, when provincial governments have taken the further step of mandating formal learning for teachers, such as the Ontario Professional Learning Program and its required 14 courses over five years, teacher resentment and organized resistance has negated any learning benefit. Both Nova Scotia and Ontario have now abandoned their mandatory PD regimes. The WALL findings that teachers overwhelmingly participate in formal learning opportunities and engage in these activities for statistically similar hours per week in each province regardless of government policy (Clark et al. 2007, p. 41) have served to inform and cement this policy reversal.

Some Canadian provinces instead have looked to work more in partnership with teacher unions to develop policies for teacher professional learning that are more effective than legislated requirements. As articulated by Levin, Fullan and Glaze (2008), all of whom were instrumental in creating the Ontario government's educational strategies from 2003 to 2009, "Ontario's strategies rest on the belief that educators have enormous skill and knowledge to contribute to school improvement," and include working with teacher federations to create "many opportunities for teacher learning at all levels, from schools to networks of schools to districts to provincial activities" (p. 277). Michael Fullan credits these strategies in part for Ontario's current ranking among the top educational systems in the world, evidenced by Ontario's placement in the top ten in the OECD's Programme for International Student Assessment (Fullan 2009). Instead of a reform agenda of attacking teacher unions, since 2003 Ontario has worked with the unions, particularly on teacher learning initiatives. The Ontario approach of sharing power in this manner was lauded at the 2011 OECD International Summit on the Teaching Profession (OECD 2011, p. 57).

There is a growing consensus about what should be done. Darling-Hammond et al. (2009) conducted a comprehensive survey of existing research into what constitutes effective professional learning, and compared US practice to examples from other industrialized countries. Some of their key findings are:

> Effective professional development is intensive, ongoing, and connected to practice; focuses on the teaching and learning of specific academic content; is connected to other school initiatives; and builds strong working relationships among teachers. However, most teachers in the United States do not have access to professional development that uniformly meets all these criteria. (p. 5)

> Other nations that outperform the United States on international assessments invest heavily in professional learning and build time for ongoing, sustained teacher development and collaboration into teachers' work hours. (p. 6)

Traditionally, teacher learning in the United States and Canada has consisted of mandated PD days and voluntary formal learning at various workshops, conferences and university courses. In the United States in 2003–04, 92 per cent of teachers engaged in one of these formal learning activities (Darling-Hammond et al. 2009, p. 19), which is very close to the 90 per cent response in Canada in the WALL teacher survey (see Chapter 4).

However, teachers have long decried these PD days, exemplified by large-scale presentations by the latest "guru," or workshops that impart good ideas but no time, resources or support for putting them into practice, as relatively ineffective and indicative of the struggle over control of the profession which characterized the education reform agendas discussed earlier in this chapter. As one teacher interviewed in 2004 for the WALL Teacher Study said:

I think you learn so much more just sitting down with your colleagues and just sharing ideas – how did this work; discipline ideas; Christmas concert ideas; managing the peer pressure in the senior grades – than you do sitting in an auditorium with 600 other teachers listening to some speaker from the States. So I think ... the trust that we are going to use these PD days to better ourselves is gone. They feel they have to fill them for us, like we might just sit and do nothing if we had a day that wasn't filled for us.

Research has shown that this teacher's perception of the value of traditional PD is correct. A study (Yoon et al. 2007) examining more than 1,300 research projects on the impact of teacher professional development identified a key problem with this traditional approach – namely, that learning of 14 hours or less in duration (the norm with the PD day model) has no effect on student learning. In contrast, Yoon et al. (2007) found that ongoing and intensive professional learning of 49 hours or more annually had a significant impact on student achievement (p. 1).

Any policy that simply focuses on what workshops are delivered during the traditional one or two days per year set aside for PD days, therefore, will not have desired results in terms of changing teacher practice. It is critical to take a balanced approach to enhancing teacher learning, one which offers what Thomas Guskey called the "optimal mix" of approaches to professional development including such activities as formal training, observing colleagues, action research, mentoring and study groups. Guskey (1995) argued that "Because of the enormous variability in educational contexts, there will never be 'one right answer'" (p. 117).

In the twenty-first century, more enlightened governments have incorporated a range of teacher professional development strategies, recognizing that there is more to teacher learning than required participation in PD workshops or the "contrived collegiality" of mandatory professional learning communities focused on meeting improvement targets (Hargreaves & Shirley 2009, p. 92). Instead, these policy makers are recognizing that change requires collaboration and learning at all levels. For example, Michael Fullan (2005) has worked extensively with others in England, Ontario's York Region and other school systems on transforming entire education systems for greater student success. Such programs encourage a mix of professional development opportunities and school-based collaborative learning focussing on improving student success. Ben Levin, an academic, served as the head bureaucrat (Deputy Minister of Education) in Ontario implementing the Liberal government's policy changes after 2003 which are described in this chapter. Among these policy changes was a reversal of the anti-teacher and anti-union agenda of the previous government by ensuring that teacher union leaders were not only directly involved in educational policy development but also provided with government funds to offer their own union-run professional learning programs (Levin 2008, p. 42).

To understand why a mix of learning options is necessary, it is instructive to examine the conceptual framework for looking at teacher knowledge advanced by Cochran-Smith and Lytle (1999) (discussed in Chapter 3). Their first category is "knowledge *for* practice," which is commonly referred to as formal knowledge or theory, and which is the type of knowledge gained in pre-service education, continuing education courses at university, formal conferences, workshops and professional reading. The second conception of teacher learning is "knowledge *in* practice," which is the practical, job-embedded knowledge gained from interactions with and learning from colleagues and job experience. This is the type of knowledge especially sought by beginning teachers, and featured in Ontario's NTIP program outlined later in this chapter and which is expanded upon in the case study described in Chapter 8. Finally, the third concept is knowledge *of* practice, which is intentional study of their work undertaken by inquiry by individual teachers, or more commonly, by learning communities of experienced teachers. This type of teacher knowledge is understood and fostered by the National Writing Project in the United States (see Lieberman & Wood 2002), and in Ontario's Teacher Leadership and Learning Program, also featured later in this chapter.

We Need to Make Time During the Work Day for Informal, Ongoing Teacher Learning

As the teachers quoted in Chapter 4 emphasize repeatedly, teachers value informal learning from their colleagues above other types of professional learning. Similarly, in their survey of over 4,000 teachers, the General Teaching Council (GCTE) for England found that "a substantial majority gain their inspiration for their most effective lessons from talking with colleagues," and further that virtually all respondents reported that "they have engaged in professional knowledge-sharing conversations with their colleagues" (GTCE 2004, p. 3). The best time and place for such informal interactions and on-the-job learning is during the school day and at the workplace, where classroom teachers have the greatest professional control and the most opportunity to implement changes immediately into their practice.

The Darling-Hammond et al. (2009) study for the US National Staff Development Council showcased a number of international models incorporating job-embedded, collaborative and ongoing teacher learning into the work day. In fact, more than 84 per cent of schools in Belgium, Denmark, Finland, Hungary, Iceland, Norway, Sweden and Switzerland build time for teachers' professional development into the daily or weekly teacher timetable. (p. 15). In Sweden, as well as teachers collaborating daily in teacher teams on curriculum development and lesson planning, 104 hours, or 15 days per year, are allocated to inservice teacher learning. A similar program in Singapore provides for 100 hours per year (p. 17). As documented in Chapters 2 and 4, lack of time is the constraint most mentioned by Canadian teachers when discussing their work and learning challenges.

Teacher informal learning is a key part of any job-embedded learning strategy. The WALL teacher survey documented that teachers spend more than four hours per week in intentional job-related informal learning (see Chapter 4). Again, teachers with fewer than ten years experience spent only slightly more time (4.5 hours/week) than those with over 20 years in teaching (3.9 hours), indicating that informal learning is valuable to all teachers and not just to beginners. Teachers

SOME POLICY IMPLICATIONS

repeatedly commented in focus groups and interviews that their most valuable learning has come from colleagues in their workplaces.

Studies of teacher informal learning in other jurisdictions have similar findings to our WALL study. Hoekstra et al. (2007), studying teachers in the Netherlands struggling with implementing new government initiatives, found that those who most embraced the reforms were those who experimented in their classrooms, received new ideas from colleagues and engaged in meaningful reflection. Lohman (2006) found that while teachers prefer interactive learning among colleagues, the amount of informal learning that occurred was constrained by lack of time, lack of funds, and lack of proximity to colleagues.

Increasingly, policy directions in teacher learning in Canada have moved towards embracing informal as well as formal learning by recognizing the important distinction between *professional learning* and *professional development*. Professional development (also called staff development) is thus conceived of more as an event that is externally planned, a set of workshops or a program with a specific (and also externally-derived) agenda and offered on one or more specific dates rather than a daily part of the job. While teachers often take away valuable tips from these workshops and programs, they may not be translated into everyday practice. Official policies that emphasize job-embedded and ongoing learning opportunities are needed.

Hannay, Wideman and Seller (2006) emphasize this point:

> It bears repeating that professional development is learning designed externally with the goal of remediation, whereas professional learning focuses on individuals taking charge of and responsibility for their own practice. (p. 15)

Fullan, Hill and Crevola in their book *Breakthrough* (2006) make this distinction an important feature of their thesis:

> We have deliberately selected the term *professional learning* over the more narrow conceptual terms of *professional development* or professional learning communities because Breakthrough means focused, ongoing learning for each and every teacher ... (p. 21)

> How, then do we make deeper daily learning a reality for teachers? Replacing the concept of professional development with professional learning is a good start; understanding that professional learning "in context" is the only learning that changes classroom instruction is a second step. (p. 25)

SOME SUCCESSFUL SYSTEM-WIDE PROGRAMS

The Ontario New Teacher Induction Program (NTIP)

One example of a policy move towards more structured informal learning which recognizes the beginning teacher's need for practical knowledge is the Ontario New Teacher Induction Program. As argued in both Chapter 3 and 6, and illustrated in our case study of the Toronto District School Board's NTIP implementation in Chapter 8, induction programs, involving release time for mentors and a range of supports including targeted professional development and one-on-one coaching for new teachers, are not only essential for teacher retention, but are increasingly recognized as an essential part of the "continuum of teacher learning." This continuum is defined by Schwille and Dembele (2007), whose policy advice for UNESCO encompasses "being concerned not only with formal teacher preparation, induction and continuing professional development programs, but also with the many informal influences on what and how teachers learn to teach" (p. 20). They note that China and ten major OECD countries, including England, France, Italy and Japan, have mandatory induction programs (p. 89). Many studies have concluded that induction programs can reduce teacher turnover (Smith & Ingersoll 2004), as well as improving teacher practice for student success if the programs are job-embedded and include appropriate mentoring (Wang et al. 2008; Darling-Hammond et al. 2009).

What makes the Ontario NTIP a model induction program is its universality. It was created in 2006 by provincial legislation, after consultation with stakeholders including teacher unions. Under this program, all publicly-funded school boards in the province were required to offer a three-part induction program to all new teachers. New teachers were defined as:

> All teachers certified by the Ontario College of Teachers (including teachers trained out-of-province) who have been hired into permanent positions – full-time or part-time – by a school board, school authority, or provincial school ("board") to begin teaching for the first time in Ontario. (Ontario Ministry of Education 2006)

Since its inception almost 28,000 teachers have benefitted from the induction program. The three mandatory elements are:
– Orientation for all new teachers to the school and school board;
– Mentoring for new teachers by experienced teachers (the most critical component); and
– Professional development and training (PD) appropriate for new teachers.

Orientation typically starts even before the beginning teacher encounters her/his first class. The mentorship pairing is also done quickly and allows choice on both sides so that both mentor and beginning teacher can become comfortable with each other, undergo appropriate professional learning to assist the process, and embark on their ongoing relationship. Mentors are experienced teachers who either volunteer for the task or are approached by the school principal. Funding is provided by the ministry for both mentors and beginning teacher partners for release time for such activities as co-planning and peer observation. A safe exit procedure must be set up by each board so that either partner can back out of the mentor relationship in cases of incompatibility. The targeted professional learning opportunities offered within the NTIP program requirements[11] includes a range of "core content" areas for new teacher learning, including such topics as:
– Classroom management;
– Planning, assessment, and evaluation;

- Communication with parents;
- Teaching students with special needs and addressing the varied challenges of meeting the needs of diverse learners; and
- Literacy, numeracy, student success and safe schools province-wide initiatives.

Not only is participation compulsory for school boards, but also for new teachers. Participation in the NTIP, including the mentoring and learning targeted to the new teacher's specific needs, is required, but it is not evaluated, because the beginning teacher must be assured of the confidentiality of the mentor relationship. Successful completion of the program is noted, however, in their professional record at the College of Teachers. In addition, each new teacher undergoes two appraisals of her/his teaching performance during the school year, and the supports from the NTIP induction elements may lead to more successful evaluations.

Success of any legislated initiative depends on funding and ongoing review of the initiatives to ensure that the program is working. Provincial funding was provided to each Ontario school board to implement this program, based upon the number of new hires in each jurisdiction, and some flexibility within the NTIP framework allowed boards to differentiate the supports they offer, based on their assessments of local conditions and needs.

Ruth Kane and colleagues from the University of Ottawa were hired to review the program over three school years from 2006–07 through 2008–09. They invited all new beginning teachers, mentors and principals who participated in the NTIP to complete web-based questionnaires, and conducted individual interviews of new teachers, mentors and principals in 13 selected school boards, in each of the three years. They found that new teachers were generally satisfied with the induction program, and especially with the mentorship component, and that their mentors and principals believed that teachers who went through the NTIP were more confident and effective teachers than previous cohorts. The most positive experiences took place in collegial relationships, where mentor pairings took place early in the school year with input from both parties and where they had congruent teaching assignments, preferably in the same school. There were some unsuccessful experiences where the school culture left the beginner feeling relatively isolated and unsupported (Kane et al. 2010).

The Ontario Ministry of Education adopted recommendations for improving the program that had been made by the review team. For example, in 2009–10, after the review, the ministry broadened the scope of the program and its funding to also include newly hired long-term occasional teachers (those whose contracts provide for more than 97 teaching days) and allowed boards to expand the program to second year permanent hires if they wished.

The Teacher Learning and Leadership Program (TLLP)

Another ground-breaking Ontario government initiative, the Teacher Learning and Leadership Program, started in 2007,[12] is putting millions of dollars into funding grassroots projects developed by experienced classroom teachers[13] so that their personal knowledge about how to improve one or more aspects of student learning or teacher learning can be developed and shared with their peers. In its first four years of existence, 401 projects were funded, covering approximately 2,400 teachers (statistics provided by project leader, Ontario Ministry of Education 2011). While the program is entirely government-funded, each year the Ontario Teachers' Federation (the umbrella union for over 120,000 teachers) is invited to plan and mount the training conference for new project participants and "summit" sessions where groups who have finished the one-year action research phase of their project share their learning and plan how to extend the learning to other teachers, schools and school boards.

The goals of the TLLP are:

- To support experienced teachers who undertake self-directed advanced professional development[14] related to improved student learning and development;
- To help classroom teachers develop leadership skills for sharing learning and exemplary practices on a board-wide and/or provincial basis; and
- To facilitate knowledge exchange by building a provincial network for the sharing of teacher expertise.

Participants have been extremely positive about the experience, and projects have addressed new approaches to all teaching subjects, innovative programs to improve literacy, numeracy or education for students at risk, and action research into improving professional learning communities in schools. What makes these projects distinctive as an approach to professional learning is exemplified by one project leader's comment about her group's TLLP experience in the Ontario Teachers' Federation DVD *Taking the Lead*.[15]

> We're not sitting in a room just discussing theories, or just reading research or just talking about practice. We go back into the classroom and put it in practice.

> It's grounded in research; it's grounded in best practice. And we get, as much as we're trying to really dig deep into our own practice and be honest, we get fresh eyes coming in and giving us feedback.

The Ontario Teacher Learning and Leadership Program is an example of inquiry-focussed, collaborative professional learning aimed at increasing teacher knowledge *of* teaching (from the framework outlined by Cochran-Smith & Lytle 1999). Such models of professional learning give more power to the individual teacher over his/her own learning, rather than having the school principal, school district or the state determine what teachers need to learn. Ann Lieberman, drawing on her experience with the National Writing Workshop (Lieberman & Wood 2002), has been instrumental during the TLLP training session in contextualizing the program for each cohort of teachers whose projects are funded for the program. Lieberman's comments on this program (Lieberman 2010) include the following:

> TLLP provides us with a rethinking of the professional development paradigm that goes for compliance rather than collaboration, disparaging teacher unions rather than building shared solutions, thinking of professional development from the "outside" without participation and partnership from

SOME POLICY IMPLICATIONS

the "inside," and research imposed on teachers without the practice that roots new knowledge in the everyday work of teaching and learning.

Both Ontario programs, the TLLP and the NTIP, are putting the emphasis on individual professional learning and networking rather than on PD days, and are worthy of further research to discover the extent to which teacher learning and ultimately student learning are actually enhanced by the shift away from externally-designed traditional professional development programs to ongoing, collaborative, teacher-selected and job-embedded learning activities. Evidence to be provided in Chapter 8 certainly supports this shift in the power dynamics of decisions over teachers' professional learning, as do the dozens of quotes from teachers interviewed in all provinces of Canada as part of the WALL 2004 focus groups and later interviews of beginning teachers and occasional teachers, featured in this book in Chapters 4, 5 and 6.

Similar programs to Ontario's job-embedded, teacher-initiated learning do exist elsewhere. For example, in Scotland since 2001, special roles within the teacher union called "learning representatives" have increasingly been able to use government funding to facilitate continuing professional development opportunities for teachers (Alexandrou & O'Brien 2007). Another program similar to the TLLP has been in place in New Zealand since 2004, called the INSTEP (In-Service Teacher Educator Practice) Project. Action research projects and job-embedded teacher learning, with teachers taught by peers, are featured in this program. A 2009 review of the program concluded that, while results are uneven, the INSTEP project demonstrated

> that when they examined their practice collaboratively, challenged each other's ways of working and shared and discussed ways in which they determined effectiveness of their work, they were able to achieve far greater engagement from teachers in the professional development and learning. (Sankar 2009)

The Ontario TLLP program and New Zealand's INSTEP both resemble the Japanese "lesson study" and Chinese teachers' research group approaches that Schwille and Dembele (2007) describe as exemplary teacher-focussed professional learning models. As they note (p. 111), there is a widespread international consensus that defines what constitutes effective professional development, yet few examples of countries that implement such a program. The Japanese and Chinese programs share these important features:
- They use the teachers' own classroom as laboratories for professional development;
- They emphasize teachers working together;
- They use target lessons to discuss and investigate broader goals of schooling;
- They rely on action research with teachers writing reports to disseminate their learning;
- They emphasize the need to understand student thinking; and
- There is a balance between individual teacher initiative and leadership, and outsider advice and guidance. (pp. 112–113)

All of these features are present in the Ontario Teacher Learning and Leadership Program. This program, and hopefully others to come, will accomplish the pendulum swing, called for by progressive researchers such as Ann Lieberman, towards "policies that enable schools to build the capacity of teachers to seriously engage in transforming their school community" (Lieberman & Miller 2004, p. 13). While the struggles for control of the educational agenda that are documented throughout this book will remain, the success of the two Ontario programs and others featured here may yet be jeopardized by changing policy if different governments are elected, funding is withdrawn or government attitudes towards teachers and their unions change. However, the evidence is strong that control of professional learning, at least, should increasingly be ceded to the teachers themselves. Providing teachers with greater autonomy over their own professional learning will have positive benefits not only for teachers, but, most importantly, also for their students.

JIM STRACHAN

8. CASE STUDY

Job-Embedded Learning for Beginning Teachers in the Toronto District School Board

EDITORS' NOTE

Chapters 6 and 7 have outlined the importance of a mandatory teacher induction program for beginning teachers and ultimately for their students as well. This chapter constitutes a case study of how one very large school board has implemented and expanded upon the legally-mandated Ontario New Teacher Induction Program (NTIP). It is important to note that the chapter is written by the co-ordinator of the program, so the account is necessarily subjective. Nevertheless, the extremely high teacher retention rates, the positive comments by participants, and the evaluations of the model emphasizing collaborative learning, networked communication fostering continuous informal learning, active knowledge construction, and empowering teacher choice and differentiation in formal learning opportunities all produce empirical evidence of an exemplary induction program.

PURPOSE AND GOALS OF THE BEGINNING TEACHERS PROGRAM

I'm impressed with the depth and breadth of support being offered to new teachers. I have received a tremendous amount of support and feel extremely fortunate to have begun my career with the TDSB. (First year teacher)[1]

A beginning teacher walks into a school for the first time ... What are the initial and ongoing structures that will allow for the "intentional" sharing of knowledge and practice?

Job-embedded Learning has been at the heart of our work with beginning teachers and mentors in the Toronto District School Board (TDSB). The TDSB is the largest school board in Canada and the fourth largest in North America, serving over 260,000 students with 175 nationalities and 75 languages represented in our 558 schools. Since 2005–06, the TDSB has hired over 4,600 beginning teachers. This represents over 25 per cent of the entire teaching population of the board.

In my role as Program Coordinator–Beginning Teachers, I have worked in collaboration with Family of Schools superintendents, school administrators, Employee Services, Special Education and Program departments, beginning teacher coaches, mentors, and our partners in the teacher federations, faculties of education, and the Ontario Ministry of Education. In alignment with the Ministry of Education's New Teacher Induction Program (NTIP – explained in detail in Chapter 7), our shared goal has been to develop job-embedded supports for beginning teachers that go beyond retention and survival and focus on developing instructional excellence in the classroom.

The four key goals of the TDSB Beginning Teachers Program are to:
- Build instructional excellence to support improving student achievement;
- Support nurturing and caring relationships in our classrooms with our students;
- Create a sustainable system-wide mentoring culture across the TDSB; and
- Ensure the TDSB retains outstanding teacher leaders.

Underlying our vision is a strong belief that our beginning teachers possess tremendous strengths and attributes including energy, enthusiasm, and an ability to form authentic connections with students. By providing beginning teachers with a continuum of job-embedded professional learning and growth opportunities for the first five years, our goal is to directly impact upon the human development and learning of our students.

This chapter will focus on what we've learned from beginning teachers via online data collection, focus groups, and classroom visits and the key aspects of the job-embedded support and mentorship we provide. In addition, our vision for supporting beginning teachers along a continuum of professional learning and growth for their first five years will be highlighted.

BEYOND SURVIVAL: THE RETENTION MYTH

"The first year is all about survival" is a common refrain in both faculties of education and staff rooms. "Don't 50 per cent of new teachers quit or burn out?" is sadly a question this writer has been asked on numerous occasions. This popular conception is based largely on US data, where indeed in some jurisdictions retention of new teachers is a huge concern. For example, Liu and Ramsey (2008) found that roughly half of all teachers leave the profession within the first five years of their career.

Our TDSB data, as shown in Table 8-1, demonstrates that very few beginning teachers actually leave the school board, let alone the teaching profession. Throughout the 2005–10 period, TDSB retained over 98 per cent of our first year hires.

Our tracking of second-, third-, fourth- and fifth-year teachers reveals similarly high rates of retention to TDSB for each subsequent year. Of the 1,240 teachers who began their careers with TDSB in 2005, 94 per cent were teaching in TDSB in 2010. Debunking the myth of low retention is an essential starting point in getting away from a 'deficit model' for looking at beginning teachers and focusing instead on professional learning and growth. The goal of the programs and job-embedded supports we offer is not simply to keep teachers but instead to develop instructional excellence in the classroom.

Table 8-1. TDSB retention of first year teachers

	2005–2006	2006–2007	2007–2008	2008–2009	2009–2010
No. of first year permanent hires	1240	1239	1061	670	467
No. of teachers returning to TDSB	1218	1223	1051	666	462
Rate of retention	98.23	98.71	99.05	99.40	98.93

STRATEGIES/ACTIONS TAKEN

Based on our data collection from beginning teachers, TDSB has designed a "layered" approach to providing opportunities for formal and informal learning that has evolved considerably since the inception of this initiative in 2004. Over this time, we have steadily moved away from the traditional "one size fits all" workshop model of professional development to the creation of professional learning structures that allow for differentiation, choice, and ongoing job-embedded support. Table 8-2 provides a succinct overview of the approach that has informed our program design.

Table 8-2. TDSB Program Design

Traditional professional development ⟶	*Job-embedded mentorship*
• Outside consultants	• Inside professionals
• Ministry or Board workshops	• Capacity building learning communities
• System centred	• Student centred
• Participation is mandated	• Participation is by invitation
• Passive knowledge consumption	• Active knowledge construction
• Individual implementation	• Collaborative implementation, Mentorship
• Authoritarian communication	• Networked communication

Source: Adapted from Gibbs & Ushijima (2008, p. 125)

LEVELS OF SUPPORT

Our model in TDSB provides intentional support for the first five years of a beginning teacher's career through a variety of job-embedded structures to support ongoing learning and professional growth. A layered program design offers supports at the school, at the regional (family of schools) level, and system-wide. A critical element of the model is the opportunity for each beginning teacher to choose the supports that best meet her/his learning needs.

Level 1: School-Based Mentoring

Throughout our work, the importance of school culture is a recurring theme. Simply put, the support of the principal, teachers, and other staff members at school plays a defining role in the experiences of beginning teachers. Providing structures and programs to support school – based mentorship is fundamental to our vision for beginning teachers.

Job-Embedded Learning Initiative (JELI) and Job Associated Mentoring (JAM)

> *I love the gift of time that JELI days provide. Being able to go and visit an exemplary classroom and bring back ideas to use in my own classroom was very important to me this year. In my second year, I feel less overwhelmed by the day-to-day parts of teaching I am more able to benefit from JELI days.* (second-year teacher)

> *JELI and JAM provide an opportunity to get the sort of on-the-job training previously inaccessible to teachers that other workplaces take for granted.* (fourth-year teacher)

Using funding from the Provincial Ministry of Education's New Teacher Induction Program and the TDSB, release time is provided for beginning teachers in their first five years, including newly hired long term occasional (LTO) teachers. First and second year teachers receive four "JELI days" with newly hired LTO teachers receiving three days. This job-embedded structure continues with third-, fourth-, and fifth-year teachers accessing two "JAM days."

Beginning teachers may choose to use their JELI and JAM days for:
- School-based planning and professional learning with mentors;
- Central TDSB professional learning sessions;
- Example classroom visits – classrooms identified within the beginning teacher's own school or family of schools for observational visits; and
- Demonstration classroom learning – focused observation, debriefing, action planning, and co teaching opportunities guided by a program team member (details in next section).

Table 8-3 represents how 2,210 Beginning TDSB teachers used their JELI and JAM days from September 2010 to May 2011.

Table 8-3. How time release days are used by beginning teachers (1–5 years of experience)

School-based professional learning with mentors	Classroom observation (example & demonstration classrooms)	Central PD
48.9%	45.2%	5.9%

Demonstration classroom learning Here are two beginning teachers speaking on the value of demonstration learning:

> *So much PD is all theory – but the demo classroom allows us to see the theory in practice, which is critical. As teachers we rarely get to see other teachers at work – we may talk about teaching, but there's a real value in seeing it. And the demo classroom is authentic and allows us to witness things that work and things that may not. The chance to have constructive collaboration and debriefing is so valuable.* (first-year teacher)

> *I would recommend attending an observation demo class to not only beginning teachers but also to veteran teachers. Being able to see first hand how teachers are applying different strategies and seeing the reaction of the students is phenomenal.* (second-year teacher)

Lois Brown Easton (2005, p.55) describes powerful professional learning as possessing the following characteristics or attributes:
- Arises from and returns benefits to the real world of teaching and learning;
- Focus is on what is happening with learners (both student and adult) in the classroom, school, and district;
- Collaborative or has collaborative aspects;
- Establishes a culture of quality; and
- Slows the pace of schooling, providing time for the inquiry and reflection that promote learning and application.

In 2008–09, the TDSB began to explore the concept of demonstration classrooms. Through our own action research and by examining a variety of professional learning models from other districts during our 2008–09 pilot year, we were afforded the opportunity to develop a research-based model unique to the needs of the TDSB. In the third year of implementation, the TDSB hosted over 380 demonstration classrooms representing every grade level (including combined grades), and all subject areas (see Table 8-4).

Table 8-4. Evolution and scope of TDSB demonstration classrooms

	2008–2009	2009–2010	2010–2011
No. of demonstration teachers	2 (pilot year)	288	384
No. of classroom visits	12	558	762
No. of visiting teachers	70	1956	2915

Each demonstration classroom learning experience aligns with Easton's (2005) powerful designs model and includes:
- *Orientation* – an opportunity for each visiting teacher to connect with a guide (centrally assigned TDSB coach or instructional leader), guiding the visit and to share specific learning goals for the Observation day – focused observation and authentic professional learning in the actual classroom, led by the Guide;

- *Debriefing* – an opportunity to reflect upon the classroom experience, ask questions, and share ideas with colleagues, the demonstration classroom teacher, and the Guide;
- *Action planning* – structured 'so what/now what' action planning for applying the learning to each participants' specific teaching context; and
- *Follow up* – direct assistance from the guide in implementing the ideas and strategies back in the visiting teacher's own classroom.

This opportunity is available to all TDSB teachers (regardless of years of service) and represents a real shift away from the concept of professional development via a workshop to the intentional sharing of knowledge and practice via job-embedded ongoing professional learning, coaching and mentorship. By learning together in grade, division, subject area, school or small Family of School teams, new ideas, strategies and approaches can be discussed and reflected upon and then tailored, modified, and differentiated to the local needs of the children being served.

The diagram below (Table 8-5) summarizes this approach and emphasizes the importance of follow up and support for implementation that is an integral part of this structure.

Our demonstration classroom registration data from 2011 indicates that over 45 per cent of teachers participating in demonstration classroom visits are beyond their first five years of teaching, again speaking to the power of this approach to encourage intentional sharing of knowledge and practice for all teachers.

Multiple models of mentoring In the TDSB, mentors are colleagues of beginning teachers teaching at the same school:

I've had tremendous support – not just from my mentor. The entire school has offered their expertise and has been very willing to listen to my thoughts and opinions. (first-year teacher)

I had many great mentors at my school who helped me throughout my first couple of years. I really liked the fact that there was someone to turn to for bouncing off ideas, strategies, and/or just plain networking. It is nice to have that added support without feeling you are "bothering" someone. Now I am currently mentoring a 1st year Teacher! (fifth-year teacher)

Mentors volunteer for their role and/or are asked by their school administrator to support a beginning teacher. Mentors do not evaluate or judge performance; rather, their goal is to develop internal capacity for learning and growth in the beginning teachers they support. They do this via consulting (offering support and providing resources); collaborating (creating challenge and encouraging growth); and coaching (facilitating professional vision). They share the job-embedded release time described earlier in this chapter with the beginning teacher they are supporting.

In the initial stages of our work, we paid specific attention to the idea of each beginning teacher being matched on a one to one basis with a mentor at their school. In our early data collection (2004–05 and 2005–06), we asked beginning teachers the following question: "Do you have a mentor at your school?"

Table 8-5. Beyond the workshop

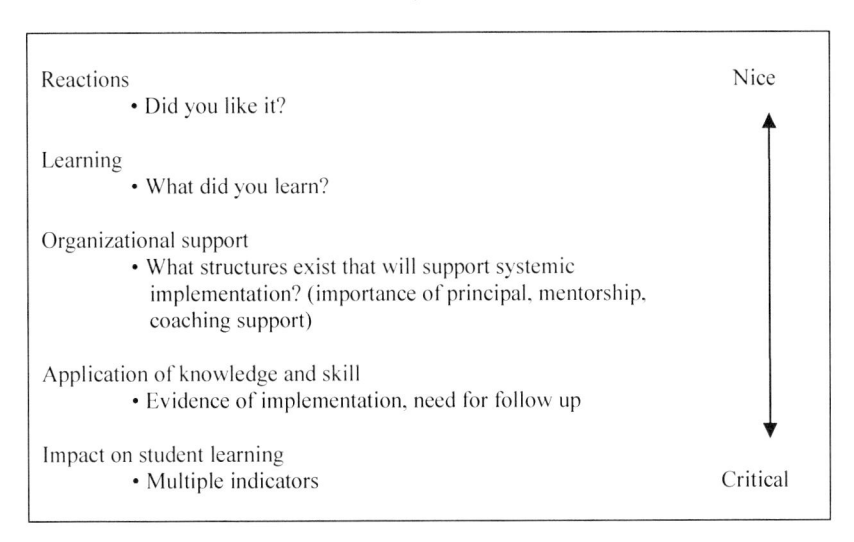

Reactions	Nice
• Did you like it?	↑
Learning	
• What did you learn?	
Organizational support	
• What structures exist that will support systemic implementation? (importance of principal, mentorship, coaching support)	
Application of knowledge and skill	
• Evidence of implementation, need for follow up	↓
Impact on student learning	
• Multiple indicators	Critical

Source: Adapted from Guskey (2000, p. 82)

What we realized from our data collection is that we were actually asking the wrong question. Having a formally identified mentor did not necessarily mean a beginning teacher was being mentored. As a result, in subsequent years we have changed the question to: "Are you being mentored at your school?"

This change in question acknowledges that, while a one-to-one mentoring relationship can be very powerful, mentorship can exist in many forms and each beginning teacher is an active participant in the mentoring process. Our goal is that beginning teachers are directly involved in determining what mentoring supports will best meet their unique learning needs.

Table 8-6 reflects our understandings regarding the multiple models that can exist in any school. It is worth noting that multiple models of mentorship can co-exist in the same school, often to the benefit of the beginning teacher.

Layer 2: Family of Schools Mentoring

I am the only Grade 5 teacher at my school so the Family of Schools supports gave me the chance to connect with dedicated teachers, beginners or veterans and share our learning. This was very meaningful. (second-year teacher)

As we continue to move towards a professional learning model that is responsive to the needs of beginning teachers, the Family of Schools (FOS) has become an increasingly important layer of support.

Table 8-6. Models of mentoring

Broker mentor
Role • Mentor provides orientation to school logistics and culture • Mentor brokers involvement of colleagues as needs arise from protégé Considerations • Consultant-type relationship, fewer opportunities for collaboration and coaching • May be initial support until other mentoring relationships are established or ongoing throughout the year
One-to-one mentor matching
Role • Mentor is site-based and is matched on an individual basis with a protégé • Mentor adopts consultant, collaboration and coaching stances based on the needs of the Protégé Considerations • Mentor/protégé relationships that flourish are reciprocal – both parties learn and grow • Greater "ownership" if the mentor has volunteered and if protégé has been involved in the determination of which person will be their mentor
Group mentoring
Role • Mentor works with 2 or more protégés or protégé may have 2 or more mentors • School Mentoring Committee plans formal support and professional learning opportunities for both mentors and protégés Considerations • Provides flexibility if school has large number of beginning teachers (or mentors) • This model is often embedded in a school-wide "mentoring culture" where all staff are mentors or protégés (or both)
Informal mentoring
Role • Protégé informally connects with a variety of staff members as needs arise • Mentor/protégé roles are fluid – often referred to as Peer Mentoring as in many cases the informal mentors are beginning teachers themselves Considerations • Spontaneous, informal nature of relationship can lend itself to collaboration • Protégé may feel isolated and/or "disconnected" if not part of any informal relationships
Online mentoring
Role • Using online conferencing protégés can participate in discussion and sharing with both experienced teachers and other beginning teachers Considerations • Enables access to a variety of resources and perspectives beyond the school site • Not all protégés feel comfortable sharing issues and concerns in this "public" forum

In the TDSB there are 24 Families of Schools, each consisting of approximately 20 to 25 elementary and secondary schools located in some geographic proximity. Each of the Families of Schools has a beginning teachers team consisting of principals and vice-principals, mentors, and centrally assigned coaches and instructional leaders. This team works closely with each Family of Schools superintendent and the Beginning Teachers Program Coordinator to ensure alignment of support and responsiveness to local needs.

The smaller scale of the Family of Schools provides more focused professional learning that can be tailored to specific needs expressed by beginning teachers. Examples of FOS professional learning opportunities and themes include:
– orientation/welcome events/celebrations;
– classroom management;
– diversity of learners;
– assessment and evaluation;
– FOS initiatives and priorities; and
– networking work smart groups and idea shares with teachers of similar assignments and mentors.

In many Families of Schools professional learning opportunities focus on the intentional sharing of knowledge and practice between colleagues rather than knowledge consumption. For example, rather than attending a literacy assessment workshop, a small group of primary teachers and mentors from nearby schools may meet together with their Family of Schools literacy coach to facilitate the sharing assessment and evaluation strategies amongst the group.

Our data reveal that this type of knowledge construction and networking has proven especially valuable if school based mentorship is not proving meaningful for an individual beginning teacher. In this sense, the Family of Schools level can provide a meaningful "second layer" of support.

Level 3: Central System Mentoring

Central mentorship provides an additional layer of support and is available to both beginning teachers and mentors via face-to-face and online professional learning.

Summer Institute An important component of our approach is the Summer Institute:

Thank you for the warmth, strength and inspiration the Summer Institute provided. Hearing the different perspectives from three different French Immersion teachers was so valuable and seeing the classroom set up first hand was amazing! (second-year teacher)

In late August, before schools open, beginning teachers are able to spend three days in grade/home groups led by experienced teachers who currently teach their actual teaching assignment. In 2010, over 700 participants chose from over 30 assignment-specific sessions held in actual classrooms across the TDSB.

The Institute is voluntary and focuses on practical ideas for the first day, first week and first month of school. Strategies to build inclusion and create a positive classroom environment for learning are shared and structured opportunities to network and make connections with colleagues, mentors, and Family of Schools beginning teacher teams are provided. Grade/home group facilitators provide follow up support throughout the year both online and via demonstration classroom visits.

Online sharing Using the TDSB's First Class conferencing system, beginning teachers are able to share resources, dialogue with mentors and collaborate with each other in grade and subject specific conferences:

> *All the posting of information and ideas on our New Teachers.TEL conference has been very helpful. When you have so much to teach in what seems like not much time, then there is no time to re-invent the wheel. I LOVE the sharing that goes on. I also liked the inspirational words of support from your weekly e-mails throughout the year. It helped you to realize that you are not alone in your struggles at times.* (fifth-year teacher)

Beginning teachers can access their "TEL" conferencing both at school and at home. A weekly "Happy Thursday" blog[2] is sent directly to over 4,000 beginning teachers, mentors, and administrators highlighting practical classroom ideas and professional learning opportunities.

Professional learning for mentors Job-embedded release time is available for mentors via the JELI and JAM programs highlighted earlier in this chapter. Beginning teachers can 'share' their JELI/JAM days with mentor(s) in order to foster collaboration, mentorship, and professional learning.

As school-based mentorship is a key component of the supports we offer, the TDSB provides central professional learning for both new and experienced mentors in addition to the JELI/JAM days. These full day sessions focus on a personal examination of the mentor's role in addition to the development of the knowledge and skills necessary for mentors to support the professional growth and development of beginning teachers.

Our goal is to provide in-depth opportunities for mentors to broaden their personal repertoire of effective mentoring strategies and to enhance professional practice both with colleagues and with students. Over 1,950 TDSB teachers have attended these central professional learning opportunities over the past seven years. By providing ongoing support for mentors we are acknowledging the commitment to the profession they demonstrate and the direct impact of their support on the professional learning and growth of beginning teachers.

IMPACT/EVIDENCE/RESULTS

Table 8-7 reflects data collected from 652 TDSB beginning teachers in May 2011 regarding their perception of the impact on the learning of their students of each aspect of the beginning teachers program.

Table 8-7. Impact on student learning

Layers of Support	Not meaningful	Somewhat meaningful	Meaningful	Very meaningful	Meaningful + very meaningful
Job Associated Mentoring (JAM)	0%	4%	22%	74%	96%
Job-embedded Learning Initiative (JELI)	1%	5%	25%	69%	94%
Demonstration classroom learning	1%	9%	25%	65%	90%
Being mentored at your school	7%	11%	29%	53%	82%
Summer institute	0%	19%	34%	47%	81%
Family of Schools Professional Learning	5%	17%	39%	39%	78%
Online sharing	7%	14%	41%	38%	79%
Other TDSB workshops	22%	27%	32%	19%	51%

ANALYSIS: PERSONALIZATION, CHOICE AND AUTHENTICITY

Job-embedded learning (JELI & JAM) are clearly reported by beginning teachers to have the greatest impact both on teaching practice and the learning of their students. Fundamental to the JELI/JAM program are the concepts of personalization and choice. The challenges of a first year Grade 10 Applied English teacher may (or may not) be different from a fifth year kindergarten teacher, but in consultation with their principal and mentor(s) both are able to use their JELI/JAM days to best meet individual learning needs and goals.

Looking at the bottom row of Table 8-7 we see the relatively less popular traditional "one size fits all" workshop and must wonder what opportunities for choice and authenticity exist in this professional learning setting. Without follow-up coaching and mentorship, our data reveals 'stand alone' types of professional development sessions do not significantly impact upon teacher practice and student learning for a very large percentage of participants in our induction program.

Demonstration classroom learning represents an approach to professional learning that is personal. Because we have over 380 demonstration teachers, virtually any teacher can find a match to their current teaching assignment. That said, although all the visiting teachers may teach the same grade or subject, it is not uncommon for each of the visiting teachers to reveal different learning goals for the day during the goal setting conversation with the guide.

One person may be focused on classroom management, another be interested in how the demonstration teacher structures their Guided Reading program, and still another may want to learn more about how inclusion is fostered with the students. Demonstration classroom learning provides a venue for each participant to observe authentic "real world" teacher practice and student learning that aligns with their unique learning goals.

These concepts of choice and differentiation also emerge in the school-based mentorship data. While the overall data indicate mentorship at school is meaningful to most beginning teachers, it is worth noting that for 18 per cent this was not the case. We have been gathering these data for the past five years and have consistently found that these "disconnects" in the mentoring relationship fall into three categories:

(1) Mentor does not want to be a mentor:
- "Voluntold" by school administrator;
- Same strong people often asked to do multiple roles in school.

(2) Mentor stuck in consulting stance:
- Lack of trust and rapport;
- Protégé feels judged and/or evaluated.

(3) Complex dynamics of human interaction:
- Wonderful people do not always "click."

In all three categories, beginning teachers reported seeking out informal mentoring from other teacher colleagues. Often these colleagues were themselves recently hired teachers. Beginning teachers report successful mentoring relationships when they have been active participants in determining what mentoring supports will best meet their unique learning needs.

While school-based mentoring alone may not be meaningful for every beginning teacher, we have found that a "layered" program design featuring multiple models of school-based mentoring, local Family of Schools support, central professional learning, and online conferencing is more likely than a one size fits all approach to meet the diverse learning styles and learning needs of our beginning teachers.

CHALLENGES AND LEARNING

The remainder of this chapter consists of personal reflections and ideas to consider in the design of meaningful induction programs for beginning teachers based on our experiences in the TDSB.

School culture Our centrally designed programs create supportive structures, but it is in the classroom and school each day where the difference is made in the learning of both students and adults. While our goal is that mentorship and the intentional sharing of knowledge and practice becomes the norm in each of the 558 schools in our district, an ongoing challenge is to respond to the considerable variation both within and between schools. For a beginning teacher it is a common desire to adapt to and adopt the norms of the dominant school culture and it is a considerable challenge if these norms do not align with his or her own emerging personal beliefs about teaching and learning. While a beginning teacher may well be assigned a 'formal' mentor, we strongly encourage connecting with as many colleagues as possible in order to build and create a professional learning network that is meaningful, supportive and responsive to their learning needs and goals.

Learning of mentors and demonstration teachers Of all the discoveries we have made in the past few years, this one is perhaps the most gratifying. In short, although the role of the mentor and/or demonstration teacher is to model and provide learning for others, they themselves report tremendous personal and professional growth themselves. Below is a summary of the learning themes that have emerged via focus groups with over 260 mentors and demonstration classroom teachers:

– Increased reflection on current practice:

> *I developed a greater awareness of my personal teaching philosophy; a stronger desire to incorporate more varied learning strategies to reach my students.*

> *Working with my protegé has opened me up to possibility of growth and to the potential new ideas ... this has helped me become more reflective about my own practice.*

– Fostered inspirational connections with colleagues:

> *I highly valued opportunity to make new connections with other TDSB teachers and also to work closely with our Math coach throughout the school year.*

> *Mentoring has improved my relationships with other teachers (not just beginning teachers). I have become more aware of the value of other teachers on staff, and more encouraged to share.*

– Impacted teaching practice and learning of students:

> *I take seriously the high yield strategies in my own practice and as a result of being a demonstration teacher I reflected about how I could use them on a daily basis.*

> *The sharing of effective practices served to improve student learning in my own classroom not just when visiting teachers came to visit but every other day too!*

Importance of a continuum of support over five years When the New Teacher Induction Program (NTIP) was introduced in 2006, the Ontario Ministry of Education defined a new teacher as a newly hired first year permanent teacher. In 2009, the Ministry broadened the use of NTIP funding to also include newly hired Long-Term Occasional (LTO) teachers who are teaching longer than 97 days and second-year permanent hires.

JIM STRACHAN

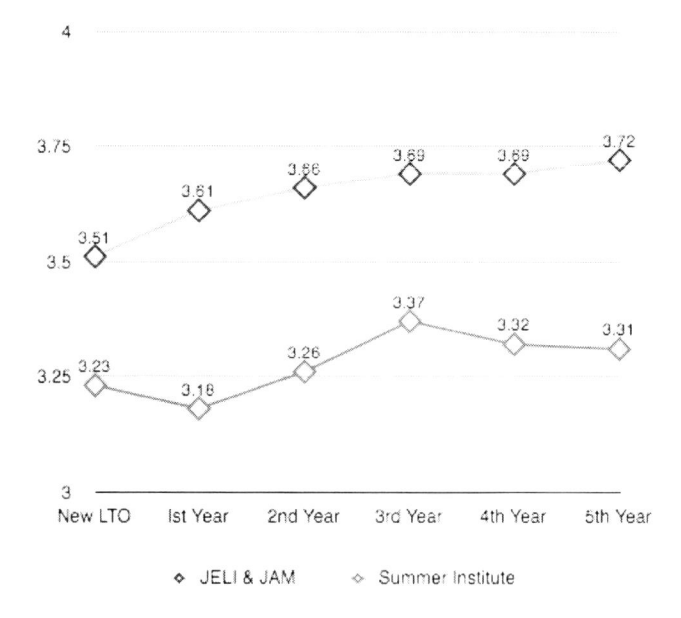

Figure 8-1. Impact of induction program on student learning, years 1–5

Our data presented in Figure 8-1 reinforce this idea of extending supports beyond the first year. It is of interest to note that as beginning teachers gain more experience and context for their learning, the job-embedded supports become more meaningful. When asked for their opinions on the impact of JELI and JAM, beginning teachers in their fifth year of teaching reported the greatest impact on student learning, while newly hired LTOs reported the lowest impact.

Interestingly, this same pattern was found regarding our Summer Institute, which is geared directly to brand new hires with its focus on the first days and weeks of school. When asked about the impact of the Summer Institute on the learning of the students in their classroom, the groups who reported the least impact were newly hired LTOs and first-year teachers. By comparison, second-, third- and fourth-year teachers, with their context of prior teaching experiences, reported significantly higher response averages. Beginning teachers report that as they gain actual teaching experience they move beyond "survival mode" and begin to more deeply examine their teaching and apply ideas and strategies in their classroom practice. This input is directly responsible for the TDSB extending the supports it offers to the first five years of teaching.

Learning from beginning teachers: The Attributes-Based Approach One of the most interesting discoveries I made early on in my role was that while everybody I met had very clear ideas about what beginning teachers needed, none of the people giving me advice about program design were actually beginning teachers! For the past seven years I have spent every Monday morning in the classroom of a beginning teacher. They invite me, usually after hearing me speak at a large group session or in response to a weekly blog I have sent out. These Monday visits have been the greatest source of my personal and professional learning, as I am able to see and hear firsthand the issues, challenges and successes encountered from Kindergarten all the way through to Grade 12.

What I have learned can be summed up in what I call the "Attributes-Based Approach." The attributes-based approach is a lens through which we can choose to view beginning teachers (and students). We can look at beginning teachers and note all the deficits and challenges, or we can look at those same professionals and purposefully seek out and identify their strengths. If we believe that our beginning teachers have strengths and positive attributes, we will intentionally structure opportunities for them to learn from and with each other – and for us to learn from them.

Scaling the attributes-based approach to a system level means providing choice and acknowledging that beginning teachers know more about their personal learning goals and needs than I do. Effective professional learning is not something that is "done" to teachers. When the agenda of learning is held outside the circle of learners, implementation of learning rarely occurs. Opportunities for authentic knowledge construction and personalization of learning must be constructed by the learners themselves and explicitly connected to the "real world" of classroom practice and student learning.

By embedding choice of formal and informal learning opportunities into the daily experiences of our beginning teachers, we are giving both our teachers and our students a valuable gift. Our students will be in classrooms where their teachers are not only provided with resources, but are also part of a learning community where challenge is created and professional vision is encouraged.

Providing ongoing consulting, collaborating and coaching opportunities for our mentors and beginning teachers models the very learning community we would like beginning teachers to create and promote in their own classrooms. It is here that we have come full circle, as the beginning teachers we are currently supporting will become the mentors for our next generation of new hires as well as mentors of the students they teach.

SUMMARY OF EVOLUTION AND SCOPE OF THE TDSB BEGINNING TEACHERS PROGRAM

Table 8-8. Summary of programs

	2005/2006	2006/2007	2007/2008	2008/2009	2009/2010	2010/2011
NTIP	\multicolumn{6}{l}{• Orientation, mentoring, professional learning in key areas of need for beginning teachers • Teacher Performance Appraisal (twice in first 12 months) • NTIP Steering Committee (NTIP Superintendent, NTIP Contact, Employee Services, Faculties, Federations, VP/Ps, new teachers, mentors)}					
TDSB program initiatives	• Support extended to 2nd Year & New LTO's	• JELI for 1st, 2nd Year and New LTO's	• Special Ed & FSL Coaches	• JAM for 3rd, 4th, 5th Year	• Demonstration Classroom Learning	
No. of beginning teachers supported	1st –1240 2nd –710 LTO– 190	1st – 1239 2nd –1218 LTO–273	1st – 1061 2nd –1223 LTO–290	1st – 670 2nd –1051 LTO–448 3rd– 1185 4th –1150 5th – 653	1st – 467 2nd – 666 LTO– 376 3rd – 1039 4th –1161 5th –1127	1st –665 2nd –462 LTO– 206 3rd – 652 4th – 1018 5th –1138

ROSEMARY CLARK, D.W. LIVINGSTONE
& HARRY SMALLER

CONCLUSION

Reconsidering Teacher Learning and Power

INTRODUCTION

The recognition of knowledge is intimately related to the exercise of power. In class societies, ownership of the means of production enables rewarding, punishing or ignoring the knowledge of workers without such ownership. In feudal economies, craftsmen who were able to band together in guilds gained sufficient power to guard and gain reward for their specialized knowledge, whereas serfs who had intimate complex knowledge of the land remained tied to their lords with little reward. In capitalist economies, workers have been freer to seek diverse forms of knowledge and different employers. Widening democratic access to many forms of previously exclusive knowledge has been a progressive feature of these market-based economies.

Although the emergence of "knowledge-based economies" has been widely heralded, the extent of recognition of workers' knowledge has remained dependent on the prerogative of their employers or their own collective negotiating power. Even among professionals who have reached the highest levels of formal educational attainment and certification, recognition of their specialized knowledge continues to be conditioned by either the power of ownership of means of production or negotiating power with their employers. Doctors and lawyers have been the most evident examples of occupations with specialized knowledge that organized themselves in guild forms, retained ownership of their services and continued to shape recognition and reward of their knowledge, even with increasing state oversight of all forms of knowledge. The predominance of ownership power among them has ensured that they have been widely regarded as "professionals" rather than "workers." Admittedly, professional status diminishes as many doctors become salaried employees in public institutions.

Behind their classroom doors, contemporary teachers must try to communicate vibrant and changing curricular knowledge while nurturing, counselling and evaluating diverse groups of students. Effective teaching continues to be one of the most complex and demanding of all jobs. This complex array of tasks requires a high degree of discretion, as well as continual experiential learning on the job, in order to be performed adequately. This is why in the present study we have found teachers to be the professionals who perceive the greatest autonomy in their own workplaces. Teachers' other motives for doing their jobs may be as commonplace as for any job. But this sense of personal autonomy is jealously guarded by most teachers to ensure performance of the central mission of the teaching profession – helping their students to become fully developed human beings – even as a growing array of standardized regulatory duties are externally imposed upon them. There may be differences between Canada and other countries in the extent to which regulatory authorities effectively support teachers' mission. But this sense of power within the classroom appears to contrast greatly with teachers' relative lack of involvement in organizational-level decision-making in most countries.

In the period of economic instability since the mid-1970s, as in most such prior periods in capitalist societies (see Curti 1935), the schools have been looked to as sources of economic salvation. There is now a widespread notion that economies are becoming increasingly knowledge based, and development of learning capabilities is seen as a heightened priority to ensure individual and societal success. The failures of society to provide sufficient jobs, sustainable growth and healthy lives are visited upon schools across the globe, and the schools are admonished to do more to resolve such problems. The "great recession" of 2008–09 has probably increased these expectations. But, unfortunately for many advocates of school reform, the schools are not the root of the problem. In spite of being blamed for many economic and social problems that are really the responsibility of the larger society, schools are already producing more well qualified people than the larger society has been able to accommodate in meaningful employment. As Livingstone (2010b, p. 227) has observed:

> Educational systems will continue to try to improve the relevance of their programmes in response to growing economic and social demands. Formal educational qualifications may continue to be primary proxy criteria for entry into many jobs … But economic production would be more sustainable if the current labour force were more highly valued for capabilities to develop and use [already attained] reserves of abilities. Economic reforms, including redistribution of paid work and workplace democratisation, are more sustainable measures to address these systemic limits than are appeals for still greater learning efforts by already highly educated and knowledgeable labour forces.

As Anyon (1995) put it: "Educational reforms cannot compensate for the ravages of society" (p. 88).

Nevertheless, a neo-liberal school reform agenda now prevails in most advanced capitalist societies. The basic assumption is that schools would be better run like private businesses driven by competitive market pressures. Both school and teacher performance are to be increasingly measured by students' scores on standardized tests and with future resources rewarded accordingly. Parents are encouraged to shop for schools for their children based on such criteria while freer choices among types of schools are also promoted. In the United States at least, this business-oriented school reform movement is now led by large philanthropic organizations such as the Gates and Walton Foundations that invest aggressively in public schools to convert them to more "businesslike" practices. As Foster (2011) notes:

The Gates Foundation has poured hundreds of millions of dollars into the support of educational advocacy groups meant to pressure public policy, all aimed at restructuring public education, promoting charter schools, encouraging privatization, and breaking teachers' unions. (p. 7)

However, such neo-liberal school reform efforts have most often led to diminishing educational services to those least able to pay for them directly, and to demonizing teachers for failing to deliver such diminishing services.

But any *public* education worthy of the name must try to respond to democratic demand. At the same time as neo-liberal political forces try to manufacture parental demand for regressive businesslike school reforms, popular demand for continuing access to advanced formal education has never been greater: progressive forces in many communities are mobilizing to defend remaining educational entitlements.[1] Part of the response of teachers and their unions to the narrowing of their central mission and intensification of other assigned tasks surely must be to ally with democratic community forces to ensure that schools are accessible and responsive to the needs of all people.[3] It would be both in the self-interest of teachers and for the greater good of the larger community if the centralizing, standardizing trend in educational decision-making were to be reversed and if teachers as well as representatives of significant community groups were to become fuller participants. If teachers gain greater roles in shared organizational decision-making while retaining strong commitment to their central mission, educational programs are likely to become more effective in responding to real needs.

TEACHERS AS PROFESSIONALS AND PROFESSIONAL LEARNERS

The most pertinent example of relations between learning and power in terms of this book is formal professional development programs. By dint of their collective bargaining power, teachers' participation rate in PD programs is higher than most other professionals. But their complaints about the irrelevance of most established programs are legion; most teachers consider such programs to be of minor importance compared to informal learning by themselves and with colleagues. Those few teachers who have been delegated greater roles in organizational decision-making relating to school level and system-wide policies and practices do tend to engage more effectively in formal professional development programs and integrate what they learn there with their everyday work and ongoing informal learning. If most teachers were empowered to play meaningful roles in the design and development of their formal professional development (as some other, self-regulating professions have been able to do), the more effective integration of their informal and formal learning practices would very likely lead to more effective classroom teaching and fuller development of their students.

Many advocates of a knowledge-based economy envisage it as thriving on "freer expression, better feedback between rulers and ruled, more popular participation in decision-making" (Toffler 1990, p. 364). Further teacher empowerment that brings their delegated organizational decision-making roles into

179

fuller accord with their classroom autonomy could be a very constructive step toward the realization of a genuine knowledge-based economy.

It may be that teachers' fixation on their presumed classroom autonomy is one of the greatest obstacles to their fuller engagement in progressive social change movements. Canadian teachers' perceived autonomy may be somewhat greater than that of teachers in some other countries that have experienced greater centralized regulatory control. Canadian teachers express a nearly unanimous sense of design control of their own classrooms but also a greater discrepancy between personal autonomy and organizational decision-making power than most other professionals. The neo-liberal attack on established government social services and public sector unions threatens equitable access to education and many other social services. Teachers are among the most well-organized and resourced to lead the fight for equity. But equity concerns appear to take low priority in relation to their other immediate practical concerns for their own job security and autonomy (see Table 4-7). Recent advocates of the knowledge economy (e.g., Cortada 1998) presume that professionals in this economy have their autonomy and immediate control over their work preserved by their specialized knowledge. However, we have found that a sense of autonomy in designing one's own work is increasingly shared by majorities in all occupational groups, with professionals becoming indistinct from other occupations. One interpretation of this change is that an ideology of discretionary control has become widespread in the labour force even among those who have relatively little actual power. As suggested in Chapter 4, preoccupation with retaining 'teacher empowerment' in the classroom may be becoming both a technique of self-regulation, as well as of teachers' disempowerment beyond the classroom in relation to struggles for more democratic education.

Our posited claims about teachers' work and learning have largely been confirmed by our research over the past 15 years, sounding out thousands of classroom teachers across Canada through survey questionnaires, focus groups, time-study diaries and one-on-one interviews. First, and perhaps foremost, we found that teachers generally very much prize what they see as their workplace autonomy – perhaps best evidenced through their concerns over what they see as increasing encroachment on this professional freedom by administrative fiat. Secondly, it is clear that virtually all teachers are engaged in their own further professional learning. Over 90 per cent reported having taken at least one formal course or works in the previous year, with an overall average of four courses/workshops each. Teachers also engaged, on average, in four hours per week of intentional informal, job-related learning activity. Overall, the dominant themes have been increasing workload and limited opportunities for meaningful professional learning. At the same time, differences of gender, age and/or geographic location did sometimes arise in relation to themes such as workload, or engagement in formal and informal learning activity.[2]

As noted in Chapter 5, the labour market for teachers in Canada experienced declining demand over the course of our research – a situation which seems to be increasingly the case in other countries as well. This declining demand may have accentuated the boundaries separating off two specific groups of otherwise duly

CONCLUSION: TEACHER LEARNING & POWER

certified and employed teachers. One of these disparities lay between teachers with five or more years of teaching experience, and those new to the "front of the classroom." The other very acute difference lay between those teachers who had permanent teaching positions, and the increasing number of those in Canada now able to find only "occasional" work – many on a day-to-day basis or at best with short-term contracts. While all three groups were employed teaching students in classrooms in public schools across the country, their conditions of work and the ways in which they were able to take up their own further professional learning, differed – sometimes dramatically.

As compared to their more senior colleagues, new teachers reported longer weekly hours of work. This was not surprising, given that they saw themselves as having to struggle with a very different set of conditions and expectations than they had previously experienced and known as students themselves. The numerous anecdotal comments made during our interviews and focus groups certainly illustrated this challenge, sometimes in very dramatic ways. New teachers (similar to new workers generally) also seemed to be most aware of the need for ongoing professional learning. Perhaps not surprisingly, the informal learning which new teachers' did engage in leaned heavily to those themes supporting their immediate classroom needs – classroom management, inclusion and special education, and student extra-curricular activities.

One further difference separating newer from more senior teachers was their perception concerning the possibility of being transferred to other schools or grade panels within their board, or even being laid off by the employer as surplus to school board needs. This job uncertainty also affected formal learning choices; an additional pursuit for many was enrolment in second language courses, typically French, a subject area in which there is a continuing shortage of teachers in many Canadian school jurisdictions. While this situation may well be similar to other workers during tough times, the case of public schooling not having an ongoing and effective renewal of its teaching force may certainly increase problems of needed continuity and change in the years ahead, and further underscore the importance of fully funding new teacher induction programs to help with retention rates, as indicated by the model program described in Chapter 8.

In some respects, non-permanent "occasional" teachers evidenced even starker differences compared to their permanently-employed experienced counterparts. For most occasionals, access only to intermittent day-to-day work meant much less financial security. In addition, being sent into different classrooms each day meant there was little or no opportunity to develop relationships with students – something which these teachers saw as severely limiting their ability to engage in meaningful and efficacious teaching-learning routines. Further, a number of these teachers noted that these poor relationships extended also to the regular teachers in the school – lack of respect for them as teachers, and the particularly difficult work routines in which they found themselves. Therefore, occasional teachers' learning needs centre around obtaining jobs and navigating the school system rather than long-term planning for new curriculum or teaching strategies.

Similar to new teachers, the specific motivations for occasional teachers engaging in further professional learning also reflected both the unique conditions of their work as well as their individual backgrounds. Internationally educated occasional teachers (IETs) spent more time engaged in formal and informal activity related to gaining a deeper understanding of the Canadian school system – school structures, curriculum, student assessment and expectations of teachers, both in and outside the classroom. However, both IETs and Canadian-educated occasional teachers hoping for more permanent positions also focused much of their informal learning pursuits on networking and gaining further knowledge about how, and where, this more long-term teaching employment might be found.

EMPOWERING TEACHERS FOR GREATER PROFESSIONAL LEARNING

As noted in the Introduction, the Canadian federal state has limited regulatory authority for formal education in relation to provincial governments. It is possible that Canadian teachers in general retain greater workplace power and engage in greater professional learning than those in some other countries. We doubt it. But since no other comparable studies yet exist, we hope that our findings on both issues stimulate further research on the range of teachers' and other professionals' learning practices and the influence of professionals' power on these practices.

In 2011, education ministers, teachers and union leaders from sixteen countries and regions whose education systems were deemed by the Organization for Economic Co-operation and Development (OECD) to be "rapidly improving and high-performing" met for the first ever International Summit on the Teaching Profession (OECD 2011). What made this conference unique was the acknowledged need to *share power* between governments and teacher unions with respect to positive future outcomes in terms of teacher professionalism, recruitment and retention, professional learning, and successful education reform. Ontario was one of the high-performing regions singled out as a policy model by the OECD (p. 57).

As outlined in Chapters 3, 4 and 7, Ontario and other Canadian provinces feature strong teacher unions that are governed by an array of educational legislation. Teachers in Canada have retained a robust sense of autonomy and solidarity, even while they have dealt with imposed neo-liberal education reforms during the 1990s and early 2000s, including periodic governmental manipulation of colleges of teachers in Ontario and British Columbia in attempts to undermine the negotiating power of teacher unions. In several provinces, including Ontario, these neo-liberal policies included mandatory professional development regimes that were resented by teachers and ultimately abandoned by subsequent governments. As Reid (2003) and others argue, reforms such as high-stakes standardized testing and rewritten state curricula are key elements of control by the state. The ultimate example of such a state agenda for reform and control, the American *No Child Left Behind Act*, set an impossible goal of "proficiency for all," and instead of directing more resources to help schools in high-poverty areas with failing students, punishes such schools and sets them on a path towards the firing of unionized teachers and potential closure of thousands of public schools. Neo-liberal attacks on teachers and their unions continued aggressively in American states such as Wisconsin in 2011, although the OECD report (2011) argues strongly that "without the active and willing engagement of teachers, most educational reforms fail" (p. 52).

After the election of 2003, however, the new Ontario government adopted a very different attitude towards teachers and their unions, at least in respecting teacher professionalism and including teacher unions in policy discussions, and pouring millions of dollars into job-embedded, individualized professional learning programs. Two of the most successful of these professional learning programs, described in Chapter 7, are the New Teacher Induction Program (NTIP) and the Teacher Learning and Leadership Program (TLLP). The Ontario NTIP is both mandatory and centrally funded, providing release time for mentorship, targeted professional learning and individualized supports for beginning teachers. To recognize the value of experienced teachers who remain in the classroom yet are leaders in their schools and their profession, the TLLP funds action research projects with the added component of requiring the funded teachers to share their learning and their practical knowledge with their peers in their schools, in their local regions or elsewhere in the province.

Chapter 8 is an extended case study of how the province's largest school board, the Toronto District School Board (TDSB), implemented and expanded upon the NTIP program. The TDSB program for beginning teachers features multiple models of school-based mentoring and mentoring within a Family of Schools (FOS) to ensure that each teacher's needs are met, because TDSB beginning teachers identify learning from mentors as the most meaningful source of professional learning. Funded time release facilitates the mentoring process as well as other sources of learning such as visits to demonstration classrooms, and a comprehensive online sharing site allows beginning teachers to work through their issues and share ideas with colleagues. With retention rates of 99 per cent, and thousands of new teachers assisted in their transition to the profession, the TDSB program appears to be a worthwhile example of a successful induction program.

In a knowledge society, where schools are expected to adapt quickly to the rapid pace of change and students are to be taught to become lifelong learners, teachers must also be lifelong learners. Greater focus on ongoing professional learning and educational reforms which take teacher opinions into fuller account are both necessary policy directions. One positive example is the 2003 negotiated workforce remodelling agreement in England which, while subject to more criticism (see p. 71), did provide more support staff to allow teachers to concentrate on their central mission of teaching. In addition, the recognition in such diverse areas of the world as Finland, Singapore, Japan and Sweden that time is needed during the workday for teachers to meet with colleagues, to plan together and learn informally from each other is a hopeful sign.

Our research group surveyed, interviewed and studied classroom teachers for over 15 years and we have overwhelmingly been told that learning from single events such as professional development day workshops is inferior to ongoing, job-embedded, self-chosen professional learning, including informal learning from colleagues. Results from the Toronto District School Board's beginning teachers (see Table 8-7) have quantified this discrepancy; only 19 per cent reported very meaningful learning from such workshops, compared to a 74 per cent "very meaningful" rating for job-associated mentoring. Traditional professional development programs may continue to be imposed on teachers by their employers or state authorities as a symbol of the power that these authorities have over educational policy, curriculum and their employees. However, for a true knowledge economy to be realized, teachers need to be empowered in their learning as they are in their autonomy over the classrooms they teach in – empowered to learn continuously, from multiple sources including each other, making professional choices for enhancing not only their own learning but that of their students.

The growing gap between the ample rewards and secure lives of the very rich and the increasingly wasted education and withering work of most of the population could provoke profound social upheaval. The outcomes could range from the growth of a more authoritarian shareholder capitalist society run by a technocratic elite to the emergence of a movement toward economic democracy. Demands among an increasingly underemployed labour force for more opportunities to use their increasing knowledge in rewarding work, and popular resistance to neo-liberal government moves to make public education less accessible, suggest that hard political choices are imminent. As we conclude this book, the leader of Canada's largest teachers' union is calling on members to fight for public schools as equalizers against poverty and injustice (Brown 2011). In fighting for more democratic decision-making in schools, teachers and their unions could both ensure more effective strategies of learning and continuing development within the teaching profession, and also contribute to more democratic education for all.

In any event, the bulk of the evidence gathered here points to one overriding conclusion. Both more integrated professional development programs and fuller development of the talents of the next generation of students will be more effectively realized through teachers' greater participation in educational decisions beyond their classrooms. Optimally, these decisions will involve genuine co-operation both with those educational officials who now have most of the delegated power and with representatives of all the communities they are supposed to serve. These communities are the ultimate source of both democratic power and continuing development of knowledge.

APPENDIX

Research Methodology

WHO WE ARE

The NALL and WALL teacher projects were conducted through the Centre for the Study of Education and Work (CSEW) at the Ontario Institute for Studies in Education of the University of Toronto (OISE/UT). The New Approaches to Lifelong Learning (NALL) network conducted its research between 1998 and 2002. The NALL network developed an expansive framework for (paid and unpaid) work and (formal and informal) learning studies, and conducted the first national survey in the world (*N*=1,562) of all these forms of learning and work in 1998, as well as a series of over 30 exploratory case studies.[1]

The Work and Lifelong Learning (WALL) research network conducted its field research from 2003 to 2008. The WALL research team conducted a large-scale, country-wide 2004 survey and 12 related case studies to provide unprecedented documentation of lifelong learning and work relations. The 2004 WALL survey sample, using a similar questionnaire as the NALL survey, contained 9,063 adult respondents aged 18 and over, who spoke English or French, and resided in a private home (not old age/group homes/penal or educational institutions) with a telephone. All households and individuals within households were given an equal chance of selection using random-digit dialling. The general response rate was 51 per cent of the eligible households – 58 per cent if we exclude the households whose eligibility was not determined. The data presented here are weighted by known population characteristics of age, sex and educational attainment to ensure profiles are representative for Canada as a whole. A summary of the basic 2004 findings on demographic background, paid and unpaid work and the continuum of adult learning practices, as well as most case studies, may be found in Livingstone and Scholtz (2010). A further national survey of work and learning (*N*=2,028) addressing the same issues was conducted in 2010 in conjunction with Livingstone's Canada Research Chair in Work and Lifelong Learning. All three of these surveys were administered by the Institute for Social Research (ISR) at York University. Further information on the interview schedules, codebooks, the ISR technical reports on the survey samples, as well as many other publications using these data, are now available.[2] Fuller analysis of the 2010 survey will appear in *Knowledge and Power in Workplaces* (forthcoming).

While both the NALL and WALL research networks combined survey and case study research methods, the teachers' work and learning project was distinctive in being the only continuing project to combine both methods throughout the entire life of the network. Harry Smaller (York University) and Rosemary Clark (Ontario Secondary School Teachers Federation [OSSTF]) were the Principal Investigators on both the NALL and WALL projects. The core teacher research group has consisted of university faculty members, graduate students, and representatives from teacher unions and school boards whose work involved teacher learning and

APPENDIX

teacher professional development. In addition, our research group decided early in the planning process to approach the Canadian Teachers' Federation–Fédération canadiennes des enseignantes et des enseignants (CTF–FCE), the umbrella organization of the teachers' federations in the ten provinces of Canada, to seek their involvement in this study. We saw their input into planning the study from teachers' perspectives as being highly important, as well as assisting with access to teachers' names and addresses for the survey and for providing legitimacy for the study in the eyes of the participants. Given their overall interests in teachers' learning on the one hand, and their concerns about effects of increasing state control over teacher development regimes on the other, the federation welcomed the opportunity to participate, and to assist in developing a data-base, both of teachers' existing involvement in their own learning, as well as their further interests in that regard. The provincial teacher federations also contributed financially towards the printing and mailing costs of the initial survey. Without their assistance, these first national surveys of the formal and informal learning activities of Canadian school teachers would not have been possible. The federations were also invaluable in assisting with logistics and lunches for the focus groups we conducted in a number of provinces.

THE TEACHER PROJECT RESEARCH METHODS

Over the course of the project, several specific research methods, both qualitative and quantitative, were employed in gathering data on themes related to teachers' work and learning. The comparative analyses of teachers' work and learning and that of those in other professional occupations were based on the general national surveys as detailed in Chapters 1 and 2. The specific methods used in the teachers' projects included the following:

National Survey Questionnaires

Two national teacher survey questionnaires were developed and undertaken, the first one in 1998 and the second in 2004. In each case, these questionnaires were developed in tandem with the above-mentioned general national surveys on work and learning involving representative samples of the entire national population. Names and addresses for potential teacher respondents were randomly and proportionately sampled from the membership lists of the teacher unions in each of the ten Canadian provinces. (Given the mandatory membership legislation or regulation in place in all provinces, virtually every teacher working in a publicly-funded elementary and secondary school in Canada is included in these data-bases).

Each survey consisted of an eight-page booklet, with questions grouped into five sections involving their formal schooling and continuing education courses, as well as questions about their own informal learning in the community, informal learning in the workplace, informal learning in the home, and other informal learning issues and approaches. In addition, there was a final section involving background/demographic questions, workplace matters and computer/internet use.

APPENDIX

(Copies of the questionnaires may be found on the NALL and WALL network websites). These questionnaires were mailed out to the individual sampled teachers at their home or school address, along with a pre-addressed return envelope and a one-page letter on the letterhead of the respective provincial teachers' federation over the signature of the president or equivalent of that organization. In total, 1,945 questionnaires were mailed out at the end of October, 1998, and 2,040 were sent out in the second round in early 2004. Response rates varied considerably across Canada. In 1998, returns by province ranged from 31 per cent to 46 per cent, with somewhat higher response rates in the western provinces, for a total effective sample of 817 respondents. The response rate for the second survey in 2004 was somewhat better, with almost 50 per cent of the forms being completed and returned, for an effective sample of 1,011 respondents. In both cases, these respondents closely reflected the backgrounds of the larger Canadian teaching population, with the exception of some under-representation of new teachers.

Time-Study Diaries

The research method of asking respondents to maintain diaries to collect data on their daily activities has been used successfully in a number of jurisdictions, with a range of respondent types (teachers, other workers, housewives, etc.), for a number of research purposes. The prior work of a number of researchers in this area was drawn upon to conceptualize and plan this component of the overall project (Peters & Raaijmakers 1998; Michelson 1998; Harvey 1984). In November 1999, a purposive subsample of 19 Ontario[3] secondary school teachers, all of whom had completed the 1998 survey and agreed to participate, was sent survey packages (copies are available on the NALL network website). Participants were asked to use the diary forms provided to keep track, on an hourly basis, of all of their activities 24 hours a day, for seven consecutive days. In addition, they were asked to make note of any learning which took place as a result of their engagement in each of these activities. Thirteen completed logs were returned, and three months later (February 2000), this group was sent another package, with a request to repeat the same exercise for second seven-day interval during that month. From this second round, ten completed sets were received (two of the other three teachers having retired in the interim), for a total of 23 sets of weekly diaries from the thirteen respondents.

These diaries provided rich and detailed pictures of one week in the lives of these teachers – their paid and unpaid work, as well as other home, community and recreational activities. Many of the notations in the column 'things learned' required some interpretation, and general agreement among our research group about guidelines for this interpretation. For example, how should one construe the response of one respondent who reported that he/she had attended a three-and-a-half hour night class as part of a professional development program, but wrote nothing in the 'learning' column? Problematic also were the many occasions when some respondents reported explicitly on learning having occurred as a result of reading a newspaper or viewing a documentary, while other respondents reported engagement in the same activities but with no 'learning" comment.' Did this constitute an actual, and self-perceived, difference in self learning processes? Or, were these simply differences in understanding the purpose of the survey, or perhaps differences in circumstances and/or motivation to fill out a form at any given instance?

In-Depth Telephone Interviews

For the purposes of further exploration of the data provided in the first two phases of the project, four 'diarists' were randomly selected by categories of gender and age (male/female; younger/older). When contacted by telephone, all agreed to participate in individual telephone interviews. These interviews, conducted during September of 2000 by one of the authors of the project, ran between 45 and 60 minutes. All were taped and subsequently transcribed. In order to provide a context for exploring issues of learning in depth with these four teachers, the interview questions were based on events which had occurred in during the previous three years – a period of provincial government enactment of sweeping changes to the province's school system. Among many changes affecting secondary schools, teachers and students, the following reforms were referenced during the interviews: a) the complete revision of syllabi and all courses for secondary schools in the province; b) preliminary introduction of a new compulsory, standardized student assessment process, including revised standardized report cards; c) introduction of provincial regulation requiring mandatory teacher involvement in student extracurricular activities; d) establishment of a provincial statutory body to control teacher selection, training, examining, certification, registration, standards of practice, professional development and discipline; and e) an earlier, and short-lived, provincial government initiative to de-stream grade 9 programs in the high school system. In many respects, these government reforms served as a useful medium for exploring issues of teacher learning – they were universally applied across the province, and certainly well-known to all teachers.

After some preliminary opening questions, interviewees were asked to identify one or more provincial government reform measures which they felt were particularly notable – if none came spontaneously to mind, then the five above programs were mentioned and the respondent asked to select one. They were asked first to explain their understanding of these reforms, and then to reflect on the ways in which they themselves had come to learn about these initiatives. Subsequently, they were also asked to explore how it might have been that their colleagues in their respective schools came to be knowledgeable about, and engaged in, these initiatives.

During this part of the interview there was considerable prompting to elicit reflections on ways in which learning may have taken place – formal opportunities such as workshops, meetings, presentations, circulars, and school announcements, as well as the more informal discussions among teachers, administrators, students and parents. In particular, interviewees were asked to comment on how the opinions of colleagues about these reform initiatives were being expressed and exchanged, and the ways in which teachers were attempting to learn about and understand what these reforms might mean in relation to change in the school and classroom curriculum and materials and teaching practice, as well as the overall effects on students themselves.

Focus Groups

In the second survey questionnaire form distributed in 2004, respondents were asked to consider possible further involvement in the study. Approximately 35 per cent of respondents so indicated. For the first round of nine focus groups, eight cities in four provinces were designated – Ontario (Toronto [2 groups], London, North Bay), Nova Scotia (Halifax, Sydney), Alberta (Calgary, Edmonton) and British Columbia (Vancouver). The first three provinces were chosen because in 2003 they all had teacher learning requirements of varying degrees spelled out in provincial legislation or regulations.

The focus groups were each made up of five to seven participants. They were conducted by one or two of the project researchers, and generally lasted about two to three hours. Participants were initially asked to respond individually to a standard protocol of questions relating to their engagement in and opinions about formal and informal learning, as well as the ways in which social and material relations in their workplaces, and in their homes, intersected with their ability to pursue such learning. As the group process progressed, participants interacted with each other on these and related issues – questioning, clarifying, and posing alternative opinions and beliefs. All of the proceedings were audio recorded, and subsequently transcribed.

Face-to-Face Individual Interviews

A number of different sets of individual face-to-face interviews were undertaken during the latter phases of the WALL project (2005 to 2008). Two sets involved relatively new teachers, in their first and second years of teaching, while another set involved teachers who did not hold permanent contracts, but rather worked as "occasional" or "supply" teachers in the school system.

The first major set of interviews of new teachers was undertaken at a particularly propitious moment in the careers of these teachers. All new teachers in the Toronto District School Board were given the opportunity of participating in an all-day institute on the first Friday of October 2005 at the end of their fourth week "on the job." At this event, the teacher research team spread out material describing the project with release forms on a designated table, and then asked teachers as they walked by if they were willing to engage in a short, two-question interview. Virtually all of those asked were willing to be audiotaped, while approximately half of those requested agreed to be videoed. The two audio-interviewers each completed about 45 interviews over the course of the morning, and a further 25 teachers were interviewed on videotape. Basically, each interview consisted of only two questions: "What has been most challenging for you, in your first four weeks in the classroom?" and then "Have you sought out any assistance to help you meet these challenges?" Following their response to this second question, if no mention had been made of use of any written or computer-based

APPENDIX

sources, they were asked the supplementary question, "Did you seek out any help from a book or from the internet?" For the most part, interviews lasted for somewhere between one and two minutes in length. Both the audio and video interviews were subsequently transcribed verbatim for analysis.

A second major set of interviews took place during several one-day workshops held for groups of 20 to 30 relatively new teachers during the 2007–08 school year. Teachers had been offered a roster of different programs, with the possibility of signing up for one which was of most interest to them (topics ranged from grade-specific literacy programs to more general science and social studies curriculum). At each workshop, a member of the teacher research group set up a small interviewing table in the corner of the large room where the workshop was occurring, or in an adjacent room, and teachers were invited to volunteer to come over to the table whenever it was free, to participate in the interview. Each interview lasted about five to ten minutes, and was audio-recorded. Questions focused on the reasons why they were participating in the day-long workshop, and a general inquiry into their first year of teaching, their successes and challenges, and the ways in which they had sought out assistance to deal with specific issues that had arisen, as well as more general issues relating to unit and lesson planning, classroom pedagogy, assessment of students, and so on.

The study of occasional teachers employed a qualitative research methodology. Semi-structured interviews were conducted with non-permanent teachers working for English-speaking public school boards in southern Ontario during the 2006–07 school year. The study employed convenience and purposeful sampling procedures. Personal contacts at local teacher unions provided names of possible participants. A snowball sampling technique was also employed; those occasional teachers who did participate were asked at the end of the interview if they knew of others who might be interested in participating in the study, and a number of them provided the names of other potential participants.

A total of eighteen semi-structured interviews were conducted; eight were held face-to-face in a research room at a local university, while the other ten were interviewed by phone. In all fifteen occasional teachers from the southern Ontario region and three others who had knowledge of occasional teachers and teaching – a union representative who bargained on behalf of occasional teachers, an employee from the Toronto District School Board and a past staff member of a bridging program for internationally trained teachers seeking work in Ontario – participated in the study. While the main purpose of the study was to explore occasional teachers' access to the teaching profession, participants indicated when they were interviewed that their professional learning was a very important part of accessing the teaching profession. During the interview process, occasional teachers were asked to describe what steps they took to get on the "eligible to hire" list, to detail some of the strategies used to get on the occasional teacher list and to get occasional teaching work, and to identify some of the barriers that they faced. As part of these responses, participants described in detail how they engaged in both formal and informal aspects of professional learning. Interviews were audio recorded and transcribed for data-analysis.

APPENDIX

RESEARCH LIMITATIONS

It is a tricky matter to infer social relations through survey questionnaires and semi-structured interviews with individuals who will necessarily respond from their own personal viewpoints. Participant observation and observational ethnographic methods could address this limitation somewhat. These methods were largely beyond the scope of our project, except for occasional school site visits and the experience of those on the research team who were former or current teachers. It is also very challenging to effectively combine survey and more qualitative case study methods, as the WALL network generally and this project in particular have attempted to do throughout their endeavours. In particular, ensuring both representative selection and valid interpretation in the same study remains extremely difficult. But the quest to combine statistical surveys that address the extent of the human conditions such as systemic discrimination in work and learning practices with case studies that tell compelling human stories will continue. Hopefully, the case studies, survey findings and reflections reported here offer some resource materials for further combined or mixed method studies of teachers' work and learning. As Livingstone (2010) has observed with regard to the WALL network research generally:

> However successful future studies are in combining case study and survey research methods, they are unlikely to grasp the full extent of learning in work in all its dynamic complexity. If nothing else, the current research should suggest the vast scope of these processes. But even within these limits, the research points to a wider extent and deeper ingenuity of workers' learning than most prior studies. (p. 238)

Research methods involving self-reporting by respondents are also always subject to speculative interpretation. Who did we get to hear from, who not, and in what contexts? For example, as already noted above, we found it quite difficult to encourage newer teachers to participate in our focus groups, which were often located distant from their homes. Based on their comments in our phone calls to them, the extra pressures of coping and learning as new teachers, and the many extra-curricular activities they believed that they had to engage in, mitigated against their taking the time out to participate in our study.

A more specific limitation is the uncertainty of time estimates provided by teachers self-reporting on the work and learning that they undertook. What does it mean when we ask teachers (or any workers) to self-report on the number of hours they spend per week in work or in learning activities? In what ways, and with what significance, might under- or over-reporting of hours occur? In the case of our questionnaires, asking teachers (most of whom were undoubtedly attempting to complete the extensive, eight-page form as expediently as possible, in the midst of their daily routine) to reflect back on their "average" work week and to calculate numbers of hours involving a large range of activities, would understandably evoke a variety of responses. Similarly, asking teachers in a collaborative focus group situation involving total strangers (or, for that matter, colleagues in the same school/town), to delve significantly into work-related activities and events, some of which might be very personal in nature, is again to introduce complexities into the data analysis process. Further, it is possible that teachers who agreed to participate in such activities might represent the more "engaged" or "interactive" teacher, rather than the "average" teacher.

In any event, our research did provide us with one intriguing insight into the issue of the potential accuracy or otherwise of self-reported data, particularly as it related to the possibility that workers (from any occupational group) might (consciously or unconsciously) over-report the amount of work which they undertook in any given week. This resulted from a comparison we were able to make between the ways in which a specific group of 17 teachers reported on the survey questionnaire, and how the same group of teachers filled out the time-study diary a few months later. Virtually every one of these respondents reported significantly more hours worked for those weeks in their daily diaries entries (an average of ten per cent more) than the average weekly hours they had reported on their individual questionnaires. Two respondents – both mothers with school-aged children – underestimated their average school-related work week in their questionnaires by 35 per cent. As Livingstone and Scholtz (2010) note in a report on paid and unpaid work and learning based on the general WALL survey:

> [C]hildcare responds to the needs of the child. For many mothers this is a constant labour of varying intensity, but it is inherently different than the time measured by a plant or office time clock. Even in terms of clock-time measures, mothers with small children are among those who work the longest hours. If they also happen to be employed, clock-time fails utterly to grasp the extent of their labours. (p. 27)

Overall however, the data collected from one source or using one instrument, very much complemented (rather than contradicted) data collected in other ways. Quantitative data from survey questionnaires, pointing to the increasing amounts of time needed for student assessment or increasing levels of reported stress, meshed closely with the anecdotal comments made during interviews and focus groups, covering the same themes.

As a final contextual note, our initial study was undertaken during a time of much upheaval in schools, with government-initiated and imposed restructuring projects in full swing in a number of provinces. In Ontario, for example, the first phase of our study was undertaken shortly after virtually all of the elementary and secondary schools in the province were closed for two weeks by 125,000 teachers on an unofficial strike in protest over new government regulations and unilaterally imposed changes. In addition to whatever ways these conflicts and disruptions affected teachers, students and parents, they provided a serendipitous opportunity for examining teachers' informal learning. As Jean Lave (1993) has noted, learning occurs through "situated activity," and often through "conflict [which] is a ubiquitous aspect of human existence" (p. 15). In undertaking the interviews across Canada in the most recent phase of the study, we were also able to invoke discussion of specific informal learning, learning that had been situated not just within the complex and ubiquitous routines of "normal" school activity, but also in a context of rapid change in teachers' working conditions. These changes, and the disruptions they cause, seem not to have abated.

ENDNOTES

INTRODUCTION

[1] The North American term 'professional development' (PD) is used in this book rather than 'continuous professional development' (CPD) used in some other countries.

[2] For documentation of most of these facts, see Livingstone (2010). On knowledge management, see Luque (2001).

[3] Those who are involved more directly in developing and implementing teacher learning/professional development programs may also wish to consult our earlier publications for additional insights and ideas: *Beyond PD days: Teachers' work and learning in Canada* (Clark et al. 2007) and the associated DVD, *No two alike: PD that works*, available from the Ontario Teachers Federation.

CHAPTER 1

[1] From interview transcript of teacher case study in the Education and Job Requirement Matching (EJRM) Project (see Lordan 2009).

[2] It should be noted that some current unions of skilled trades workers are like medieval craft guilds in being recognized as having specialized knowledge, but their unions do not have self-regulating autonomy and they are distinguishable from professions in that such knowledge is typically not acquired predominantly by extensive academic preparation.

[3] For a recent review of this literature, see Adams (2010).

[4] See Derber, Schwartz and Magrass (1990) for a broad historical account of development of similar employment statuses among professionals.

[5] Life insurance personnel may not be generally regarded as requiring very specialized knowledge. Their entry requirements do not now include a university education; associational membership has been weak and self-regulation even weaker. This is an illustration that the inclusion of many newer occupations in "emerging professional" or "semi-professional" groupings remains very controversial.

[6] These terms both refer to the loss of control of working conditions. Deprofessionalization is more specific to those with credible prior claims to professional status and will be used generally in the rest of this text.

[7] The contested roles of colleges of teachers will be examined in later chapters.

[8] All differences reported in this chapter are significant at the .05 level of confidence.

[9] The 2004 WALL Survey contained the following numbers of cases for respective professional occupations: doctors and lawyers (67); teachers (149); nurses (115); engineers (102); computer programmers (136); and other professionals (859). The total employed labour force was 5,800. Doctors and lawyers were combined because of their similar patterns on most variables and relatively small numbers in the sample. The much smaller sample size for the 1983 CCS survey ($N=2577$) prohibited any detailed analysis for specific professional occupations.

[10] For a detailed examination of contingent work in teaching, see Chapter 5.

[11] In the WALL 2004 teacher survey, teachers likely under-reported their weekly work hours by omitting their unpaid overtime. See Smaller et al. (2005) for more detailed explanation of teachers' unpaid overtime.

[12] Part-time workers include respondents who reported working less than 30 hours per week. A 30-hour work week (four days of 7.5 hours per day) was deemed sufficient for full-time status in terms of job control and learning variables. For the most part, this cut-off point produces part-time percentages for the occupations close to Statistics Canada (Pyper, 2004) data with one exception – nurses. For a more detailed depiction of the part-time and contingent workforce in nursing, please see Canadian Nurses Association (2009).

BIBLIOGRAPHY

[13] Adams (2010) provides a detailed account of the timing of legislated regulation of many professions and other selected occupations in Canada up to 1961, with the notable exception of any information on teachers.

[14] There were insufficient numbers in the other smaller national surveys to provide statistically significant information for respondents in specific occupational groups.

[15] For a general comparative analysis of this class model and several other variants of Marxian and Weberian class theories, see Livingstone and Mangan (1996). Two empirical limitations must be noted. The large employer or corporate capitalist class is not adequately distinguished in large-scale surveys because of their very small numbers. Also, the much larger underclass of chronically unemployed and otherwise excluded from the wage labour force but dependent on the capitalist mode of production is also poorly represented in sample surveys, and they are beyond the scope of the present analysis.

[16] It should be noted that our class model is similar to Wright's rendition in his (1980) article. The main difference is that professional employees are not distinguished by Wright. He established a large grouping of 'semi-autonomous employees' identified by their subjective sense of personal discretion and decision-making roles in their jobs (Wright 1980, p. 202), which would presumably include many professional employees as well as other employees. On the basis of his survey evidence, Wright therefore concluded that teachers were roughly equally divided between his 'semi-autonomous employees' and 'workers' categories (p. 205).

[17] There is now a great deal of discussion about the extremely high remuneration of top managers in comparison with much lower workers' wages and in relation to company asset value, and some research on the way that managers act to increase share values in their own interest has been undertaken, but little scrutiny of their labour process has been conducted. There is virtually no attention to the work of owners.

[18] See Ingersoll (2003) for an extensive assessment of the control exercised by teachers and others over different aspects of their work, based on US national surveys and case studies.

CHAPTER 2

[1] From transcript of interview in teacher case study in the Education and Job Requirement Matching Project (see Lordan 2009).

[2] All survey data reported in this chapter are drawn from the 2004 WALL general population survey. See the Appendix, this volume, for further details.

[3] From transcript of interview in teacher case study in the Education and Job Requirement Matching Project (see Lordan 2009).

[4] It should be noted that almost all public school teachers have a degree beyond an *undergraduate* degree (i.e., a Bachelor of Education [BEd]).

[5] From interview transcript of computer programmer case study in the Education and Job Requirement Matching Project (see Weststar 2009).

[6] From interview transcript of teacher case study in the Education and Job Requirement Matching Project (see Lordan 2009).

CHAPTER 3

[1] See, e.g., a recent "independent" report on the British Columbia College of Teachers, commissioned by the College, which criticized the BC Teachers' Union for interference in college affairs, at http://www.bcct.ca/documents/TC/TCMagazine_Current.pdf.

[2] (1) Commitment to students and student learning; (2) professional knowledge; (3) teach-ing practice; (4) leadership and community; and (5) ongoing professional learning.

[3] By comparison, this same study found that a provincial sample of teachers had a very strong preference for self-directed PD.

[4] To be sure, these opinions do vary, based on the class, ethnic and racial backgrounds of parents.

ENDNOTES

5. Even the titles of some of the more well-known volumes make this clear, almost from the beginning of the recent push for change: *The myth of educational reform* (Popkewitz et al. 1982); *Tinkering toward utopia* (Tyack & Cuban 1995) and *Left back: A century of failed school reforms* (Ravitch 2000).
6. The 'Fourth Way' refers to a proposed change and improvement from Tony Blair's purportedly more centrist 'Third Way,' which itself was supposed to be an advance from the traditional left–right politics of the post-War era.
7. For more general recent research studies and discussion of the relations between formal and informal aspects of learning in relation to paid and unpaid work, see Livingstone 2010.
8. For a review of literature relating to teacher empowerment, see Bogler and Somech 2004.
9. See, e.g., http://www.arkansased.org/pd/renewal.html.

CHAPTER 4

1. Both the demands of teaching and "acting professionally" as perceived by teachers at the micro levels are shaped by such external realities as the official curriculum and the social values and norms advanced in public discourses.
2. It should be noted also that the majority of teachers' who agreed to participate in interviews were veteran teachers.
3. "Neo-liberal government rests on *self-managing* institutions and individuals, in which free agents are empowered to act on their own behalf but are 'steered from a distance' by policy norms and rules of the game" (Marginson 1997, p. 63).
4. See the Appendix to this volume for further information on the WALL teachers' survey, focus groups, in-depth follow-up interviews and time diaries.
5. Although it is important to note that teachers' negotiating 'power' via their union is not insignificant across the multiple levels.
6. We might consider a whole set of historically inflected depictions here, as: the morally uprighteous role model, the (feminine) caregiver, the disciplinary 'gate-keeper,' the professional ...
7. All survey data reported in this chapter are drawn from the 2004 WALL teacher survey. See the appendix for further details.
8. Including job and non-job related formal courses.
9. One of the explanations for the reduced participation by more experienced workers is that they have attained greater levels of workplace knowledge or competence.
10. As with formal learning, there were no major differences in the *content* of teachers' informal learning across the different provinces surveyed.
11. As other chapters illustrate, these findings are consistent with *all* teacher groups participating in our research study.
12. In spite of these pressures, however, among full-time respondents, 29 per cent reported that they were "very satisfied" with their jobs, while a further 56 per cent were at least "somewhat satisfied." By comparison, only nine per cent were "dissatisfied" and two per cent "very dissatisfied" with their job.
13. This finding also aligns with research in adult education on workplace learning more generally (Livingstone, Stowe & Raykov 2003)
14. As found in the Lohman study, increased administrative tasks and the perception of having to support students with greater needs were two of the most significant changes reported by teachers in their working conditions in recent years.
15. Storey (2007) suggests that we may want to consider teacher "creativity" rather than "autonomy" given that the traditional "control versus autonomy" construct might have diminishing relevance under new contexts of performativity.
16. 'Governmentality,' which owes much to the oeuvre of Michel Foucault, refers to the "conduct of the self" and, in this case, how organizations (can) control or influence worker subjectivities not by overt methods of rewards and punishments, but by shaping the worker–learner's individual desires

BIBLIOGRAPHY

and actions that are ultimately productive in the context of organizational efficiency and output. It is the individual that appears to choose for him or herself the conduct that is also useful to the organization.

[17] We do heed post-modern insights that trouble the separability of means versus ends, but the point here is that, at least conceptually, we can differentiate between valuing increased autonomy as a good in itself as opposed to a tool for increasing efficiency.

[18] A few teachers commented on the significant importance of the principal in supporting teachers under the shifting demands of their work. Without such administrative support, teachers seem to perceive less room to negotiate how they respond to new demands.

[19] As later chapters suggest, there seems to be growing support, most especially for beginning teachers in induction programs, to get (more) release time for classroom observation, PD, and mentoring.

[20] For readers cognizant of recent changes in Ontario, the rejection and renegotiation of Ontario's Professional Learning Program of the early 2000s illustrates the lack of teacher support for mandated, top-down professional development. Nevertheless, demands for teacher accountability and lifelong professional learning have not diminished, and it may be that the government elected in 2003 has been more attuned to steering from a distance and control by self-conduct.

[21] It is worth noting also that Storey (2007) finds that new "mid-career" entrants to teaching seem more aligned with "new professionalism" with its "target setting" and performance management techniques. Her study in the UK finds that these teachers may find ways to be creative (rather than 'deskilled' as the more traditional critique goes) within the new demands of professionalism. Forrester (2000) also found in her study that: "The more recently qualified teachers in this study appear more ready to accept the managerial control in education. Longer serving teachers feel they have experienced a loss of professional autonomy" (p. 149).

CHAPTER 5

[1] All names are pseudonyms.

[2] 'Underemployment' signifies that, when they were employed, their qualifications exceeded the requirements of their jobs. For fuller discussion, see Livingstone (2009).

[3] *TeachinOntario* is no longer an active program due to its low priority on the current government's agenda. Even so, the website for the program is still accessible through the Ontario College of Teachers' website. Begun in 2004, the project was originally funded by the Ministry of Training, Colleges and Universities. In 2005 the funding responsibility was transferred to the Ontario Ministry of Citizenship and Immigration. The Ontario College of Teachers was the lead recipient in the funding agreement and formed partnerships with the Ontario Teachers Federation, Local Agencies Services, and Skills for Change. This program lasted until March 31, 2010 (Ontario College of Teachers 2007).

[4] See www.teachinontario.ca.

[5] New teachers are defined as "all new teachers (including teachers trained out-of-province) certified by the Ontario College of Teachers who have been hired into permanent positions – full-time or part-time – by a school board, school authority or provincial school to begin teaching for the first time in Ontario" (Ontario Ministry of Education 2010).

CHAPTER 6

[1] Taken from transcripts of beginning teachers interviewed for this WALL project.

[2] A complex matter, to be sure. Recent reports suggest that in the United States, one-third of teachers leave after three years, and one-half leave after five (Schwartz 2011; see also Dickson 2006; Guarino et al. 2006; Boe et al. 2008). However, Canada seems to have much lower new teacher dropout rates (see, e.g., McIntryre 2010).

[3] We are cognizant that evaluation can be a strategic element of 'classroom management;' perhaps then both of these fundamental concerns link to deeper concerns around control and authority.

ENDNOTES

4 Another reason may well have related to the manner in which we were able to draw on our sample of respondents through teacher union databases, which may have experienced some months lag in receiving and compiling new teacher updates from boards of education.
5 As noted in Chapter 4, a 'governmentality' perspective troubles this theme, questioning the extent to which personal job autonomy is, or is increasingly becoming, anything more than self-regulation of organizational objectives.

CHAPTER 7

1 All italicized quotations in this chapter, unless otherwise noted, are from teachers interviewed in focus groups conducted across Canada in 2004.
2 See www.bctf.ca and www.bcct.ca for more details of the 2003 campaign and the 2010 report.
3 See, e.g., www.nytimes.com/2011/02/16/education/16education.html.
4 See www.teachers.ab.ca for a more detailed history.
5 See http://education.alberta.ca/admin/funding/accountability.aspx.
6 See www.bced.gov.bc.ca/schools/sdinfo/acc_contracts/achievement-guidelines-10.pdf.
7 In March 2011, President Obama predicted that the number could reach 80 per cent of schools (Cooper 2011).
8 Nova Scotia and Ontario, chosen because of the schemes mentioned in this paragraph, plus Alberta, chosen for its relatively benign program of having teachers submit an annual learning plan to the school principal. See the Appendix, this volume.
9 Five studies of teacher work hours in Canada undertaken between 2000 and 2005 documented average work hours per week of over 50 hours, while three studies done in the 1990s ranged from 47 to 49.4 hours (Clark et al. 2007, p. 48).
10 In 2010, for example, 43,749 of the 230,000 members of the Ontario College of Teachers, or 19 per cent, took Additional Qualifications (AQ) courses at university faculties of education to add to their credentials on their own time and at their own expense (Ontario College of Teachers 2010).
11 For the complete NTIP requirements, see www.edu.gov.on.ca/eng/teacher/induction.html.
12 Complete TLLP program details are available at www.edu.gov.on.ca/eng/teacher/tllp.html.
13 It is important to note that the legislated Ontario professional learning regime for experienced teachers includes ongoing staff development in locally determined PD days, plus an Annual Learning Plan completed by each teacher outlining individual professional learning objectives for the year, including both formal and informal learning activities. The TLLP is not legislated, but rather an adjunct program.
14 The Ministry of Education in Ontario uses different definitions than used in most of this book. Traditional "professional development" or PD Days are called "staff development" in this Ontario lexicon, while "professional development" is a broader term corresponding to the term "professional learning" used in this book and others.
15 This DVD is available from the Ontario Teachers' Federation.

CHAPTER 8

1 All quotations in this chapter are from on-line data collection and surveys of TDSB Beginning Teachers.
2 For the blog, see http://web.me.com/btintdsb.

CONCLUSION

1 For an example of a community group mobilizing to defend education, see the Save Our Schools web site (www.saveourschool.ca).

BIBLIOGRAPHY

[2] From our survey data and other assessments, it is clear that a vast majority of Canadian teachers still do not reflect the increasing racial/cultural diversity of the country. In that regard, we were unable to assess with statistical accuracy, any differences which the relatively few teachers of colour may have expressed in responding to our surveys.

APPENDIX

[1] Most of these case studies are now available through the NALL website: www.nall.ca.
[2] See www.wallnetwork.ca.
[3] Ontario teachers were selected because research funding for this component of the overall study was made available by the Ontario Secondary School Teachers' Federation (OSSFT).

BIBLIOGRAPHY

Achinstein, B., & Bartlett, L. (2004). (Re)framing classroom contexts: How new teachers and mentors view diverse learners and challenges of practice. *Teachers College Record, 106*(4), 716–746.
Acker, S. (1994). Gender and teachers' work. Unpublished paper, OISE/University of Toronto.
Acker, S. (1999). *The realities of teachers' work: Never a dull moment.* London: Cassell.
Adams, T. (2010). Profession: A useful concept for sociological analysis? *Canadian Review of Sociology, 47*(1), 49–70.
Alexandrou, A., & O'Brien, J. (2007). Union learning representatives: Facilitating professional development for Scottish teachers. *International Electronic Journal for Leadership in Learning,* 11. Retrieved from www.ucalgary.ca/iejll/vol11/brien.
Allan, P., & Sienko, S. (1998). Job motivations of professional and technical contingent workers: Are they different from permanent workers? *Journal of Employment Counseling, 35:* 169–178.
Althouse, J.G. (1929). *The Ontario teacher: a historical account of progress, 1800–1910.* Unpublished doctoral thesis, Toronto, University of Toronto.
American Educational Research Association (AERA). (2011). *Social imagination: Education research for the public good.* Washington, DC: AERA.
Anyon, J. (1995, Fall). Race, social class and educational reform in an inner city school. *Teachers' College Record:* 69–88.
Apple, M. (1988). Facing the complexity of power: For a parallelist position in critical educational studies. In M. Cole (Ed.), *Bowles and Gintis revisited: Correspondence and contradiction in educational theory* (pp. 112–130). Philadelphia: Falmer.
Apple, M. (1996). Power, meaning and identity: Critical sociology of education in the United States. *British Journal of Sociology of Education, 17*(2), 125–144.
Ashton, P.T. (1996). Improving the preparation of teachers. *Education Researcher, 25*(9), 21–22, 35.
Atkins, L., & Lury, C. (1999). The labour of identity: Performing identities, performing economies. *Economy and Society, 28*(4), 598–614.
Aziz, A. (2004). Sources of perceived stress among American medical doctors: A cross-cultural perspective. *Cross Cultural Management, 11*(4), 28–39.
Ball, S., & Goodson, I. (Eds.). (1985). *Teachers' lives and careers.* London: Falmer.
Ball, S. (2003). The teacher's soul and the terrors of performativity. *Journal of Education Policy, 18*(2), 215–228.
Barlin, D., & Hallgarten, J. (2001). Supply teachers: Symptom of the problem or part of the solution? Retrieved from http://www.ippr.org/articles/index.php?article=26.
Bartel, K., & Beckstead, K. (1998). *Annual report of labor market information. 1998.* Salt Lake City: Utah Department of Workforce Services.
Bartlett, L., & Johnson, L.S. (2010). The evolution of new teacher induction policy: Support, specificity, and autonomy. *Education Policy, 24*(6), 847–871.
Bascia, N., & Jacka, N. (2001). Falling in and filling in: ESL teaching careers in changing times. *Journal of Educational Change, 2,* 325-346.
Becker, H.S. (1952). The career of the Chicago public school teacher. *American Journal of Sociology, 57*(5), 470–477.
Beijaard, D., Korthagen, F., & Verloop, N. (2007). Editorial: Understanding how teachers learn as a prerequisite for promoting teacher learning. *Teachers and Teaching,* 13(2), 105–108.
Belanger, P., & Larivière, M. (2005). The dynamics of workplace learning in knowledge economy: Organizational change, knowledge transfer and learning in the pharmaceutical and biotechnology industry. Retrieved from www.wallnetwork.ca/resources/Belanger-Lariviere_Workplace_Learning_Jun2005mtg.pdf.
Bell, D. (1976). *The coming of post-industrial society: A venture in social forecasting.* New York: Basic.

BIBLIOGRAPHY

Betcherman, G., McMullen, K., & Davidman, K. (1998). *Training for the new economy*. Ottawa: Canadian Policy Research Networks.

Betts, R. (2006). *Lived experiences of long-term supply beginning teachers in New Brunswick: A hermeneutic phenomenological approach*. Unpublished doctoral dissertation, Fredericton, University of New Brunswick.

Billett, S. (2003). Workplace mentors: Demands and benefits. *Journal of Workplace Learning, 15*(3), 105–113.

Billett, S. (2004). Workplace participatory practices: Conceptualising workplaces as learning environments. *Journal of Workplace Learning, 16*(6), 312–324.

Bjorkquist, D.C., & Kleinhesselink, J. (1999). Contingent employment and alienated workers. *Journal of Industrial Teacher Education, 36*(2), 1–11.

Boe, E., Cook, L., & Sunderland, R. (2008). Teacher turnover: Examining exit attrition, teacher area transfer, and school migration. *Exceptional Children, 75*(1), 7–31.

Bogler, R., & A. Somech. (2004). Influence of teacher empowerment on teachers' organizational commitment, professional commitment and organizational citizenship behavior in schools. *Teaching and Teacher Education, 20*, 277–289.

Booth, D., & Rowsell, J. (2007). *The literacy principal: Leading, supporting, and assessing reading and writing initiatives*. Markham, ON: Pembrooke.

Borko, H. (2004). Professional development and teacher learning: mapping the terrain. *Educational Researcher, 33*(8), 3–15.

Brine, J. (2006). Lifelong learning and the knowledge economy: Those that know and those that do not—the discourse of the European Union. *British Educational Research Journal, 32*(5), 649–665.

Briscoe, C., & Peters, J. (1997). Teacher collaboration across and within schools: Supporting individual change in elementary science teaching. *Science Education, 81*(1), 51–65.

Broad, K., & Evans, M. (2006, October 20). A review of literature on professional development for experienced teachers. Unpublished document prepared for the Ontario Ministry of Education.

Brown, L. (2011, August 18). Union leader urges teachers to get political. *Toronto Star*.

Buffum, A., & Hinman, C. (2006). Professional learning communities: Reigniting passion and purpose. *Leadership, 35*(5), 16–19.

Bushaw, J., & McNee, J. (2009). The 41st annual Phi Delta Kappa/Gallup poll of the public's attitudes toward the public schools. *Phi Delta Kappan, 91*(1), 8-23.

Campbell, E. (2000). Professional ethics in teaching: Towards the development of a code of practice. *Cambridge Journal of Education, 30*(2), 203–221.

Canadian Nurses Association (CNA). (2009). *2007 workforce profile of registered nurses in Canada*. Retrieved from www.cna-aiic.ca/CNA/documents/pdf/publications/2007_RN_Snapshot_e.pdf.

Carey, M. (2007). White-collar proletariat? Braverman, the deskilling/upskilling of social work and the paradoxical life of the Agency Care Manager. *Journal of Social Work, 7*(1), 93–114.

Carlaw, K., Oxley, L., & Walker, P. (2006). Beyond the hype: Intellectual property and the knowledge society/knowledge economy. *Journal of Economic Surveys, 20*(4), 633–658.

Carmeli, A., & Freund, A. (2004). Work commitment, job satisfaction, and job performance: An empirical investigation. *International Journal of Organization Theory and Behavior, 7*(3), 289–309.

Carnoy, M., & Rhoten, D. (2002). What does lobalization mean for educational change? A comparative approach. *Comparative Education Review, 46*(1), 1–9.

Carnoy, M., & Levin, H. (1985). *Schooling and work in the democratic state*. Stanford: University of Stanford Press.

Carter, B. (1997). The restructuring of teaching and the restructuring of class. *British Journal of Sociology of Education, 18*(2), 201–215.

Center for Workforce Development. (1998). *The teaching firm: Where productive work and learning converge*. Newton: Education Development Center.

Centre for Teacher Development OISE/UT & Ontario Ministry of Education. (2007). *Teacher induction, mentoring and renewal: Supporting new teacher induction in Ontario*. Retrieved from www.curriculum.org/NTIP/home.shtml.

BIBLIOGRAPHY

Chan, K., Lai, G., Ko, Y., & Boey, K. (2000). Work stress among six professional groups: The Singapore experience. *Social Science and Medicine, 50*(10), 1415–1432.

Cheetham, G., & Chivers, G. (2001). How professionals learn in practice: An investigation of informal learning amongst people working in professions. *Journal of European Industrial Training, 25*(5), 246–292.

Church, K., Bascia, N., & Shragge, E. (2008). *Learning through community: Exploring participatory practices.* New York: Springer.

Clark, R., & Antonelli, F. (2009). *Why teachers leave: Results of an Ontario survey 2006–08.* Paper presented at AERA 2009, Ontario Teachers' Federation.

Clark, R., Antonelli, F, Lacavera, D, Livingstone, D.W., Pollock, K., Smaller, H., Strachan, J., & Tarc, P. (2007). *Beyond PD days: Teachers' work and learning in Canada.* Toronto: Ontario Teachers' Federation/Ontario Institute for Studies in Education, University of Toronto.

Clarke, J., & Newman, J. (1997). *The managerial state.* London: Sage.

Clement,W., & Myles, J. (1994). *Relations of ruling: Class and gender in postindustrial societies.* Montreal: McGill–Queen's University Press.

Clifton, R.A., & Rambaran, R. (1987). Substitute teaching: Survival in a marginal situation. *Urban Education, 22*(3), 310–327.

Cochran-Smith, M. and Lytle, S.L. (1999). Teacher learning in communities. *Review of Research in Education, 24*(1), 249–305.

Collins, R. (1979). *The credential society: An historical sociology of education and stratification.* New York: Academic.

Connell, R.W. (1982). *Making the difference: Schools, families and social division.* Sydney: George Allen and Unwin.

Connelly, C.E., & Gallagher, D.G. (2004). Emerging trends in contingent work research. *Journal of Management, 30*(6), 959–983.

Cooper, H. (2011, March 14). Obama urges education law overhaul. *New York Times.*

Corrie, L. (1995). The structure and culture of staff collaboration: Managing meaning and opening doors. *Educational Review, 47*(1), 89–99.

Corson, D. (1986). Primitive semantic notions about hierarchical structures: Implications for educational organizations and educational knowledge. *Journal of Educational Administration, 24*(2), 173–186.

Cortada, J. (1998). *Rise of the knowledge worker.* Boston: Butterworth-Heinemann.

Curti, M. (1935). *The social ideas of American educators.* Paterson, NJ: Littlefield, Adams.

Curtis, B. (1988). *Building the educational state: Canada west, 1836–1871.* London: Falmer.

Curtis, B., Livingstone, D.W., & Smaller, H. (1992). *Stacking the deck: The streaming of working class kids in Ontario schools.* Toronto: Our Schools/Our Selves Educational Foundation.

Dale, R., & Robertson, S. (2002). Local states of emergency: The contradictions of neo-liberal governance in New Zealand. *British Journal of Sociology of Education, 23*(3), 463–482.

Daley, B. (2001). Learning and professional practice: A study of four professions. *Adult Education Quarterly, 52*(1), 39-54.

Daley, B. (2002). Context: Implications for learning in professional practice. *New Directions for Adult and Continuing Education, 96,* 79–88.

Damianos, M. (1998). *Substitute teachers in elementary schools and their professional discourse.* Unpublished master's thesis, Toronto, University of Toronto.

Darling-Hammond, L. (1998). Educating teachers for the next century: Rethinking practice and policy. In National Society for the Study of Education (NSSE) (Ed.), *Yearbook 1998* (pp. 221–256). Washington, DC: NSSE.

Darling-Hammond, L. (2007, May 21). Evaluating "No Child Left Behind." *The Nation.*

Darling-Hammond, L., & Sykes, G. (Eds.). (1999). *Teaching as the learning profession: Handbook of policy and practice.* San Francisco: Jossey-Bass.

Darling-Hammond, L., Chung Wei, R., Andree, A., Richardson, N., & Orhanos, S. (2009). *Professional learning in the learning profession: A status report on teacher development in the United States and abroad.* N.p.: National Staff Development Council.

BIBLIOGRAPHY

Darling-Hammond, L., & Sclan, E. (1996). Who teaches and why: Dilemmas of building a profession for twenty-first century schools. In J. Sikula, T.J. Buttery, & E. Guyton (Eds.), *Handbook of Research on Teacher Education* (2nd ed.) (pp. 67–101). New York: Macmillan.

Day, C. (1999). *Developing teachers, the challenge of lifelong learning*. London: Falmer.

Day, C., Fernandez A, Hauge, T.E., & Moller J. (Eds.). (2000). *The life and work of teachers*. New York: Falmer.

Dehli, K., & Fumia, D. (2002). *Teachers' informal learning, identity and contemporary education "reform."* Retrieved from http://oise.utoronto.ca/depts/sese/csew/nall.

Densmore, K. (1987). Professionalism, proletarianism and teacher work. In T. Popkewitz (Ed.), *Critical studies in teacher education*. London: Falmer.

Department for Education and Employment (DfEE). (1998). *Teachers: Meeting the challenge of change*. London: DfEE.

Department for Education and Skills (DfES). (2003). *The induction support programme for newly qualified teachers*. London: DfES.

Derber, C. (1983). Managing professionals: Ideological proleterianization and post-industrial labor. *Theory and Society, 12*(3), 309–341.

Derber, C., Schwartz, W., & Magrass, Y. (1990). *Power in the highest degree: Professionals and the rise of a new mandarin order*. New York: Oxford University Press.

Dewey, J. (1916). *Democracy and education: An introduction to the philosophy of education*. New York: Macmillan.

Dickens, G., Sugarman, P., & Rogers, G. (2005). Nurses' perceptions of the working environment: A UK independent sector study. *Journal of Psychiatric and Mental Health Nursing, 12*(3), 297–302.

Dickson, C.B. (2006). *Strengthen teacher quality: Improving the quality of teachers in the classroom*. Retrieved from www2.ed.gov/admins/tchrqual/learn/nclbsummit/dickson/index.html.

DiNatalie, M. (2001). Characteristics of and preference for alternative work arrangements, 1999. *Monthly Labor Review, 124*(3), 28–49.

Donmoyer, R. (1995). *The very idea of a knowledge base*. Paper presented at the Annual Meeting of AERA., San Francisco.

DuFour, R. (2004). Schools as learning communities. *Educational Leadership, 61*(8), 6–11.

Duggleby, P.A. (2007). Real teachers: Real jobs. *SubJournal, 8*(1), 15–22.

Duggleby, P.A., & Badali, S. (2007). Expectations and experiences of substitute teachers. *Alberta Journal of Educational Research, 53*(1), 22–33.

Duman, D. (1979). The creation and diffusion of a professional ideology in nineteenth century England. *Sociological Review, 27*(1), 113–138.

Dymoke, S., & J. Harrison (Eds.). (2006). *Reflective teaching and learning: A guide to professional issues for beginning secondary teachers*. London: Sage.

Easthope, C., & Easthope, G. (2000). Intensification, extension and complexity of teachers' workload. *British Journal of Sociology of Education, 21*(1), 43–58.

Easton, L.B. (2005). Power plays: Proven methods of professional learning pack a force. *Journal of Staff Development, 26*(2), 54–57.

Easton, L.B. (2008). From professional development to professional learning. *Phi Delta Kappan, 89*(10), 755–759, 761.

Easton, L.B. (2009). *Protocols for professional learning*. Alexandria, VA: Association for Supervision and Curriculum Development.

Education Act, R.S.O. 1990, c.E2.

Education Act, R.S.O. 1997, c.31.

Elementary Teachers' Federation of Ontario (ETFO). (2002). *Professional beginnings: An induction resource guide*. Toronto: ETFO.

Elmore, R.F. (1995). Structural reform and educational practice. *Educational Researcher, 24*(9), 23–26.

Engestrom, Y., Miettinen, R., & Punamaki, R.-L. (Eds.). (1999). *Perspectives on activity theory*. New York: Cambridge University Press.

Eraut, M. (2000). Non-formal learning and tacit knowledge in professional work. *British Journal of Educational Psychology, 70*(1), 113–136.

BIBLIOGRAPHY

Eraut, M., Alderton, J., Cole, G., & Senker, P. (2000). Development of knowledge and skills at work. In F. Coffield (Ed.), *Differing visions of a learning society* (pp. 231–259). Bristol: Polity.
Eraut, M., Alderton, J., Cole, G., & Senker, P. (1997). *Development of knowledge and skills in employment*. Swindon: Economic and Social Research Council.
Evetts, J. (2002). New directions in state and international professional occupations: Discretionary decision-making and acquired regulation. *Work, Employment and Society*, 16(2), 341–353.
Evetts, J. (2003). The sociological analysis of professionalism: Occupational change in the modern world. *International Sociology*, 18(2), 395–415.
Evetts, J. (2006). Short note: The sociology of professional groups. *Current Sociology*, 54(1), 133–143.
Filson, G. (1988). Ontario teachers' deprofessionalization and proletarianization. *Comparative Education Review*, 32(3), 298–317.
Fleming, W.G. (1972). *Ontario's educative society*. Toronto: University of Toronto Press.
Forrester, G. (2000). Professional autonomy versus managerial control: The experience of teachers in an English primary school. *International Studies in Sociology of Education*, 10(2), 133–151.
Forrester, G. (2005). All in a day's work: Primary teachers "performing" and "caring." *Gender and Education*, 17(3), 271–287.
Foster, J.B. (2011). Education and the structural crisis of capital. *Monthly Review*, 63(3). Retrieved from http://monthlyreview.org/2011/07/01/education-and-the-structural-crisis-of-capital.
Foucault, M. (1980). *Power/knowledge: Selected interviews and other writings, 1972–1977*. (Trans. C. Gordon). Toronto: Random House.
Freidson, E. (1984). The changing nature of professional control. *Annual Review of Sociology*, 10(1), 1–20.
Freidson, E. (1986). *Professional powers: A study of the institutionalization of formal knowledge*. Chicago: University of Chicago Press.
Freidson, E. (1994). *Professionalism reborn: Theory, prophecy, and policy*. Chicago: University of Chicago Press.
Freire, P. (1970). *Pedagogy of the oppressed*. New York: Continuum.
Friedman, A., & Phillips, M. (2004). Continuing professional development: Developing a vision. *Journal of Education and Work*, 17(3), 361–376.
Fullan, M. (1995). The school as a learning organization: Distant dreams. *Theory into Practice*, 34(4), 230–235.
Fullan, M. (2005). *Leadership and sustainability: Systems thinkers in action*. Thousand Oaks, CA: Corwin.
Fullan, M. (2009). Large-scale reform comes of age. *Journal of Educational Change*, 10, 101–113.
Fullan, M., Hill, P., & Crevola, C. (2006). *Breakthrough*. Thousand Oaks, CA: Corwin.
Fulton, K., Yoon, I., & Lee, C. (2005). *Induction into learning communities*. ERIC Document, ED494581. ERIC Clearinghouse.
Furlong, J., Barton, L.S.M., & Whitty, G. (2000). *Teacher education in transition*. Buckingham: Open University Press.
Gall, M.D., & Renchler, R.S. (1985). *Effective staff development for teachers: A research-based model*. ERIC Clearinghouse.
Galloway, S., & Morrison, M. (1994). *The supply story: Professional substitutes in education*. London: Falmer.
Gardner, P. (1984). *The lost elementary schools of Victorian England*. London: Croom Helm.
Gariety, B.S., & Shaffer, S. (2001). Wage differentials associated with flextime. *Monthly Labor Review*, 124(3), 68–75.
Garrick, J., & Usher, R. (2000). *Flexible learning, contemporary work and enterprising selves*. Retrieved from http://epe.lacbac.gc.ca/100/201/300/ejofsociology/2000/v05n02/content/vol005.001/garrick-usher.html.
Gear, J., McIntosh, A., & Squires, G. (1994). *Informal learning in the professions*. Hull: Higher Education Funding Council for England University.
General Teaching Council for England (GTCE). (2004). *Survey of teachers' opinions*. Retrieved from www.gtce.org.uk/TeacherSurvey04.

205

BIBLIOGRAPHY

Gibbs, J., & Ushijima, T. (2008). *Engaging all by creating high school learning communities.* N.p.: CenterSource Systems.

Gibson, S., & Olberg, D. (1998). Learning to use the internet: A study of teacher learning through collaborative research partnerships. *Alberta Journal of Educational Research, 44*(2), 239–242.

Glassford, L.A., & Salinitri, G. (2007). Designing a successful new teacher induction program: An assessment of the Ontario experience, 2003–2006. *Canadian Journal of Educational Administration and Policy, 60*. Retrieved from www.umanitoba.ca/publications/cjeap/articles/glassfordsalinitri.html.

Gleeson, D., & Husbands, C. (2003). Modernizing schooling through performance management: A critical appraisal. *Journal of Education Policy, 18*(5), 499–511.

Golden, L. (2001). Flexible work schedules: What are we trading off to get them? *Monthly Labor Review, 124*(3), 50–67.

Goodlad, J. (1984). *A place called school.* New York: McGraw-Hill.

Goodman, J. (1995). Change without difference: School restructuring in historical perspective. *Harvard Educational Review, 65*(1), 1-29.

Goodson, I. (1994). Studying the teachers' life and work. *Teacher and Teacher Education, 10*(1), 29–37.

Gopee, N. (2002). Human and social capital as facilitators of lifelong learning in nursing. *Nurse Education Today, 22*(8), 608–616.

Gorelick, S. (1982). Class relations and the development of the teaching profession. In D. Johnson (Ed.), *Class and social development: A new theory of the middle class* (pp. 202–223). Beverly Hills: Sage.

Granstrom, K. (1996). Decentralization and teachers: Professional status cannot be granted, it has to be acquired. In J. Chapman (Ed.), *The reconstruction of education: Quality, equality and control.* London: Cassell.

Grimmett, P., & Echols, F. (2000). Teacher and administrator shortages in changing times. *Canadian Journal of Education, 25*(4), 328–343.

Grimshaw, D., Earnshaw, J., & Hebson, G. (2003). Private sector provision of supply teachers: A case of legal swings and professional roundabouts. *Journal of Education Policy, 18*(3), 267–285.

Guarino, C., Santibanez, L., & Daley, G. (2006). Teacher recruitment and retention: A review of the recent empirical literature. *Review of Educational Research, 76*(2), 173–208.

Guskey, T. (1995). Professional development in education: In search of the optimal mix. In T. Guskey, & N. Huberman (Eds.), *Professional development in education: New paradigms and practices* (pp. 114–132). New York: Teachers College Press.

Guskey, T. (2000). *Evaluating professional development.* Thousand Oaks, CA: Corwin.

Hanlon, G. (1999). The changing nature of professionalism and the fracturing of the service class. *International Review of Sociology, 9*(1), 87–99.

Hannay, L., Wideman, R., & Seller, W. (2006). *Professional learning to reshape teaching.* Toronto: Elementary Teachers Federation of Ontario (ETFO).

Hargreaves, A. (2003). *Teaching in the knowledge society: Education in the age of insecurity.* New York: Teachers' College Press.

Hargreaves, A. (2000). Four ages of professionalism and professional learning. *Teachers and Teaching, 6*(2), 151–182.

Hargreaves, A., & Shirley, D. (2009). *The fourth way: The inspiring future for educational change.* Thousand Oaks, CA: Corwin.

Hargreaves, A., & Levin, B. (2008, February). *Do educators need targets to hit the mark? Changing Perspectives.* Ontario Association for Supervision and Curriculum Development (OASCD).

Hargreaves, A., & Goodson, I. (1996). Teachers professional lives: Aspirations and actualities. In I. Goodson, & A. Hargreaves (Eds.), *Teachers' Professional Lives* (pp. 1–27). London: Falmer.

Hargreaves, A., & Shaw, P. (2000). *The paradox of improvement and reform: Four schools' experience of Ontario's secondary school reform.* Toronto: OISE/UT Centre for International School Improvement.

BIBLIOGRAPHY

Hargreaves, D. (1994). The new professionalism: The synthesis of professional and institutional development. *Teacher and Teacher Education, 10*(4), 423–438.

Hargreaves, D., & Dawe, R. (1990). Paths of professional development: Contrived collegiality, collaborative culture and the case of peer coaching. *Teaching and Teacher Education, 4*(2), 227–241.

Hargreaves, D., & Jacka, N. (1995). Induction or seduction? *Peabody Journal of Education, 70*(3), 41–63.

Harrison, J.K. (2002). The induction of newly qualified teachers in secondary schools. *Journal of In-Service Education, 28*(2), 255–275.

Hart, D., & Livingstone, D.W. (2007). *Public attitudes towards education in Ontario 2007: The 16th OISE/UT survey*. Ontario Institute for Studies in Education, University of Toronto. Retrieved from http://www.oise.utoronto.ca/OISE-Survey/2007/survey_final_final.pdf.

Hart, D., & Livingstone, D.W. (2010). *Public attitudes toward education in Ontario: The 17th OISE/UT Survey*. Toronto: OISE Press.

Hart, G., & Rotem, A. (1995). The clinical learning environment: Nurses' perceptions of professional development in clinical settings. *Nurse Education Today, 15*(1), 3–10.

Harvey, D. (2000). *The condition of postmodernity*. Malden, MA: Blackwell.

Hatcher, R. (2001). Getting down to business: Schooling in the globalised economy. *Education and Social Justice, 3*(1), 45–59.

Haug, M. (1973). Deprofessionalization: An alternate hypothesis for the future. *Sociological Review Monograph, 20*(1), 195–211.

Haug, M. (1975). The deprofessionalization of everyone? *Sociological Focus, 8*(3), 197–213.

Hawley, W., & L. Valli (1999). The essentials of effective professional development: A new consensus. In Darling-Hammond, L., & Sykes, G. (Eds.), *Teaching as the learning profession: Handbook of policy and practice* (pp. 151–80). San Francisco: Jossey Bass.

Herbert, B. (2004, January 26). Education is No Protection. *New York Times*.

Hipple, S. (2001). Contingent work in the late 1990s. *Monthly Labor Review, 124*(3), 3–27.

Hodkinson, H., & Hodkinson, P. (2005). Improving schoolteachers' workplace learning. *Research Papers in Education, 20*(2), 109–131.

Hodkinson, P., & Hodkinson, H. (2004). The significance of individuals' dispositions in workplace learning: A case study of two teachers. *Journal of Education and Work, 17*(2), 167–182.

Hoekstra, A., Beijaard, D., Brekelmans, M., & Korthagen, F. (2007). Experienced teachers' informal learning from classroom teaching. *Teachers and Teaching, 13*(2), 191–208.

Hoekstra, A., Northagen, F.A.J., Beijaard, D., Brekelmans, M., & Imants, J. (2009). Experienced teachers' informal workplace learning and perceptions of workplace conditions. *Journal of Workplace Learning, 21*(4), 276–298.

Holmes Group (1990). *Tomorrow's schools: A report of the Holmes Group*. East Lansing, Michigan: Holmes Group.

Hopkins, R.A. (1969). *The long march: A history of the Ontario Public School Men Teachers' Federation*. Toronto: Baxter.

Hord, S., & Sommers, W. (2008). *Leading professional learning communities: Voices from research and practice*. Thousand Oaks, CA: Corwin. Retrieved from http://www.cna-aiic.ca/CAN/documents/pdf/publications/2007_RN_Snapshot_e.pdf.

Hughes, G.W. (1936). *The social and economic status of the elementary school teacher in England*. Unpublished masters thesis, Manchester, University of Manchester.

Illinois State Board of Education. (2010). *Educator certification*. Chicago: Illinois State Board of Education. Retrieved from www.isbe.state.il.us/certification/Default.htm.

Ingersoll, R.M. (2003). *Who controls teachers' work? Power and accountability in America's schools*. Cambridge: Harvard University Press.

Jensen, K. (2007). The desire to learn: An analysis of knowledge-seeking practices among professionals. *Oxford Review of Education, 33*(4), 489–502.

Jensen, K. (Ed.). (2012). *Professional learning in the knowledge society*. Rotterdam: Sense.

BIBLIOGRAPHY

Johnson, M. (2001). Making teacher supply boom-proof. In M. Johnson, & J. Hallgarten (Eds.), *From victims of change to agents of change: The future of the teacher profession* (pp. 125–149). London: Central.

Joyce, B.R., Howey, K., & Yarger, S. (1976). *I.S.T.E. report 1*. Palo Alto: CA: Stanford Center for Research and Development in Teaching.

Jurasaite-Harbison, E. (2008). Teachers' workplace learning within informal contexts of school cultures in the United States and Lithuania. *Journal of Workplace Learning*, *21*(4), 299–231.

Kane, R. et al., (2010). *Induction can make a difference to teacher practice and ministry policy: evidence from a province-wide evaluation*. Paper presented at AERA.

Katz, M.B. (2001). *The irony of early school reform: Educational innovation in mid-nineteenth century Massachusetts*. New York: Teachers College Press.

Katzenmeyer, M., & Moller, G. (1996). *Awakening the sleeping giant: Leadership development for teachers*. Thousand Oaks, CA: Corwin.

Keller, B. (2007, October 4). New York shifts strategy on mentoring new teachers. *Education Week*.

Kelner, M., Wellman, B., Boon, H., & Welsh, S. (2004). Responses of established healthcare to the professionalization of complementary and alternative medicine in Ontario. *Social Science and Medicine*, *59*(5), 915–930.

Kennedy, P. (2010). The knowledge economy and labour power in late capitalism. *Critical Sociology*, *36*(6), 821–837.

King, M.B. (2002). Professional development to promote schoolwide inquiry. *Teaching and Teacher Education*, *18*(3), 243–257.

Klein, P. (1996). Preservice teachers' beliefs about learning and knowledge. *Alberta Journal of Educational Research*, *42*(4), 361–378.

Knight, J. (2009). Coaching: The key to translating research into practice lies in continuous job embedded learning with ongoing support. *Journal of Staff Development*, *30*(1), 18–20.

Knight, P. (2002). A systemic approach to professional development: learning as practice. *Teaching and Teacher Education*, *18*(3), 229–241.

Knowles, M. (1975). *Self-directed learning: A guide for learners and teachers*. New York: Association Press.

Kohl, H. R. (1967). *36 children*. New York: New American.

Kohl, H. R. (1974). *Half the house*. New York: Dutton.

Kozol, J. (1967). *Death at an early age: The destruction of the hearts and minds of Negro children in the Boston public schools*. Boston: Houghton Mifflin.

Krause, E. (1996). *Death of Guilds: Professions, States and the Advance of Capitalism, 1930 to the Present*. New Haven: Yale University Press.

Kyriacou, C. (2001). Teacher stress: Directions for future research. *Educational Review*, *53*(1), 27–35.

Labaree, F.D. (1992). Power, knowledge and the rationalization of teaching: A genealogy of the movement to professionalize teaching. *Harvard Educational Review*, *62*(2), 123-132.

Larson, M.S. (1980). Proletarianization and educated labour. *Theory and Society*, *9*(1), 131–175.

Lave, J. (1993). The practice of learning. In S. Chaiklin (Ed.), *Understanding practice: Perspectives on activity and context*. Cambridge: Cambridge University Press.

Lave, J., & Wenger, E. (1991). *Situated learning: Legitimate peripheral participation*. New York: Cambridge University Press.

Lavoie, M., Roy, R., & Therrien, P. (2003). A growing trend toward knowledge work in Canada. *Research Policy*, *32*(5), 827–844.

Lawn, M. (1987). What is the teachers' job? Work and welfare in elementary teaching, 1940–1945. In M. Lawn, & G. Grace (Eds.), *Teachers: The culture and politics of work*. Baskingstoke: Falmer.

Lawn, M. (1996). *Modern times? Work, professionalism and citizenship in teaching*. London: Falmer.

Lawrence, J. (1988, August). On the fringe. *Education*, *19*, 175–176.

Leicht, K., & Fennell, M. (1997). The changing organizational context of professional work. *Annual Review of Sociology*, *23*(1), 215–231.

Leithwood, K. (2008). *Teacher working conditions that matter: Evidence for change*. Toronto: Elementary Teachers Federation of Ontario (ETFO).

BIBLIOGRAPHY

Levin, B., Glaze, A., & Fullan, M. (2008). Results without rancor or ranking: Ontario's success story. *Phi Delta Kappan, 90*(4), 273–280.

Levin, B. (2008) *How to change 5000 schools: a practical and positive approach for leading change at every level.* Cambridge, MA: Harvard Education Press.

Lewis, J.M., Marjoribanks, T., & Pirotta, M. (2003, March). Changing professions: General practitioners' perceptions of autonomy on the frontline. *Journal of Sociology, 39*(1), 44–61.

Lewis, K.S. (1999). Rethinking school improvement. In Murphy, J., & Lewis, K.S. (Eds.), *Handbook of research on educational administration* (pp. 251–276). San Francisco: Jossey-Bass.

Lieberman, A. (2010). Teachers, learners, leaders: joining practice, policy and research. *Educational Leadership, 67*(9). Retrieved from www.ascd.org/publications/educational-leadership/summer10/vol67/num09/Teachers,-Learners,-Leaders.aspx.

Lieberman, A., & Miller, L. (2001). *Teachers caught in the action: Professional development that matters.* New York: Teachers College Press.

Lieberman, A., & Miller, L. (2004). *Teacher leadership.* San Francisco: Wiley.

Lieberman, A., & Wood, D (2002). *Inside the national writing project: Connecting network learning and classroom teaching.* New York: Teachers College Press.

Lieberman, M. (1993). *Public education: An autopsy.* Cambridge, MA: Harvard University Press.

Lingard, H. (2003). The impact of individual and job characteristics on "burnout" among civil engineers in Australia and the implications for employee turnover. *Construction Management and Economics, 21*(1), 69–80.

Lipton, L., & Wellman, B. (2003). *Making mentoring work: An ASCD action tool.* Alexandria, VA: Association for Supervision and Curriculum Development.

Lipton, L., Wellman, B., & Humbard, C. (2003). *Mentoring matters: A practical guide to learning-focused relationships* (2nd ed.). Sherman, CT: Mira Vira.

Livingstone, D.W. (1999a). Lifelong learning and underemployment: A North American perspective. *Comparative Education, 35*(2), 163–186.

Livingstone, D.W. (1999b). Exploring the icebergs of adult learning: Findings of the first Canadian survey of informal learning practices. *Canadian Journal for the Study of Adult Education, 13*(2), 49–72.

Livingstone, D.W. (2004). *The education-jobs gap: Underemployment or economic democracy.* Aurora, ON: Garamond.

Livingstone, D.W. (2005). Expanding conception of work and learning: Recent research and policy implications. In Bascia, N., Cumming, A., Datnow, A., Leithwood, K., & Livingstone, D.W. (Eds.), *International handbook for educational policy* (pp. 52–71). New York: Springer.

Livingstone, D.W. (2007). Re-exploring the icebergs of adult learning: Comparative findings of the 1998 and 2004 Canadian surveys of formal and informal learning practices. *Canadian Journal for the Study of Adult Education, 20*(2), 1–24.

Livingstone, D.W. (2009). *Education and jobs: Exploring the gaps.* Toronto: University of Toronto Press.

Livingstone, D.W. (2010). Job requirements and workers' learning: formal gaps, informal closure, systemic limits. *Journal of Education and Work, 16*(3), 201–225.

Livingstone, D.W. (2011). *WALL 2010 codebook: National Survey of Work and Lifelong Learning.* Toronto: Centre for the Study of Education and Work, Ontario Institute for Studies in Education, University of Toronto.

Livingstone, D.W. (Ed.). (2010). *Lifelong learning in paid and unpaid work.* New York: Routledge.

Livingstone, D.W., & Antonelli, F. (2007). How do teachers compare to other workers? *Professionally Speaking.* Retrieved from http://professionallyspeaking.oct.ca/march_2007.

Livingstone, D.W., & Mangan, J. (1996). *Recast dreams class and gender consciousness in Steeltown.* Aurora, ON: Garamond.

Livingstone, D.W., Hart, D., & Davie, L.E. (2001). *Public attitudes towards education in Ontario 2000: The 13th OISE/UT Survey.* Toronto: OISE Press.

Livingstone, D.W., & Sawchuk, P. (2004). *Hidden knowledge: Organized labour in the information age.* Washington: Rowman and Littlefield.

BIBLIOGRAPHY

Livingstone, D.W., & Scholtz, A. (2010). Work and learning in the computer era: Basic survey findings. In D.W. Livingstone (Ed.), *Lifelong learning in paid and unpaid work* (pp. 15–56). London: Routledge.

Livingstone, D.W., Stowe, S., & Raykov M. (2003). *Annotated bibliography on the changing nature of work and lifelong learning*. Retrieved from www.csew.ca/resources/wallwp02.pdf.

Lohman, M.C. (2000). Informal learning in the workplace: A case study of public school teachers. *Adult Education Quarterly*, 50(2), 83-101.

Lohman, M.C. (2003). Work situations triggering participation in informal learning in the workplace: A case study of public school teachers. *Performance Improvement Quarterly*, 16(1), 40–54.

Lohman, M.C. (2005). A survey of factors influencing the engagement of two professional groups in informal workplace learning activities. *Human Resource Development Quarterly*, 16(4), 501-527.

Lohman, M.C. (2006). Factors influencing teachers' engagement in informal learning activities. *Journal of Workplace Learning*, 18(3), 141–156.

Lortie, D. (1975). *Schoolteacher: A sociological study*. Chicago: University of Chicago Press.

Louis, K.S., Kruse, S.D., & Marks, H.M. (1996). Schoolwide professional community. In F.M.A. Newmann (Ed.), *Authentic Achievement: Restructuring schools for intellectual quality*. San Francisco: Jossey Bass.

Luque, E. (2001). Whose knowledge (economy)? *Social Epistemology*, 15(3), 187–200.

Maaranen, K., Kynäslahti, H., & Krokfors, L. (2008). Learning a teacher's work. *Journal of Workplace Learning*, 20(2), 133–145.

Machlup, F. (1980). *Knowledge, its creation, distribution, and economic significance*. Princeton: Princeton University Press.

Mahony, P., Mentor, I., & Hextall, I. (2003). *Edu-business: Are teachers working in a new world?* Paper presented at the annual meeting of the American Educational Research Association, Chicago.

Malloch, M., Cairns, L. Evans, K., & O'Connor B. (Eds.). (2010). *The Sage handbook of workplace learning*. Los Angeles: Sage.

Marginson, S. (1997). Steering from a distance: Power relations in Australian higher education. *Higher Education*, 34(1), 63–80.

Marks, H.M., & Seashore Louis, K. (1999). Teacher empowerment and the capacity for organizational learning. *Educational Administration Quarterly*, 35(Supplemental), 707–750.

Marsick, V.J., & Volpe, M. (1999). The nature and need for informal learning. *Advances in Developing Human Resources*, 1(3), 1–9.

Marx, K. (1867). *Capital*. New York: International.

McIntyre, F. (2007). *Transition to teaching 2006 report*. Toronto: Ontario College of Teachers.

McIntyre, F. (2010, March). Transition to teaching, 2009. *Professionally Speaking*.

McIntyre, F. (2011, March). Transition to teaching 2010: Determined new teachers face increased wait times. *Professionally Speaking*: 30–34.

McNally, J., Blake, A., & Reid, A. (2009). The informal learning of new teachers in school. *Journal of Workplace Learning*, 21(4), 322–333.

Medina, J. (2008, January 21). New York measuring teachers by test scores. *New York Times*. Retrieved from www.nytimes.com/2008/01/21/nyregion/21teachers.html.

Michelson, W., & Harvey, A. (1999, August 8). *Is teachers' work never done? Time-use and subjective outcomes*. Paper presented at the American Sociological Association, Chicago.

Mills, C.W. (1951). *White collar*. New York: Oxford University Press.

Moir, E. (2005). Launching the next generation of teachers through quality induction. In H. Portner (Ed.), *Teacher mentoring and induction: The state of the art and beyond* (pp. 59–74). Thousand Oaks, CA: Corwin.

Morrison, M. (1999a). Running for cover: Substitute teaching and the secondary curriculum. *Curriculum*, 14(2), 125–139.

Morrison, M. (1999b). Temps in teaching: The role of private employment agencies in a changing labour market for teachers. *Journal of Education Policy*, 14(2), 167–184.

BIBLIOGRAPHY

Murphy, P., DeArmond, M., & Guin, K. (2003). A national crisis or localized problems? Getting perspective on the scope and scale of the teacher shortage. *Education Policy Analysis Archives, 11*. Retrieved from http://epaa.asu.edu/ojs/article/view/251.

Ontario College of Teachers (OCT). (1999). *Standards of practice*. Toronto: OCT.

Ontario College of Teachers (OCT). (2001, September). State of the teaching profession, 2001. *Professionally Speaking*.

Ontario College of Teachers (OCT). (2007, September). State of the teaching profession, 2007. *Professionally Speaking*.

Ontario College of Teachers (OCT). (2008). *Professionalism in teaching: Ontario College of Teachers 2008 annual report*. Toronto: OCT.

Ontario College of Teachers. (OCT). (2008). *The ethical standards for the teaching profession*. Toronto: OCT.

Ontario College of Teachers (OCT). (2008). *Transition to teaching, 2008*. Toronto: OCT

Ontario College of Teachers (OCT). (2010). *Ontario College of Teachers annual report*. Retrieved from www.oct.ca/annual_report/2010/en/stats_qualifications.html.

Ontario College of Teachers (OCT). (2011). *Transition to teaching 2010*. Toronto: OCT.

Ontario Government. (2000). *Ontario Teacher Testing Program*. Toronto: Ontario Ministry of Education.

Ontario Ministry of Education. (2007). Unpublished survey of occasional teachers in Ontario. Toronto: Ministry of Education.

Ontario Ministry of Education (2009a). *New teacher induction program resource handbooks*. Retrieved from www.edu.gov.on.ca/eng/teacher/induction.html.

Ontario Ministry of Education (2009b). *New Teacher Induction Program: Induction elements manual*. Toronto: Ministry of Education.

Ontario Ministry of Education. (2010). *The New Teacher Induction Program (NTIP)*. Retrieved from www.edu.gov.on.ca/eng/teacher/induction.html.

Ontario Royal Commission on Education. (1950). *Report of the Ontario Royal Commission on Education*. Toronto: B. Johnston.

Oppenheimer, M. (1973, December). The proletarianization of the professional. *Sociological Review Monograph, 20*, 213–227.

Organisation for Economic Co-operation and Development (OECD). (1996). *The knowledge-based economy*. Paris: OECD.

Organisation for Economic Co-operation and Development (OECD). (1998). *Education policy analysis*. Paris: OECD Centre for Educational Research and Innovation.

Organisation for Economic Co-operation and Development (OECD). (2001). *Teachers for tomorrow's schools*. Paris: OECD Centre for Educational Research and Innovation.

Organisation for Economic Co-operation and Development (OECD). (2005). *Teachers matter: Attracting, developing and retaining effective teachers*. Paris: OECD.

Organisation for Economic Co-operation and Development (OECD). (2009). *Creating effective teaching and learning environments: First results from Talis, table 5.3*. Paris: OECD.

Organisation for Economic Co-operation and Development (OECD). (2011). *Building a high-quality teaching profession: Lessons from around the world*. Paris: OECD.

Osterman, P. (2010). Job design in the context of the job market. *Journal of Organizational Behavior, 31*(2–3), 401–411.

Ozga, J., & Lawn, M. (1981). *Teachers, professionalism and class: A study of organized teachers*. London: Falmer.

Pankhurst, K.V. (2009). Elements of an integrated theory of work and learning. In D.W. Livingstone (Ed.), *Education and jobs: Exploring the gaps* (pp. 137–156). Toronto: University of Toronto Press.

Peters, P., & Raaijmakers, S. (1998). Time crunch and the perception of control over time from a gendered perspective: The Dutch case. *Society and Leisure, 21*(2), 417–433.

Pineo, P., Porter, J., & McRoberts, H. (1977). The 1971 census and the socioeconomic classification of occupations. *Canadian Review of Sociology, 14*(1), 91–102.

Polanyi, M. (1966). *The tacit dimension*. Garden City, NY: Doubleday.

BIBLIOGRAPHY

Pollock, K. (2009). *Occasional teachers' work engagement: Professional identity, work-related learning and access to the profession and to daily work.* Unpublished doctoral dissertation, University of Toronto, Ontario.

Pollock, K. (2010). *Occasional teachers' access to professional learning: Final report for the Elementary Teachers' Federation of Ontario.* Toronto: Elementary Teachers' Federation of Ontario.

Popkewitz, T., Tabachnick, B.R., & Wehlage, G. (1982). *The Myth of Educational Reform: A Study of School Response to a Program of Change.* Madison: University of Wisconsin Press.

Prentice, A. (1977). *The school promoters: Education and social class in mid-nineteenth century Upper Canada.* Toronto: McClelland and Stewart.

Professional Engineers of Ontario (PEO). (N.d.). Home page. Retrieved from www.peo.on.ca.

Pyper, W. (2004). *Employment trends in nursing.* Retrieved from www.statcan.gc.ca/pub/75-001-x/11104/7611-eng.htm.

Ranson, S. (2003). Public accountability in the age of new-liberal governance. *Journal of Education Policy, 18*: 459–480.

Ravitch, D. (2010). *The death and life of the great American school system: How testing and choice are undermining education.* New York: Basic.

Ravitch, D. (2000). *Left back: A century of failed school reforms.* New York: Simon & Schuster.

Redpath, L., Hurst, D., & Devine, K. (2009). Knowledge workers, managers, and contingent employment relationships. *Personnel Review, 38*(1), 74–89.

Reich, R.B. (1992). *The work of nations.* New York: Vintage.

Reid, A. (2003). Understanding teachers' work: Is there still a place for labour process theory? *British Journal of Sociology of Education, 24*(5), 559–573.

Renfrew County District School Board. (2004). *Collective agreement between Renfrew County District School Board and Ontario Secondary School Teachers' Federation, District 28, Occasional Teachers.* Pembroke, ON: Renfrew County District School Board.

Retallick, J. (1999). Teachers' workplace learning: Towards legitimation and accreditation. *Teachers and Teaching, 5*(1), 33–50.

Retallick, J., & Butt, R. (2004). Professional well-being and learning: A study of teacher-peer workplace relationships. *Journal of Educational Enquiry, 5*(1), 85–99.

Richards, E. (2002). *Positioning the elementary core French teacher: An investigation of workplace marginality.* Unpublished doctoral dissertation, University of Toronto, Ontario.

Rippon, J., & Martin, M. (2003). Supporting induction: Relationships count. *Mentoring and Tutoring, 11*(2), 211–226.

Robinson, S. (1971). *Do not erase: The story of OSSTF.* Toronto: Ontario Secondary School Teachers' Federation.

Rowan, B. (1994). Comparing teacher's work with work in other occupations: Notes on the professional status of teaching. *Educational Researcher, 23*(6), 4–21.

Ryan, J. (2003). Continuous professional development along the continuum of lifelong learning. *Nurse Education Today, 23*(1), 498–508.

Ryan, J., Pollock, K., & Antonelli, F. (2009). Teacher diversity in Canada: Leaky pipelines, bottlenecks and glass ceilings. *Canadian Journal of Education, 32*(3), 512–538.

Sachs, J. (2003). The activist teaching profession. Buckingham: Open University Press.

Schrag, P. (2007). Schoolhouse crock: Fifty years of blaming America's education system for our stupidity. *Harper's Magazine, 315*(1888), 36–44.

Schwarz, A. (2011, July 11). Union chief faults school reform from "on high." *New York Times.*

Scribner, J.P. (2003). Teacher learning in context: The special case of rural high school teachers. *Education Policy Analysis Archives.* Retrieved from http://epaa.asu.edu/ojs/article/view/240.

Sears, A. (2003). *Retooling the mind factory: Education in a lean state.* Toronto: Garamond.

Senge, P. (1990). *The fifth discipline: The art and practice of the learning organization.* New York: Doubleday.

Shillings, C. (1991). Supply teachers: Working on the margins: A review of the literature. *Educational Research, 33*(1), 3–11.

Slee, R., & Weiner, G. (1998). *School effectiveness for whom? Challenges to the school effectiveness and school improvement movements*. London: Falmer.

Smaller, H. (2005). Teacher informal learning and teacher knowledge: Theory, practice and policy. In Bascia, N., Cumming, A., Datnow, A., Leithwood, K., & Livingstone, D.W. (Eds.), *International handbook of educational policy series* (Vol. 13, pp. 543–568). New York: Springer.

Smaller, H. (2004). Teacher unions, (neo)liberalism and the state: The Perth County conspiracy of 1885. *Pedagogica Historica, 40*(1–2), 75–91.

Smaller, H. (1998). Canadian teachers unions: A comparative perspective. *Contemporary Education, 69*(4), 223–228.

Smaller, H. (1996). The teaching profession act in Canada: A critical perspective. In C. Gonick, P. Phillips, & J. Vorst (Eds.), *Labour gains, labour pains: Fifty years of PC1003*. Halifax: Fernwood.

Smaller, H., Tarc, P., Antonelli, F., Clark, R., Hart, D., & Livingstone, D.W. (2005). *Canadian teachers' learning practices and workload issues: Results from a national teacher survey and follow-up focus groups*. Retrieved from www.csew.ca/resources/Smaller_Clark_Teachers_Survey_Jun2005.pdf.

Smyth, J. (1992). Teachers' work and the politics of reflection. *American Educational Research Journal, 29*(2), 267–300.

Sorlin, S., & Vessuri, H. (Eds.). (2011). *Knowledge society vs. knowledge economy: Knowledge, power and politics*. New York: Palgrave.

Soucek, V. (1994). Flexible education and new standards of communicating competence. In J. Kenway (Ed.), *Economising education: Post-Fordist directions* (pp. 43–103). Geelong: Deakin University Press.

Spaull, A. (1997). A law unto themselves: Victorian state school teachers and the federal labour power. *Discourse: Studies in the Cultural Politics of Education, 18*(2), 185–196.

Spindler, J., & Biott, C. (2000). Target setting in the induction of newly qualified teachers: Emerging colleagueship in the context of performance management. *Educational Research, 42*(3), 275–285.

Stevenson, H., Carter, B., & Passy, R. (2007). "New professionalism," workforce remodelling and the restructuring of teachers' work. *International Electronic Journal of Leadership for Learning*. Retrieved from www.ucalgary.ca/~iejll/.

Storey, A. (2007). Cultural shifts in teaching: New workforce, new professionalism? *Curriculum Journal, 18*(3), 253–270.

Svensson, L., Ellstrom, P.-E., & Aberg, C. (2004). Integrating formal and informal learning at work. *Journal of Workplace Learning, 16*(7–8), 479–491.

Sykes, G. (1999). The "new professionalism" in education: An appraisal. In J. Murphy and K. Seashore Louis (Eds.), *Handbook of research on educational administration* (2nd ed). San Franciso: Jossey-Bass.

Sykes, G. (1990). Organizing policy into practice: Reactions to the cases. *Educational Evaluation and Policy Analysis, 12*(3), 349–353.

Tarc, P., Smaller, H., & Antonelli, F. (2006). *Illuminating teachers' informal learning: Shaping professional development and schooling reform*. Retrieved from csew.ca/resources/Tarc_Teachers_Inf_Learning_AERA06.pdf.

Teacher Training Agency (TTA). (2003). *Career entry and development profile*. London: TTA.

Thompson, C.L., & Zeuli, J.S. (1999). The frame and tapestry: Standards-based reform and professional development. In G. Sykes (Ed.), *Teaching as the learning profession: Handbook of policy and practice* (pp. 341–375). San Francisco: Jossey-Bass.

Tickle, L. (1991). New teachers and the emotions of learning teaching. *Cambridge Journal of Education, 19*(3), 319–329.

Tickle, L. (2000). *Teacher induction: The way ahead*. Buckingham: Open University Press.

Tikkanen, T. (2002). Learning at work in technology intensive environments. *Journal of Workplace Learning, 14*(3), 89–97.

Tikkanen, T., Lahn, L., Withnall, A., Ward, P., & Lyng, K. (2002). *Working life changes and training of older workers*. Trondheim: Norwegian Institute for Adult Education.

BIBLIOGRAPHY

Toffler, A. (1990). *Powershift: Knowledge, wealth and violence at the edge of the 21st century*. New York: Bantam.

Toronto District School Board (TDSB). (2009). *Mentoring 4 mentors: Blogs/podcasts/videos/resources*. Retrieved from http://web.me.com/btintdsb.

Toronto District School Board (TDSB). (2009). *Welcome to teaching and learning: 2009/2010 information and resources for beginning teachers and mentors*. Retrieved from http://schools.tdsb.on.ca/asit/standards/btstart.

Tough, A. (1978). *Major learning efforts: Recent research and future directions*. Toronto: Ontario Institute for Studies in Education.

Tough, A. (1979). *The adult's learning projects: A fresh approach to theory and practice in adult learning*. Toronto: OISE Press.

Troyna, B. (1994). The everyday world of teachers? Deracialized discourses in the sociology of teachers and the teaching profession. *British Journal of Sociology of Education*, *15*(3), 325–39.

Tuschling, A., & Engemann, C. (2006). From education to lifelong learning: The emerging regime of learning in the European Union. *Educational Philosophy and Theory*, *38*(4), 451–469.

Tyack, D.B., & Cuban, L. (1995). *Tinkering toward utopia: A century of public school reform*. Cambridge, MA: Harvard University Press.

Vongalis-Macrow, A. (2008). *The displaced agency of teachers in globalised education systems*. Rotterdam: Sense.

Vygotsky, L. (1978). *Mind in society*. Cambridge: Harvard University Press.

Waller, W.W. (1932). *The sociology of teaching*. London: Chapman and Hall.

Wang, J., Odell, S., & Schwille, S. (2008). Effects of teacher induction on beginning teachers' teaching: A critical review of the literature. *Journal of Teacher Education*, *59*(2), 132–152.

Warburton, R. (1986). The class relations of public school teachers in British Columbia. *Canadian Review of Sociology and Anthropology*, *23*(2), 210–229.

Watkins, K., & Marsick, V. (1992). Towards a theory of informal and incidental learning in organizations. *International Journal of Lifelong Education*, *11*(4), 287–300.

Weber, M. (1928). *Economy and society*. New York: Bedminister.

Weiss, E.M., & Weiss, S.G. (1999). *Beginning teacher induction*. Washington, DC: ERIC Digest.

Wikipedia. (N.d.). Hierarchy. Retrieved from http://en.wikipedia.org/wiki/Hierarchy.

Wilhelm, K., Dewhurst-Savellis, J., & Parker, G. (2000). Teacher stress? An analysis of why teachers leave and why they stay. *Teachers and Teaching: Theory and Practice*, *6*(3), 291–304.

Williams, A. (2003). Informal learning in the workplace: A case study of new teachers. *Educational Studies*, *29*(2), 207–219.

Williams, A., Prestage, S., & Bedward, J. (2001). Individualism to collaboration: The significance of teacher culture to the induction of newly qualified teachers. *Journal of Education for Teaching*, *27*(3), 254–267.

Wilson, E., & Demetriou, H. (2007). New teacher learning: Substantive knowledge and contextual factor. *Curriculum Journal*, *18*(3), 213–229.

Work and Lifelong Learning Network (WALL). (2005). Unpublished survey data. Toronto: WALL.

Wright, E.O. (1980). Class and occupation. *Theory and Society*, *9*(1), 177–214.

Wynd, C. (2003). Current factors contributing to professionalism in nursing. *Journal of Professional Nursing*, *19*(5), 251–261.

Yoon, K. S., Duncan, T., Lee, S. W.-Y., Scarloss, B., & Shapley, K. (2007). *Reviewing the evidence on how teacher professional development affects student achievement*. Issues & Answers Report, REL 2007-No. 033. Washington, DC: U.S. Department of Education, Institute of Education Sciences, National Center for Education Evaluation and Regional Assistance. Retrieved from http://ies.ed.gov/ncee/edlabs/regions/southwest/pdf/REL_2007033.pdf.

York Region District School Board (YRDSB). (2004). *Collective agreement between York Region District School Board and the Ontario Secondary School Teachers' Federation*. Aurora, ON: YRDSB.

Young, B. (2002). The Alberta advantage: DeKleining career prospects for women educators. In C. Reynolds (Ed.), *Women and school leadership: International perspectives* (pp. 75–92). Albany, NY: SUNY Press.

Young, B., & Grieve, K. (1996). *Negotiating time: Reduced work employment arrangements for teachers*. Paper presented at the Annual Meeting of the American Educational Research Association, New York.